W9-BDL-818

DAILY LIFE ALONG

the Mississippi

Recent Titles in the
Greenwood Press "Daily Life Through History" Series

Civilians in Wartime Early America: From the Colonial Era to the Civil War
David S. Heidler and Jeanne T. Heidler, editors

Civilians in Wartime Modern America: From the Indian Wars to the Vietnam War
David S. Heidler and Jeanne T. Heidler, editors

Civilians in Wartime Asia: From the Taiping Rebellion to the Vietnam War
Stewart Lone, editor

The French Revolution
James M. Anderson

Daily Life in Stuart England
Jeffrey Forgeng

The Revolutionary War
Charles P. Neimeyer

The American Army in Transition, 1865–1898
Michael L. Tate

Civilians in Wartime Europe, 1618–1900
Linda S. Frey and Marsha L. Frey, editors

The Vietnam War
James E. Westheider

World War II
G. Kurt Piehler

Immigrant America, 1870–1920
June Granatir Alexander

DAILY LIFE ALONG

the Mississippi

GEORGE S. PABIS

The Greenwood Press "Daily Life Through History" Series

Daily Life in the United States
Randall Miller, Series Editor

GREENWOOD PRESS
Westport, Connecticut • London

Library of Congress Cataloging-in-Publication Data

Pabis, George S.
Daily life along the Mississippi / George S. Pabis.
p. cm. — (The Greenwood Press Daily life through history series. Daily life in the United States)
Includes bibliographical references and index.
ISBN 978-0-313-33563-1 (alk. paper)
1. Mississippi River Valley—Social life and customs. 2. Mississippi River Valley—Social conditions. 3. River life—Mississippi River Valley—History. 4. Country life—Mississippi River Valley—History. 5. City and town life—Mississippi River Valley—History. 6. Mississippi River—History. I. Title.
F351.P22 2007
977—dc22 2007027012

British Library Cataloguing in Publication Data is available.

Library of Congress Catalog Card Number: 2007027012
ISBN-13: 978-0-313-33563-1
ISSN: 1080-4749

First published in 2007

Greenwood Press, 88 Post Road West, Westport, CT 06881
An imprint of Greenwood Publishing Group, Inc.
www.greenwood.com

Printed in the United States of America

The paper used in this book complies with the Permanent Paper Standard issued by the National Information Standards Organization (Z39.48–1984).

10 9 8 7 6 5 4 3 2 1

Contents

Series Foreword

The books in the *Daily Life in the United States* series form a subset of Greenwood Press's acclaimed, ongoing *Daily Life Through History* series. They fit its basic framework and follow its format. This series focuses on the United States from the colonial period through the present day, with each book in the series devoted to a particular time period, place, or people. Collectively, the books promise the fullest description and analysis of "American" daily life in print. They do so, and will do so, by tracking closely the contours, character, and content of people's daily life, always with an eye to the sources of people's interests, identities, and institutions. The books in the series assume the perspective and use the approaches of the "new social history" by looking at people "from the bottom up" as well as the top-down. Indian peoples and European colonists, blacks and whites, immigrants and the native-born, farmers and shopkeepers, factory owners and factory hands, movers and shakers and those moved and shaken—all get their due. The books emphasize the habits, rhythms, and dynamics of daily life, from work, to family matters, to religious practices, to socializing, to civic engagement, and more. The books show that the seemingly mundane—such as the ways any people hunt, gather, or grow food and then prepare and eat it—as much as the more profound reflections on life reveal how and why people ordered their world and gave meaning to their lives. The books treat the external factors shaping people's lives—war, migration, disease, drought, flood, pest infestations, fires, earthquakes, hurricanes and tornados, and other natural and man-made disasters that disrupted and even shattered daily lives—but they understand that the everyday concerns and routines of life also powerfully defined any people. The books therefore go inside homes, workplaces, schools, churches, meeting halls, stores, and other gathering places to find people on their own terms.

Capturing the daily life of Americans poses unique problems. Americans have been, and are, a people in motion, constantly changing as they move across the land, build new communities, invent new products and processes, and experiment with everything from making new recipes to making new governments. A people always in the process of becoming does not stand still for examination of their most private lives. Then, too, discovering the daily life of the diverse American peoples requires expertise in many disciplines, for few people have left full-bodied written accounts of their prosaic but necessary daily activities and habits and many people have left no written record at all. Thus, the scholars writing the books in the series necessarily borrow from such fields and resources as archaeology, anthropology, art, folklore, language, music, and material culture. Getting hold of the daily life in the United States demands no less.

Each book at once provides a narrative history and analysis of daily life, set in the context of broad historical patterns. Each book includes illustrations, documents, a chronology, and a bibliography. Thereby, each book invites many uses as a resource, a touchstone for discussion, a reference, and an encouragement to further reading and research. The titles in the series also promise a long shelf life because the authors draw on the latest and best scholarship and because the books are included in Greenwood's Daily Life Online, which allows for enhanced searching, updated content, more illustrative material, teacher lesson plans, and other Web features. In sum, the *Daily Life in the United States* series seeks to bring the American people to life.

Randall Miller

Acknowledgments

This book would not have been possible without the support of many kind people. I thank the staff of the Georgia Gwinnett College Library who worked steadfastly to get me the materials upon which this book is based. The Writer's Institute of Georgia Perimeter College (GPC) provided me with a reduction of classes for one year to allow me to focus on this project. My chair at GPC, Ray Huebschmann, supported me every step of the way. I had many colleagues at GPC, including Elizabeth Thornton, Xuchitl Cuso, William Simson, Diane Kreutzer, and Pamela Roseman, who encouraged me throughout the process. My editor, Randall Miller, challenged me to make this book the best it could be. Of course, any errors are my own. I thank Mariah Gumpert of Greenwood Press for guiding me with great cheer and supreme patience. Most importantly, my wife, Shelli, commented on several drafts of the manuscript and never wavered in her faith in me. I dedicate this book to her and to my son, Aidan.

Chronology

9500 B.C.E. Paleolithic people using the Clovis point hunted in the upper Mississippi River.

8500 B.C.E. The Early Archaic or Dalton people hunted and lived in small settlements along the Mississippi River.

2000 B.C.E. Archaic people living in villages buried their dead with ceremonial and personal items.

1200 B.C.E. The ceremonial site of Poverty Point in Louisiana prospered.

600 B.C.E. Natives cultivated squash and gourds along the Mississippi River. The Woodland people used clay pots and buried their dead in mounds in the Ohio Valley.

500 B.C.E. Poverty Point site was abandoned.

100 B.C.E. A woodland site in Marksville, Louisiana flourished.

600 C.E. Late Woodland peoples built a thriving community at Koster site in Illinois. People first settled in the American Bottom near the Mississippi across from present-day St. Louis. The cultivation of corn became more common. Effigy Mound people settled in what today is Minnesota.

1000 Cahokia emerged as the largest Native America settlement in North America.

1200	Cahokia declined.
1250	Beans became a staple in the diet of Native Americas.
1300	Oneota people lived in villages along the upper Mississippi. The Dakota organized into a federation known as the People of the Seven Council fires.
1541	A Spanish expedition under Hernando De Soto wreaked havoc to native settlements along the lower Mississippi.
1670	The Dakota began trading directly with the French.
1673	The Quapaw at the mouth of the Arkansas River greeted the French explorers Jacques Marquette and Louis Joliet.
1699	The French made contact with the Tunica. French missionaries settled at Cahokia.
1700	The French built Fort Boulaye on the Mississippi River.
1706	Tunica was forced to move because of attacks from the English and the Chickasaw.
1717	Beginning of mass migration of 7,000 Europeans to Louisiana.
1718	French established the city of New Orleans.
1719	A flood devastated New Orleans.
1722	New Orleans became the capital of the French colony of Louisiana.
1724	French Black Code defined the status of black slaves in the colony.
1729	Natchez tribe wiped out a French settlement at Fort Rosalie. In retaliation, a French force eliminated the Natchez as an organized tribe.
1731	Arkansas Post became a permanent French settlement near the mouth of the Arkansas River.
1752	A census showed 23 individuals living in Ste. Genevieve, the first permanent French settlement on the west bank of the Mississippi River.
1757	After being expelled from Nova Scotia, the first Arcadians arrived in Louisiana.
1763	The Spanish took control of the colony of Louisiana. Black slaves outnumbered white colonists. Pierre Laclede Ligueste chose a site for St. Louis.
1779	A hurricane devastated New Orleans.

1788	A major fire wiped out 800 homes in New Orleans.
1790	With less than a hundred people in the tribe, the Tunica left the Mississippi River and established themselves in Marksville, Louisiana along the Red River.
1794	Eli Whitney patented a cotton gin.
1795	Slave rebellion in Point Coupee was brutally suppressed.
1803	The United States acquired the colony of Louisiana from Napoleon.
1812	The first steamboat plied the waters of the Mississippi River.
1815	High-pressure engines replaced low-pressure engines on steamboats.
1818	The U.S. government forced the Quapaw to cede some of their land.
1819	The U.S. government built Fort Snelling at the confluence of the Minnesota River and the Mississippi River.
1832	After the Black Hawk War, the U.S. government forced land cessions from the Sauk and the Mesquakie along the Mississippi River.
1839	The Quapaw were forced to move from Arkansas to the Quapaw Reservation in what is today Oklahoma. Joseph Smith founded the Mormon city of Nauvoo along the Mississippi River.
1841	The city of St. Paul was founded in Minnesota.
1844	A mob murdered Joseph Smith.
1846	Brigham Young led the majority of Mormans out of Nauvoo to Utah.
1849	Two fires devastated St. Louis.
1852	Louisiana's legislature forbade the freeing of slaves by their masters.
1858	Under pressure, the Dakota ceded all their lands along the Mississippi River to the U.S. government.
1861	The Civil War began.
1862	New Orleans surrendered to Union forces without a fight. A Dakota attack killed 500 settlers in Minnesota.
1863	Vicksburg surrendered after a long siege.

1865	The Civil War ended. The defeated Southern states passed Black Codes to restrict the newly freed slaves.
1866	The U.S. Congress passed the Civil Rights Act and the Freedmen's Bureau Act. A white mob attacked black delegates to the state convention in Louisiana.
1867	Congressional Reconstruction began.
1873	In St. Louis, Anheuser Company became to first brewery to distribute its beer nationally.
1874	A racist organization called the White League battled black policemen in the streets of New Orleans. The Eads Bridge linked St. Louis with the railroads of the east.
1877	The Compromise of 1877 ended Congressional Reconstruction. The Great Railroad Strike shut down rail transportation.
1878	An outbreak of yellow fever killed 4,000 people in New Orleans and 6,000 people in Memphis. The U.S. Congress authorized improvements to the upper Mississippi to create a minimum 4.5 foot channel.
1896	The Supreme Court case, *Plessy v. Ferguson*, legitimized segregation.
1900	The beginning of the so-called golden age of farming in the Midwest, which would come to an end in 1918. Minneapolis was the flour capital of the world. Jim Crow laws spread throughout the Southern states.
1904	World's Fair was held in St. Louis.
1912	The Krewe of Zulu staged its first parade during Mardi Gras in New Orleans.
1914	World War I began.
1917	The United States entered World War I. Passage of the Espionage Act of 1917, Enemy Act of 1917, and Sedition Act of 1918 brought government repression against immigrants of German descent.
1918	The United States and its allies won World War I.
1927	One of the worst floods in history hit the lower Mississippi.
1929	The Great Depression began.
1935	The governor of Louisiana, Huey Long, was assassinated. The first sugar harvesters appeared.

1938	The U.S. government took away tribal recognition from the Tunica.
1939	World War II began in Europe and revitalized the U.S. economy.
1945	The first of the baby-boomers were born.
1954	U.S. Supreme Court decision in *Brown v. Board of Education* declared that racially segregated schools were not equal.
1964	Civil rights movement's Freedom Summer took place in Mississippi. Civil Rights Act banned discrimination in public areas, education, and employment.
1965	Voting Rights Act made it illegal to require tests of voters. Herbicides and mechanical pickers were common in cotton fields. Hurricane Betsy flooded St. Bernard Parish in Louisiana.
1968	Assassination of Martin Luther King in Memphis set off race riots across the country.
1981	The U.S. government recognized the Tunica-Biloxi tribe.
1991	New Orleans' city government desegregated Carnival during Mardi Gras.
1993	The upper Mississippi flooded 20 million acres of land.
2001	Mississippi River flooded areas in Minnesota, Wisconsin, and Iowa.
2005	Hurricane Katrina flooded a large portion of New Orleans, and hundreds of thousands of people were left homeless.

Introduction

No other place along the Mississippi River embodies the history of the people who have lived and worked beside its waters better than Jackson Square in New Orleans. The statue of Andrew Jackson gazing upon such buildings as St. Louis Cathedral, the Presbytere, and the Cabildo reminds us that the French, Spanish, British, and Americans arrived here as conquerors and attempted to make this river and its fertile, alluvial soil their own. Native Americans who lived along the river had to grapple with this onslaught and carve out a new world for themselves or face extermination or removal. Yet, the magnificence of these monuments in New Orleans is dwarfed by a startling fact on the opposite side of the square. A steamboat seemingly floats high above ground level, just beyond a hill. A climb to the top of the levee solves the mystery: it is springtime and the muddy waters of the Mississippi River rush relentlessly past, several feet above the rooftops of one-story buildings in low-lying areas of the city. The levee and the city of New Orleans represent the precarious triumph of humanity over nature, but only as long as the next great flood doesn't sweep it all away. The steamboat is also a symbolic relic of an era when hundreds of them docked in the wharves that lined this section of the river. This most legendary symbol of the commercial prosperity of the region has today been relegated to serving tourists who walk along a park-like riverfront, which not too long ago bristled with sweaty dockworkers and bales of cotton. The diesel-powered ocean-going vessels that pass by are a testimony that the river continues to play its timeless role as a commercial highway and New Orleans remains a major port that links the United States to the rest of the world.

Yet, the river itself draws the attention of anyone walking along the levee. Nearly two hundred feet deep at this point, the Mississippi's strong current testifies to the power of nature. The sediment floating within its waters comes from as far away as New York, Virginia, New Mexico, Montana, and Canada. Water from a land area encompassing 41 percent of the continental United States drains into the Mississippi; only the Amazon and Congo Rivers drain a larger land area. At flood stage, 1.2 million gallons of water traveling at eighteen miles per hour pass by New Orleans each second. Even at low water, it would be foolhardy to think that one could swim across it. Despite our efforts to control and harness it, the river still runs wild.

Mark Twain called the Mississippi River and its adjacent lands "the body of the nation."[1] Similarly, Stephen Ambrose and Douglas Brinkley believed that the river "does not divide the United States in half but rather draws the country together, that it is the spine of America."[2] Because the Ohio, Missouri, and hundreds of other rivers link up with the Mississippi, the histories of the North and South, East and West come together here. "It pulses," John Barry has written, "like the artery of the American heartland."[3] The major historical currents that have shaped the story of North America were played out along this river, and so too the mosaic of day-to-day events that make up people's lives. The Mississippi River and the people who lived along it impacted each other. Jonathan Raban eloquently expressed the sentiments of many who have experienced the Mississippi, when he described it as "big and depthless as the sky itself."[4] The same can be said of the dynamic history of the people who made the river their home.

This book explores the history of the daily life of people who have lived and worked along the Mississippi River. No one to date has attempted a social and material history of the people along the entire Mississippi River that reaches from the era of Native American settlement to modern times. Drawing on the recent work of scholars, and the writings and observations of many who lived and worked along the river over several centuries, this study is a comprehensive look at the rhythms of life, the interests and activities that shaped people's everyday experiences. It is also an extension of the thought-provoking scholarship that has preceded this work. Ultimately, its purpose is not only to inform, but also to guide readers to examine the secondary and primary sources for themselves so they can further their understanding of the river and its people.

A host of related forces has shaped the daily lives of individuals along the Mississippi. The first and the most obvious is the environment, particularly the river. The Mississippi River ecosystem includes the water flowing in the channel; the water that used to flow in the channel but now forms lakes and swamps along it; the sediment deposited by floods to form alluvial lands; and the land sculpted by the water to create the channel, islands, bluffs, and other geological formations. The river attracted a host of plants, animals, insects, and fish, which in turn lured human beings to take advantage of its rich natural resources. And the fact that the water in the channel moves and is connected to a network of other rivers and bayous has allowed human beings to utilize the river as a source of transportation. Since 9500 B.C.E., people have exploited these natural resources. Of course, there is a price to be paid for this abundance. Floods create rich alluvial lands, but they also destroy, and the worst floods can be devastating. Lowlands and swampy areas along the river are perfect hosts to swarms of mosquitoes that spread diseases like malaria and yellow fever.

The second factor impacting the lives of people along the Mississippi is technology. One way archaeologists characterize prehistoric periods is by their technological development. Although there is a debate about the exact periodization, prehistoric Native American cultures can be divided into the following general categories: Paleolithic, Archaic, Woodland, and Mississippian. Each of these periods had technological advances in tool-making, food-production, and construction of buildings and ceremonial centers. The arrival of Europeans changed the technological dynamic. Native Americans wanted to utilize the new technology that Europeans possessed and traded with them in order to make their lives easier, give status to their chiefs, build kinship alliances with their neighbors, and protect themselves against their enemies. In exchange for furs, Native Americans often received guns, powder, flints, axes, knives, blankets, glass beads, and kettles. Over time, technological change drastically altered the lives of the American conquerors as well. The invention of the cotton gin fueled the expansion of the cotton empire and the institution of slavery in the South. Steamboats superseded the keelboats, but then they were eventually displaced by the arrival of the railroads and diesel-powered barges. These transportation revolutions fueled the economy, and the greater access to markets affected the lives of every person on the river. Great urban centers such as New Orleans, Memphis, St. Louis, St. Paul, and Minneapolis arose along its banks. Each was a link in a natural highway system that includes such tributaries as the Missouri, Ohio, Illinois, and Arkansas rivers. Enterprising capitalists found this transportation network ideal, and industry flourished along the river. Industrialization brought cheap consumer goods to millions of households and raised their standard of living. To protect these investments, the technology of flood control and navigation improvements evolved.

But there are limits to technology. The very steamboats that brought such prosperity to the region also killed thousands of people in accidents. Steamboats spurred the growth of the cotton kingdom in the South, which only entrenched the institution of slavery. As one technology superseded another, jobs were lost and the character of life changed, not always for the better. The rapid expansion of industry brought thousands of high paying jobs to the region, but pollution made the region between Baton Rouge and New Orleans a toxic nightmare. Flood control structures were prone to failure, as the flood of 1993 on the middle regions of the river demonstrated when it wiped out 55,000 homes. Improving the navigation of the upper river with dams changed the low-water ecosystem, which interfered with the spawning of many species of fish. As the United States moved into a post-industrial era, many of the industries that provided jobs left the area. Cities and small towns have struggled to find new opportunities.

Economic change is the third factor that influences the lives of people along the Mississippi. Fur traders were the vital link between the Native American and the transatlantic economies. A frontier economy developed where neither the Europeans nor the Native Americans had the military edge, which forced both sides to depend on each other. The trade caused strife as tribes competed over hunting lands to supply the European market with furs and establish kinship relationships with one European power or another to maintain the supply of valuable gifts and goods. But a new threat arose when the United States took control of the river after the Louisiana Purchase of 1803. The settlers replaced gift-giving with a credit system that put Native Americans in debt, which could only be paid off by land cession. Indian removal during Andrew Jackson's administration in the 1820s put an end to significant Native American participation in the southern economy along the lower and middle river. By 1851 the Eastern Dakotas gave the United States sole possession of the upper river.

The need to satisfy the domestic and international demand for agricultural products shaped the daily work life of American farmers, planters, slaves, and sharecroppers. Laborers on keelboats, steamboats, railroads, and tugboats made their living moving these products to transit and distribution points, which became the towns and cities along the Mississippi. Racism shaped this market economy, especially on the lower Mississippi. With a few exceptions, slavery and later the Jim Crow laws created a segregated world of work, limiting the opportunities for African Americans. Although a black middle and upper class existed in New Orleans and other cities, their opportunities for economic advancement were severely restricted. Not surprisingly, some African Americans used the Mississippi to flee to the North in a massive wave in the early twentieth century. Similarly, gender boundaries limited the economic opportunities of women along the entire Mississippi. Despite this discrimination, a few women managed to forge an economic identity, especially in the booming cities and towns along the river. Everywhere, the difference between owners and those who worked for them was real. Most workers faced the fickleness of a cyclical market economy, and when the country fell into depression, workers and their families faced terrible hardships. After 1945 industrial development along the lower river provided employment opportunities for people at the cost of environmental deterioration and negative health risks.

The history of the rural economy is central to the story of the Mississippi because the river links the agricultural heartland of the United States with the rest of the world. The cultivation of crops was a vital component of the Native American household economy, and even more so when many tribes attempted to adapt to the European and American pressures for assimilation. But as Americans took political control of the area, a new agricultural economy arose. In Louisiana south of New Orleans, sugar became the staple crop. The alluvial lands north of New Orleans all the way to Memphis provided the foundation for a plantation economy with cotton as its chief product. Impressive plantation houses attested to the wealth of the region, but behind these mansions, the slave quarters and later the sharecroppers' huts bore witness that prosperity came from exploiting the back-breaking work of African Americans. After the Civil War, social and legal discrimination trapped many blacks in an unwelcome servitude. Falling cotton prices caused a slide into debt that few sharecroppers could avoid, and many black and white farmers tumbled into tenancy behind them. In contrast, on the upper Mississippi yeomen farmers created a thriving agricultural system based on wheat and corn. European immigrants flocked to these bountiful lands to the river north of Memphis and set up farms. The daily lives of all these people were tied to the rhythms of the seasons, the advances of technology, and the fluctuating market prices of the agricultural products.

Another factor shaping the daily life along the Mississippi was community: the agglomeration of social ties that bound individuals to everyone else. Native Americans based their societies on kinship ties that extended to outsiders through the exchanges of gifts and creation of fictive relationships. In most native societies, the chief was never more than a figurehead who took care of his people by distributing food and goods to those submitting to his authority. For the American conquerors, homes, churches, schools, courthouses, county stores, and taverns were places where people met and formed social bonds that enforced or resisted race, class, and gender boundaries. The family was the central entity for establishing identity, raising children, and ensuring the economic survival of its members. The education of children was a constant struggle for the lower classes, but disenfranchisement of African Americans made matters worse. The river provided for families, but it could take everything away in a flood, and it often did.

Ethnicity was also a key feature in people's lives. Immigrants to the Mississippi Valley brought with them ethnic traditions and languages that intermixed with native customs. The struggle to maintain the so-called old ways in the face of assimilation defined generations of immigrants. Thousands of Irish laborers were employed to work on levees. Jews settled in cities along the river and forged distinctive communities. After the Civil War, over a thousand Italians moved to the Mississippi-Yazoo Delta in a failed experiment in which planters attempted to encourage European immigrants to live as sharecroppers. Along the upper Mississippi, German and Scandinavian immigrants bought farms and prospered. Each ethnic community left its imprint on the history of the Mississippi River.

Culture is the last piece of the puzzle. In this study, culture refers to the kaleidoscope of intellectual constructs that played the duel role of justifying and reinforcing power relationships, but at the same time making the lives of people richer, deeper, and more rewarding. Race, gender, religion, and class molded every aspect of the daily lives of individuals, families, and communities along the Mississippi River. Race bound the lives of whites and blacks and defined their interaction with the rest of society. Within this framework, blacks over time created an identity for themselves and formed a world in which they could survive with dignity in an oppressive social and political arena. Similarly, gender defined the boundaries of what was acceptable in daily life. Within Native American and European societies, patriarchal systems were in place, but there were significant differences. For example, Native American women cultivated the fields. In contrast, until the twentieth century, European and white American women were generally placed in subordinate positions in terms of market forces. Despite these limits, women shaped meaningful lives in the households, and in myriad community and religious concerns, and many women fought to expand their influence beyond the limits proscribed by the men in power. Class refers to the economic power that comes from the control of the resources and technology that create wealth. Along the Mississippi River, there was the struggle between master and slave, the poor farmer and planter, industrialist and worker, and landlord and tenant farmer or sharecropper. Another vital component of culture is religion. Birth, life, and death made sense to people when they turned to their religious beliefs. Most importantly, religion provided the moral and ethical framework that molded every human interaction.

If you leave New Orleans and head up River Road that runs along the eastern bank of the Mississippi toward Baton Rouge, you will be startled by the inequities among the people living along the river. Inhabited broken-down shacks stand within eyesight of massive petrol-chemical plants. Historic mansions that have been converted to museums greet visitors, but so do the odors of chemical fumes. Pollution has been detrimental to the health of people along the river, causing many to question the long-term benefits of industrialization and the use of chemicals in agriculture. While the upper Mississippi appears to be deceptively tame because dams have slowed the current, the middle and lower Mississippi River still pose a danger to rich and poor. After the flood of 1993, the federal government provided funding for eight thousand households to leave the alluvial banks on the middle river so the river can reclaim its alluvial lands and reduce the pressure on the lower river during flood time. In 2005 Hurricane Katrina refocused national attention on the relationship of the Mississippi River and the wetlands that protect the coast. With every rain, people all along the river check the news for the latest gauge reading of the Mississippi's height, in anticipation of the next great flood. The lives of people along the river and the seasonal rhythms of the Mississippi are forever linked.

NOTES

1. Mark Twain, *Life on the Mississippi* (New York: New American Library, 2001), v.

2. Stephen E. Ambrose, Douglas G. Brinkley, and Sam Abell, *The Mississippi and the Making of a Nation: From the Louisiana Purchase to Today* (Washington, DC: National Geographic, 2002), 3.

3. John M. Barry, *Rising Tide: The Great Mississippi Flood of 1927 and How It Changed America* (New York: Simon & Schuster, 1997), 21.

4. Jonathan Raban, *Old Glory: A Voyage Down the Mississippi,* Vintage Departure Edition (New York: Vintage Books, 1998), 11.

1

Life along the Mississippi before 1492

More than eleven thousand years ago, the first Native Americans hunted along the banks of the Mississippi to take advantage of the natural bounty of the river. The alluvial lands along the banks provided a rich habitat for plants and animals and the waters of the river supplied natives with fish and other aquatic animals. The river also served as a transportation network for trade and the maintenance of kinship ties. Over time, Native American cultures borrowed ideas and technology from one another. Each culture was characterized by ever more sophisticated tools, social organization, religious ceremony, and a greater capacity for exploiting the environment. By 1000 C.E., Native Americans were planting fields of corn along the Mississippi River and thousands of people lived in a huge ceremonial center at Cahokia, just across from present-day St. Louis. However, excessive use of the forests and fields around Cahokia led to an environmental depletion that weakened the most impressive society that the natives of North America ever produced. The struggle between humanity and nature was already thousands of years old by the time Europeans entered the Mississippi Valley.

THE GEOGRAPHY OF THE RIVER

Imagine the Mississippi River before human beings changed it. Think of it without modern cities, towns, plantations, and farms lining its banks. No barges, steamboats, or keelboats traversed its waters. No artificial levees, dams, or bridges manipulated its channel. The river began as a tiny stream at Lake Itasca, but tributaries added their water to the main channel. Near present-day St. Paul, Minnesota, the river flowed over a cliff that was once 175 feet high and 2,700 feet across. The melting of snow and heavy rainfall in the spring months caused the river to overflow its banks and deposit silt that built up over time to create natural levees. Sometimes these levees were strong enough to resist the next flood and sometimes they were swept away. Fish spawned in the flooded areas, and waterfowl searched for food. Over the centuries, the river meandered and changed its channel, and in the process it sculpted the land and created new islands, lakes, and bluffs. During the most severe floods, the river expanded into a temporary fresh water sea that spread out over hundreds of square miles.

A seemingly endless cycle of high water and low water marked the seasons. Deciduous forests, prairies, and swampy areas lined its banks. River after river joined the Mississippi, making the waters deeper and the current stronger. When the clear waters of the Ohio River mixed with the muddy waters of the Mississippi, the river entered the Lower Valley. As the Arkansas and the Yazoo rivers added their waters to the channel, the Mississippi channel became a torrent of power. The river's current was calmer near its edges, but in the center of the channel, the force of the river swept everything away. Floating branches and logs went by where the Mississippi had caved in a bank and undermined the roots of trees. The Mississippi drained a portion of its waters into bayous in what today is Louisiana. At the mouth of the river, no jetties confined the channel, which meant that the force of the current was slowed down as the waters of the Mississippi broke company and spread over three wide passes, dropping sediment in the process. By the time the river reached the Gulf of Mexico, it resembled a broad lake of freshwater with hundreds of islands.

THE PALEOLITHIC AGE

The first humans moved into the Mississippi River Valley just as the last Ice Age neared its end around 9500 B.C.E. Archeologists call them the Paleolithic or the Clovis people for the fluted stone projectiles they used on their spears. Through the fog of time, we have to admit that we know almost nothing about them. They left neither dwellings nor campsites along the banks of the river, and the flooding of the river probably erased any trace of their presence long ago. We can only guess that they lived a nomadic existence as small bands of gatherers and hunters, building only temporary shelters as they migrated sometimes in search of game animals, sometimes in search of better foraging prospects. Since the Ice Age was nearing its end and most of the giant mammals of that era had already become extinct, the Clovis people hunted the diverse number of species that existed in the river valley environment, especially white-tailed deer. What archeologists know about Paleolithic people comes from the technology they left behind at their animal kill sites. They used chipped stones to scrape clean the hides of animals and cut the meat. For hunting, they used a spear with a stone fluted point, the Clovis, tied to a straight wooden stick. At the kill sites, archeologists have also found other tools made out of wood, and baskets and nets made out of plant fiber. Although no Clovis bone or ivory tools have been found in the Mississippi Valley, we know that such items were widely used in other regions of North America.

What archeologists find at the kill sites tells us almost nothing about Paleolithic society along the Mississippi. Since the Clovis point was used throughout North America and only certain rocks in particular geographic regions were used to make them, the Clovis people must have engaged in some form of exchange to acquire the necessary raw materials for tool making. Most likely, the Clovis people lived in bands of 25 related members. Marriage with the women of other bands prevented inbreeding and also created marriage alliances with neighbors. Surely, they were excellent hunters who understood the behavior of their prey and moved with herds of animals. There is no evidence to suggest that women, especially those without children, were not hunters as well. And women with children may have hunted small animals with snares and nets. Women cleaned the dead animals and most likely would have had to sharpen the Clovis scrapers when they became dull. As Elizabeth S. Chilton writes, "when we can imagine a life of smoky campfires, turtle soup, wild grapes, crying babies, dreams of the hunt, and a variety of social tensions and diversions, we have made one small step toward understanding the lives of Paleo-Indians."[1]

THE ARCHAIC PERIOD

By 8500 B.C.E., the Clovis point disappeared for reasons unknown. Instead, people along the river began using the Dalton point, an unfluted projectile that could be resharpened several times and used as a hunting weapon, a serrated knife, or a saw. For the next 1,500 years in a period known as the Early Archaic or Dalton, significant technological and social changes affected daily life. The general drying of the climate, which archaeologists call the Hypsithermal, strained the natural resources of upland areas and forced people to migrate into the river valleys. Unlike the Clovis people, Dalton people lived in more stable settlements. There are at least a thousand sites in the Central Mississippi Valley alone, most in the Arkansas lowlands north of what today is Memphis. The population of the area increased dramatically, and the Dalton peoples lived in small bands of 20 to 50 people. About three hundred people resided in the Central Valley of the Mississippi River at any given time. For their prey, these hunters focused exclusively on smaller animals such as deer, raccoons, squirrels, and rabbits. They also gathered nuts, fruits, and edible plants. Religious and cultural changes were occurring because they were burying their dead in a cemetery near their settlement. The Dalton people used the adz, a tool to trim and smooth wood and house timbers and carve out wooden utensils, as well as bowls, dugout canoes, and grave markers. They also used end scrapers, awls for making holes in wood, bone needles, edged-abraded cobbles for chopping, and grooved abraders.

During the Middle and Late Archaic Period, from 7000 B.C.E. to 600 B.C.E., the total population of Native Americans grew and settlements became larger. Along the American Bottom, which is just north of the confluence of the Mississippi and Ohio rivers in the area of today's St. Louis, native peoples lived in four different types of sites: base locales, base camps, residential extractive camps, and extractive locations. The least common were the base locales, which were permanent settlements that covered many acres of land and contained clusters of dwellings, areas for specialized work, and cemeteries. Base camps were smaller and more common. Their inhabitants lived in dwellings and dug exterior storage and processing pits, but there is no evidence of specialization of activities such as tool making. Bands of related people occupied these camps for a season, and then moved on. Residential extractive camps were temporary camps of one or more extended families whose purpose was to extract a local resource. Extractive locations were areas where a few persons exploited a resource for a short period of time, and left without building any shelters. Except for some artifacts of tools and evidence of tool maintenance, there are no other signs of residency. Overall, Archaic settlements reflected a more sedentary population compared to the Clovis people.

What people ate changed as well. Seed gathering became increasingly more important as a food source. Small bands of people moved from one camp to another in a migratory seasonal pattern to take advantage of abundant food resources. They hunted waterfowl and caught catfish and largemouth bass in the backwaters of the major river valleys, but deer, raccoon, and turkey were the principal meat sources. As food supplies became more stable, the population of the Central Valley of the Mississippi increased by five to ten times compared to the Dalton period.

At Labras Lake in the American Bottom, Native Americans collected a variety of nuts that were plentiful in the area: shagbark hickory, shellbark hickory, hazelnut, and acorns. Women roasted hickory shells in a pit. They also gathered edible seeds such as knotweed, hawthorn, and sumac. The wood fuel for their fires consists of hickory, ash, oak, elm, red cedar, maple, walnut, and honey locust. About fifty people lived in seasonal camps at any given time. By 600 B.C.E., these people cultivated squash and gourds—both imports from Mexico. The women in the camps cleaned and dried gourds, which they turned into "dippers, ladles, cups, bowls, bird houses, rattles, and masks."[2]

On Modoc Rock in southern Illinois along the Mississippi River, Native Americans had access to several ecological environments within five kilometers of their settlement, including forests, creeks, lakes, marshes, and the Mississippi River itself. Together, these varied environments provided a wide range of animal species for them to hunt. The Native Americans on Modoc Rock ate more small mammals than larger ones, including chipmunks, mice, muskrats, and cotton tails. Over time, they learned to fish with nets. They walked along the shallow pools along the river and gathered freshwater mussels and snails, and trapped crayfish. Eventually, they got better at hunting white-tailed deer, which would become their principal source of meat.

The Native Americans in the Illinois and Mississippi River Valleys occupied the same site every season and buried their dead in cemeteries, often in high level areas such as bluffs. A village of Archaic peoples consisted of kin groups. If they did have to move in search of prey or because of severe flooding on the river, they carried the decomposed bodies of their dead in bundles until they could be properly buried in a permanent cemetery. At Carrier Mills in southern Illinois, archeologists have found 157 burials, but the villagers placed tools and other items in 27 graves. The villagers were not differentiating between women and men, and none of the items buried could be characterized as valuable goods that denoted a high rank. Eight individuals did have clay placed over their burial sites, which may indicate that they were important in some way. One grave contained a man buried with eagle talons and bear's paw bones, which may denote that he was a shaman. At three other sites, the ill or injured were buried in separate cemeteries from those that were healthy.

Around 2000 B.C.E., increasing numbers of Archaic villagers buried some members of their society with ceremonial or personal items such as gorgets, hematite pestles and plummets, and tubular pipes. These valuable materials and adornments may indicate that these individuals held a higher social rank compared to others who were buried with only utilitarian items such as tools. At the Indian Knoll site in Kentucky, 1,000 people were buried in a cemetery, but only 300 had grave artifacts. And only a few of them had such exotic goods as copper that came from Lake Superior or sea shells that originated in the Gulf of Mexico. These valuable goods were interred with adults of both sexes as well as some children. The villagers may have been denoting rank not just for the achievements in one's own lifetime, but for the accomplishments of one's ancestors or immediate family.

During the Archaic period, Native Americans exchanged goods between kin groups. Bands came together to trade valuables such as marine shells from the Gulf of Mexico, copper from the areas around Lake Superior, or jasper from what today is Pennsylvania. As in earlier eras, exchanges of flint and perishable goods were common. Red ocher, a red iron deposit, was ground up and used for ceremonial functions up and down the Mississippi.

At the Koster site in Illinois, Archaic people made bone awls, which were pointed instruments for piercing materials such as leather, and bone needles made out of deer that were used in basket making. They allowed dead members of the community to decompose before they were buried in oval pits with their knees placed near their chest. In one burial, an 18-month-old infant had been dusted with red ocher before being interred. Archeologists have found three dogs buried in the village cemetery, which indicates the special affinity such Native Americans had toward domesticated canines. Within the village at Koster, 100 to 150 people resided in huts scattered over five acres. Some individuals lived into their sixties and suffered from arthritis, so their younger siblings must have taken care of them.

At Poverty Point in northeast Louisiana, the most sophisticated culture of the Archaic period arose. First settled around 1700 B.C.E., Poverty Point reached its height of influence from 1200 to 800 B.C.E. Its technologies and religious ideas spread to over 100 settlement areas in southern Arkansas, eastern and southern Mississippi, and as far north as Missouri and Illinois. These people built their villages on high ground overlooking rivers and coastal areas near lakes and marshes. The Poverty Point site was the largest at over 500 acres while the smallest sites were no more than one-fourth of an acre. The smaller sites along rivers were arranged linearly, parallel to the streams. The larger centers were organized in a semicircle. Poverty Point consisted of a series of six concentric elevated ridges. None of the sites had earthworks for protection, such as walls or fortifications, but the sites were compact, which made them defensible.

The Poverty Point site in Louisiana was distinguishable from any other Archaic site by its three monumental mounds that were built between 1000 and 800 B.C.E., just outside the six concentric ridges. Mound A, which is 70 feet high, and Motley Mound, which stands at 51 feet, include a ramp and projecting platform that served ceremonial and religious functions. Archeologists have found no burial sites at Poverty Point. The people of Poverty Point cremated some of their dead at Mound B. There are no permanent dwellings at Poverty Point, which means the site served only a religious function, and people lived in surrounding areas.

The people of Poverty Point cooked in baking pits or earth ovens, one to two feet in diameter and 9 inches to 20 inches deep. Most of the cooking took place in the northern and southern portions of the site, so the women could have ready access to water. One of the technological innovations of the Poverty Point culture involved cooking. These people heated up pebbles or balls made out of clay pottery and placed them around the food in a pit or in a leather or woven basket in order to cook it. The clay balls could be reused about ten times before they cracked. Women cooked fish, turtles, snakes, squirrels, and birds and gathered hickory nuts, walnuts, pecans, acorns, persimmons, wild grapes, chenopodiums, knotweed, doveweed, aster, hackberry seed, and squash. The women also cultivated squash and chenopodium, but these were not significant parts of the diet. Since all Poverty Point sites were located near rivers and lakes, fish were the principal source of protein.

At Poverty Point, we find other technologies that distinguish these people from those who came before, including lamellar blades and scrappers, steatite vessels, two-hole gorgets, hematite and magnetite plummets, adzes, and hoes. Ceremonial and social status items such as beads, pendants, pipes, and figurines were made from copper, fluorite, calcite, quartz, obsidian, galena, and mica. These exotic raw materials were not native to the region and had to be exchanged with other peoples using the extensive river system of the Mississippi Valley—obsidian came from the Rockies, steatite from the Appalachian Mountains, and copper from Lake Superior. The style of the figurines as well as the religious ideas for mound building and related ceremonies may indicate that the people of Poverty Point had contact with the contemporaneous Olmec culture of Mesoamerica. The residents of Poverty Point spread their technology to far-off areas as well: the baked clay balls were used by people who lived in what is today Clarksville, Indiana, and along the St. Johns River in Florida. Pottery techniques such as podal supports, punched-through nodes, clay-grit temper pottery, and rocker stamping on pottery were being copied throughout much of the southeast.

At the Poverty Point site, some form of social hierarchy must have organized construction on the site. The concentric semicircle ridges lined up perfectly behind one another, and the mounds were placed in a solar orientation. Artisans worked on the raw materials imported from other regions to create ceremonial and utilitarian objects that the elites could collect and trade. Archeologists have found no evidence of any military activity in the region. Smaller communities around Poverty Point maintained an exchange network in which they supplied the ceremonial center with food while depending upon Poverty Point for religious and civil leadership. The outlying village communities were independent and had their own elites who probably maintained kinship ties with the leaders of Poverty Point.

For unknown reasons, the Poverty Point culture declined after 800 B.C.E. Archeologists have found no evidence of an invasion or an ecological disaster. Perhaps the ceremonial site was undergoing a religious crisis and losing its relevance for people in neighboring areas that had previously supported it. People in the region continued to maintain communities along the nearby Bayou Macon, but by 500 B.C.E., Poverty Point was totally abandoned.

From 600 B.C.E. to 400 C.E., Native Americans along the Ohio River created a series of cultural and technological innovations that archeologists call the Woodlands or Marksville Period. The two most important Native American cultures of this period, the Adena and Hopewell, developed in a region centered in Ohio, but their influence spread throughout the Mississippi River Valley and from Canada to Florida. Although more settled than their predecessors, the Woodland people still migrated to areas with better food sources. They built extensive earthworks in their communities and became increasingly dependent on horticulture as an important source of food. Using hoes, they cultivated pumpkins, gourds, and various other plants. By 400 C.E., Woodland people had adopted the bow and arrow for hunting, which allowed them to kill their prey at longer ranges. Although the first known pottery in North America was crafted in South Carolina about 2515 B.C.E., it is not until the Woodland period that it reached the Mississippi Valley. Whereas the people of the Poverty Point culture had heated up clay balls and then put them into a leather or basket container to cook the food, Woodland people were able to heat their food in clay pots that they placed directly over a fire. Different types of settlements during this period reflected the changes in Native American society. Most Woodland people still lived in base camps as their ancestors did, but now they also lived in harvesting camps where they collected and processed the crops they planted. They created regional exchange centers where trade occurred and kinship ties strengthened.

The most distinguishing feature of Woodland people was their extensive mound building. From 600 B.C.E. to 200 B.C.E., the Adena people created the first society in the Ohio valley that practiced an elaborate burial ceremony, lived in permanent houses, made extensive use of pottery, and developed horticulture. Adena people resided in circular houses with single wall posts and a fire pit in the middle of the floor. They were still mainly hunters and gatherers, but they experimented with intensive cultivation of plants such as gourd, pumpkin, squash, and sunflower. They constructed between three and five hundred burial mounds in what is today Indiana and Ohio. At first, the burials were simple and showed very little evidence of rank and social status. They painted the dead body with red ochre and sprinkled some of the pigment over the grave. A dead body was buried in its entirety or allowed to decompose on a platform. The Adena people dissected or cremated other bodies before they placed the remains in a shallow pit that was lined and covered with bark and soil. As they added more bodies, a mound would form. In earlier times, they placed more utilitarian tools than ornamental objects in the burials, but this changed. Burials for those of higher social status became more elaborate—they were buried in tombs that were lined with logs, and luxury items were placed with them. At Cresap Mound near the Ohio River, villagers placed the following objects with the dead who had higher rank: round stone balls; gabbro, diorite, and hematite axe heads; gorgets of stone and copper; hematite and barite hemispheres; sandstone and fireclay pipes; a turtle effigy tablet made of fine-grain sandstone; various types of stone knives; bone awls; beads made from bone, shells, and copper; turtle shell cups; textiles and baskets; and red and yellow ochre.

Influenced by the Adena, the Hopewell people in the Ohio River Valley built an extensive number of burial mounds and elaborate earthen ridges that took animal and geometric shapes. Their villages had wall embankments. Their artisans made platform pipes, copper objects, ear spools, and tools and ornaments made from galena, obsidian, mica, and pearl. Hopewell people knew how to weave fine fabrics. To gain access to exotic raw materials, they participated in an elaborate exchange network. The tools made from obsidian originally came from the northern Rockies. Copper was used to make axe blades, headdresses, bracelets, ear spools, and ornaments in the shape of circles, fishes, bird's heads, serrated edges, antlers, bear teeth and paws, and intricate geometric designs. Hopewell artisans carved out effigy and flat platform pipes for the smoking of tobacco. In their religious ceremonies, they used animal and human effigies made out of antlers.

Hopewell's impact on the Mississippi Valley was cultural. Other Native Americans adopted their techniques to make pottery, mound burials, and other earthworks. Whereas the Hopewell people of the Ohio created elaborate mounds in geometric patterns, mounds in Illinois and on the Lower Mississippi River were a simpler conical shape. At Red Wing, Minnesota, the Effigy Mound people built over 2,000 mounds and earthworks that ranged from three to ten feet high and six to forty feet in diameter. Some of these mounds were the shape of animals such as birds and lizards. Near Helena, Arkansas, one mound contained a tomb of a female adolescent buried with the following items: a copper-and-silver covered cane panpipe, a necklace, armbands, wristbands of pearl and conch-shell beads, a belt of wolf canine teeth and shell beads that went around the waist, and bicymbal copper ear spools. Since she was so young, she must have obtained status because of her kin or marriage relations.

From 100 B.C.E. to 400 C.E., at Marksville in Louisiana, Woodland peoples lived on the edge of a high prairie near the Red River and Mississippi River. The prairie offered them prey such as rabbits, squirrels, opossum, deer, snakes, and songbirds. The floodplain added fish, waterfowl, white-tailed deer, black bear, raccoon, bobcat, red squirrel, grey fox and swamp rabbit to their diet. The Marksville site contained one large semicircle embankment that was three to seven feet high and over three thousand feet long with three large and two small openings. The Native Americans at Marksville constructed five mounds within the larger semicircle and several others outside it. Alan Toth has described the distinguishing characteristic of Marksville pottery as "small, squat tubby pots," often marked with various designs including a bird of prey, bands, and parallel lines.[3]

At the Koster site in Illinois, Middle and Late Woodland people wore down their teeth faster than modern people do. Dirt must have gotten into their food, and they probably used their teeth as tools in their day-to-day tasks. Late Woodland people also had more cavities than earlier ancestors had because they ate sweet corn, whose cultivation was introduced into the Mississippi Valley after 600 C.E. Elderly people showed evidence of arthritis, but there are differences between higher- and lower-status men. Upper-status elderly men had arthritis in the elbows, which suggest that they must have spent a great deal of time practicing throwing a spear or pulling the string on a bow. In contrast, elderly men of lower ranks had arthritis in the wrists because they worked as artisans and tool makers. Another difference between high- and low-ranking individuals was that higher-ranking men had higher frequencies of bony tumors in the cartilage of the ears. In modern medical cases, these tumors are found among frequent swimmers. Woodland men of high social status were probably the ones who dove for mussels and collected their pearls. Young men and women suffered from an epidemic of blastomycosis, a fungus that people caught from contact with the soil. As Woodland people relied more and more on the cultivation of crops, they were more at risk of contracting this disease, which leaves lesions on the spine and shortens the lifespan.

THE MISSISSIPPIAN RENAISSANCE

In the Central Mississippi Valley, the most dramatic technological, political, religious, and social transformation in Native American prehistory occurred from 700 to 1400 C.E. Mississippian culture spread from northwestern Florida to southern Illinois and from the Carolinas and Georgia to Oklahoma. Some remnants of Mississippian culture, like the Natchez and the Apalachee, lasted into the era of European contact. For the first time, Native Americans cultivated crops in fields, lived in large ceremonial centers filled with thousands and even tens of thousands of people, constructed great mounds with the residences upon them, divided their societies into rigid higher or lower ranks, and participated in elaborate religious cults. The Mississippians grew many varieties of crops, but they depended on maize for most of their calories. Generally, they ate better than their ancestors and managed to produce a surplus of grain, which contributed to the concentration of human settlement, an increase in population, and the rise of religious centers where elites gained political power. Artisans produced valuable items such as copper plates and engraved pendants and cups that elites exchanged for other luxury items and raw materials. Elites used these valuable items to legitimize their own authority and status among the general population as well as make alliances with other chiefdoms.

The emergence of the Mississippian culture was not sudden. Around 600 C.E. in the American Bottom near St. Louis, Woodland people settled in stable villages. The American Bottom is a rich alluvial plain near the confluence of the Mississippi and Missouri Rivers that is 25 miles long from north to south and 11 miles at its widest. On this fertile land, Native Americans built huts with foundations below ground so as to provide coolness in the summer and warmth in the winter. In the next couple hundred years, in what is known as the Emergent Mississippian period, a plaza became the central feature in the village of Cahokia. People built their dwellings around it. Near the center of the plaza, the villagers dug storage pits and constructed a large communal building. From 950 to 1000 C.E., the village became more densely populated and the central plaza was broken up into several smaller courtyards. Single households built structures with wall trench foundations and storage pits around their courtyard. The courtyard included a cooking and food processing area with hearths and firepits and racks for the drying of meat. The residents of the village shared communally in food preparation, storage, and rituals. They all used the centrally located cooking and processing area, the lone pit oven, a single butchering facility, granary, and sweat bathhouse. Gradually after 1000 C.E., villages in the American Bottom dissolved and Mississippian peoples either moved to individual homesteads or to religious centers that elites controlled.

In the next few hundred years, Cahokia became the largest Native American settlement in North America. Between 10,000 and 20,000 people lived within the settlement and thousands of others lived in communities nearby. The ceremonial center's population doubled or tripled during religious festivals. Cahokia encompassed five square miles, of which 2,000 acres were residential. It had a close relation with settlements within a 60 to 90 square mile area and may have had political influence over them.

The Grand Plaza and Monk's Mound were the central features of the community around which the rest of Cahokia developed. Since the planned site of the plaza originally contained residential dwellings, the elites of the ceremonial center compelled these residents to resettle away from the sacred space. Hundreds of people over the years worked to flatten a rolling hill terrain and fill in holes. The planners made sure the ceremonial

The 100 foot-high Monk's Mound at Cahokia Mounds, Cahokia, IL. Courtesy of Cahokia Mounds State Historic Site.

plaza had a slight slope to the south that allowed rainwater to drain away. Eventually, the elites called on the population to construct massive stockade walls that divided the ceremonial center from the rest of the community. Workers dug a four foot trench and then placed logs upright into it. The thickness of the logs allowed them to support raised platforms or bastions. The palisade's length reached 1.75 miles, and it enclosed a ceremonial area of 200 acres and 18 mounds. The Native Americans of Cahokia used 80,000 logs to build the four palisades. In the long run this destruction of surrounding forest would have devastating consequences to the ecology of the region.

The people of Cahokia built at least 120 mounds. The most impressive is Monk's Mound, the largest man-made structure in North America before the arrival of Europeans. It had a larger circumference than the greatest of the pyramids in Ancient Egypt. During its construction over two centuries, Mississippians used hoes to dig long pits, and then they filled baskets with the sediment, and took them to the mound site. Monk's Mound contained 22 million cubic feet of clay and dirt, which required the filling of more than 14 million baskets that held 1.5 cubic feet or 55 pounds of dirt each. The mound covered 16 acres. The people of Cahokia added terraces later. On top of the mound platform, the house of the chief of Cahokia stood as a symbol of his family's prestige. A ramp allowed access to the top of the mound, but most likely only a few people were allowed to visit. Since the mounds had no grass or other vegetation on them to keep the soil from sliding off during rainstorms, maintenance of the mounds was a constant concern.

In residential areas, the people built, repaired, and rebuilt ever larger and more architecturally diverse huts on the same lots. Families appeared to have claims on certain choice locations. These households continued to build with wall trenches, but they eventually included an indoor hearth to keep the hut warm in winter. In interior bell-shaped storage pits, they placed food, tools, and personal items. Each household complex had exterior hearths and fire pits as well. A post among the household dwellings advertised the social status of the household to the rest of the community. On the outer corner of the household complex was a small structure that may have been the women's hut where they isolated themselves during menstruation and childbirth. Overall, the houses got bigger over time—houses were 10 square meters when Cahokia was but a village, but they grew to 15 square meters in the Middle Mississippian period and as large as 20 to 40 square meters at Cahokia's height. Community sweatlodges could be as big as 100 meters square. Elites built their houses on the best lands, but as Jon Muller explained, "it seems just as much the case that the best lands *produced* the elites!"[4] Some households had sweatlodges within their household structures, and these could have been used to entertain guests and strengthen kinship ties.

Politically, Cahokia developed into a type of government known as a chiefdom, in which elites had the power to manipulate the production and exchange of surplus goods. The elites also oversaw the construction of mounds to reinforce their special kinship lineage. The people of Cahokia believed that their chiefs and his ancestors were mediators between this world and that of the cosmos. People submitted to the authority of the chief for religious reasons.

At Mound 72, archeologists have found the burial site of an elite male from a distinguished family of Cahokia. His body was placed on a platform of 20,000 shell beads that were laid out in the shape of a falcon. They also buried nearby the bodies of four females between the ages of 20 and 30 who had been sacrificed to accompany the male to the otherworld. Valuable exotic items such as a sheet of copper, bushels of mica, and hundreds of finely made arrowheads that point in one direction were included in the burial to make it known to all in the community that this individual was special. Four headless and handless bodies of men were also added to the burial. Later, the bodies of 50 women, all between the ages of 18 and 23 were placed in the mound, over time, three more mass burials of females occurred. Sixty percent of the bodies in Mound 72 were sacrificial. The women may have been tribute paid to Cahokia from distant villages it dominated. The mound and the burials symbolized to the community that this was a distinguished ancestor who gave legitimacy to the power of the elite family who resided on the platform mound.

Another way the chief and other elites kept their high status was by continually establishing and maintaining kinship ties with lesser ranking people through the exchange of valuable items. In return, people of lower rank participated in major building projects. At Cahokia, both high-ranking and low-ranking people kept a cache of valuable goods, such as pottery, hoes, and marine-shell beads that could be used if needed to improve their social standing in an exchange. Ceramics produced or inspired by Cahokia's artisans were traded as far as what today are the states of Iowa, Minnesota, Indiana, Michigan, and Mississippi. The chief did not militarily dominate any of these areas, but the exchange network provided a form of kinship ties that bound elites in a village or another chiefdom with Cahokia.

Individual farmsteads spread up and down the Mississippi and other tributaries from Cahokia for a hundred miles. These farmsteads were permanent residences of one to two buildings. Their inhabitants grew their own food and stored their surpluses in interior pits. Politically, they owed allegiance to a local chief at a mound center. Some of these small farmsteads decided to join other farmsteads to form small villages of up to fifteen households. In day-to-day activities, the people living in farmsteads were more autonomous than those Mississippians residing in or immediately around mound centers.

The emergence of agriculture was one of the most important innovations of the Mississippian period. This was especially true in Cahokia, where its people depended on maize as the principal source of their calories. Maize had several advantages over other potential crops: it had high yields and could be stored longer than oily seeds such as nuts. Agriculture techniques varied depending on the settlement. Mississippian people living in rock shelters in what today is Illinois cultivated plants in small gardens. Those in the upland areas practiced slash-and-burn agriculture in which they burned a part of the forest or prairie and planted seeds in the ashes. When the soil became infertile after a few seasons, they moved on. The people of Cahokia cleared large arable fields and planted their crops in the same fields for generation after generation. These large fields were just outside the settlement area on alluvial lands. In Cahokia itself, people worked on gardens that contained a variety of plants, including squash and gourds. Even at its height, 90 percent of the land within Cahokia did not have structures on it so there was ample space for gardening.

Although Mississippian people depended on agriculture for a significant portion of their diet, they still hunted animals for protein. Mississippians ate white-tailed deer, raccoon, fish, waterfowl, turkey, beaver, opossum, swamp rabbit and cottontail rabbit, snapping turtles, dog, fox and gray squirrel, black bear, and elk. Generally, Mississippians were healthier than peoples of earlier times. But infant mortality was higher in Mississippian societies than in the Archaic era because the people of Cahokia weaned their babies with corn mush that was not very nutritious. Nonetheless, Mississippian adults did live longer than Archaic peoples, and they were also less likely to fracture their bones during their lifetimes than those of earlier eras. Interestingly, Mississippian elites were only slightly healthier than those who ranked below them. This indicates that in terms of work and food, the daily lives of people of higher and lower rank were very similar.

One of the important sources of raw materials for tool-making in Mississippian communities was in southern Illinois, near the confluence of the Mississippi and Ohio Rivers, not far from Cahokia. Several families established a village at Mill Creek to quarry for chert, the favored stone used to make hoes. A mound center southwest of the site housed artisans who manufactured the hoes, and smaller mining sites and manufacturing workshops dotted the surrounding area. Native Americans traded the finished hoes with other mound centers, including Cahokia. Women were the principal users of the hoes in agriculture and may have been involved in the trade. At Cahokia, an artisan carved a figurine depicting a woman using such a hoe with her right hand. Hoes were useful as tools for digging trenches for dwellings, mounds, moats, and embankments. Mill Creek chert is also used for common tools such as chisels, adzes, picks, and ceremonial items like celts, maces, stone swords, and fine knives. Mill Creek chert was popular because it was speckled and came in a variety of colors. When mined, the chert nodules were large and could be made into tools of various sizes. It often came in preformed shapes that lent themselves to tool formation. The chert's edge was very resilient to heavy usage, and when it did break, it chipped into small, sharp reusable pieces. Whereas most of the exchange items in Mississippian times were ceremonial items, like copper and marine shells, hoes served a very utilitarian and vital purpose for a society based on agriculture. Not surprisingly, Mill Creek hoes were traded widely as far as Michigan, Wisconsin, Missouri, Tennessee, Kentucky, Iowa, Arkansas, and Mississippi.

The Native Americans of Cahokia considered the ceremonial center of their settlement sacred. The four plazas that surrounded Monk's Mound were laid out in the four cardinal directions—north, south, east, and west—to symbolize a four-cornered world. During the summer and winter solstice when the sun reached its most northern and southern point in the sky, a series of wooden posts in Cahokia and some of its mounds aligned with the rising sun on that particular day. Mississippian people believed in a dual world: the upper and the lower. The chief was the mediator between the two, and his family controlled the temples where sacred fires were constantly kept going. He also oversaw the production of fertility cult figurines that were exchanged with other mound centers and villages. Keeping the two worlds apart was very important in the lives of Mississippian people, for there would be chaos if the two ever crossed. The chief and other elites lived on mounds closer to the world above in contrast to the common people who lived at ground level on the flat terrain of the American Bottom. The iconography that appeared on artifacts reflected these dual worlds. The sun's rays or birds of prey represented the upper world, and snakes, frogs, and fish corresponded to the lower world. Mississippian people believed that beavers, owls, and cougars inhabited both worlds.

This dualism was found within the burial site at Mound 72. The people of Cahokia had placed the body of an elite person on the platform of beads in the shape of a falcon, the symbol of the upper world, with his face upward toward the sky. Right beneath him was another body who was facing downward. The four headless and handless male bodies buried near him may represent the cardinal directions. It is unclear whether Mississippians practiced the Green Corn Ceremony, a harvest festival originating in Mexico that involved fire and the sacrifice of four victims. The four headless bodies may be such sacrifices, but if the ceremony was done every year, there should be hundreds of such sacrifices, but only one group of four has been found. Nevertheless, Mississippians practiced some form of communal fertility cult tied to their agricultural practices.

Other major Mississippian chiefdom centers appeared in Spiro on the Arkansas River, in Moundsville in Alabama, and Etowah in Georgia. Each developed independently of Cahokia out of the local Woodland tradition, and only a few items of pottery from Cahokia reached them. In fact,

Cahokia never had political dominance over any of the other chiefdoms nor of villages and farmsteads outside the northern and central areas of the American Bottom.

Cahokia had more frequent exchanges of goods with Mississippian villages to its north. One such trading relationship was established with Native American people of the Red Wing area near today's St. Paul, Minnesota. The Red Wing area was an alluvial bottomland of several miles where the Chippewa River met with the Mississippi River. The alluvial land was ideal for the growing of maize. Since the Woodland period, the Effigy Mound peoples had settled in the region. As traders, hunters, and migrant families moved from the South into the area, exchanges of goods became more frequent with Cahokia. The Effigy people had grown maize as early as 400 C.E., but they became more dependent on it as a principal source of their calories over time. Their pottery showed a mixture of Woodland and Cahokian styles. But they never developed a ceremonial center on the model of Cahokia—there were no mounds on either side of a plaza. Rather, they built their mounds in a semicircle outside their villages. They lived in a fairly egalitarian village society with no rigid social hierarchy. Although they had no political connection to Cahokia, the Mississippian culture of the Red Wing region went into a decline at the same time Cahokia did. The climate got colder season after season and did not allow the full 140 days of warm temperatures necessary to produce a good harvest of maize. War between neighboring villages also disrupted life. Eventually, the Oneota peoples moved into the area and absorbed the local population.

By 1200 C.E., Cahokia's influence began to fade as its population decreased by roughly 40 percent. Households in Cahokia moved to the highest levels at the site, and there was no effort to erect new mounds or fix the existing ones. The dead were now buried in small stone boxes in cemeteries. The reasons for this decline are still unclear, but the population may have overexploited the wood resources of the area. Increased water runoff most likely caused sediment to block the waterways that connected Cahokia with the Mississippi River. The people of Cahokia may have cut down all the trees in a 10 to 15 kilometer radius of the town for fuel and construction. Flooding was always a problem, but now it only worsened and made agriculture in the area less productive. The region also suffered through a series of droughts between 1090 and 1100 C.E. Perhaps the lower-ranking chiefs of the settlements around Cahokia asserted their independence when the chief at Cahokia was weak because there is evidence of warfare in Illinois at this time. Several bodies have been found that were scalped. About 1300 C.E., a band of Oneota settled temporarily near Cahokia. By then, the population of Cahokia had decreased by another 35 percent. A hundred years later, Mississippian people abandoned the Cahokia site altogether. For another century, a few people clung to farmsteads in the American Bottom.

As Mississippian culture declined, the diet of people in the American Bottom actually changed for the better. The common bean became a staple of the diet of Native Americans after 1250 C.E. The bean provided people with a good source of quality protein, and in combination with maize gave people a better balance of amino acids. The bean may have allowed individual households to be more productive, and thus weaken their reliance on elites. Mississippian peoples still gathered food. The nuts they used included hickory, acorns, pecan, and less frequently walnut. Besides gourds, squash, maize, and beans, the people of the region also domesticated amaranths, marsh elder, knotweed, and chenopods, maygrass, and a little barley. They continued to gather hawthorn, blackberries, persimmon, and grapes.

Although the Mississippian world was waning, in the Upper and Central Mississippi Valley, Oneota culture was coming into its ascendancy. The Oneota people spread to Iowa, Wisconsin, Minnesota, Missouri, Kansas, and Nebraska. They lived in villages that occupied 10 to 20 acres with about 50 huts randomly placed within each settlement. There were no plazas. Wall trenches were no longer used in house construction. Instead, the huts had a wooden pole frame, and bark was tied to it to make the walls. Oneota people cultivated maize, but they did not have large fields. Whereas Mississippian people had cleared large trees by cutting them down, the Oneota people killed large trees by cutting a deep grove in the bark and then left them standing to fall down naturally. Oneota people used bone scapulas of buffalo as hoes instead of mining for chert. The women continued to gather nuts, fruits, and fresh water mussels, but the exterior storage bins were often reused as trash bins. During the summer, the Oneota people nearly abandoned their villages, as most of the men and women traveled across the prairies to hunt for bison. They buried their dead in cemeteries on ridges or mounds that were constructed during the earlier Woodland or Mississippian eras, but only a few individuals were buried with ornamental goods and tools made from copper, stone, and bone. Oneota pottery was shell-tempered, soft and easily broken, with a smooth surface that had geometric decorations etched into it. However, Oneota bone and stone tools and pipe ornaments were well made and showed a high level of craftsmanship.

CONCLUSION

For nearly ten thousand years before European contact, native peoples had hunted and settled along the Mississippi River. Although the Paleolithic people left few signs of their passing, they were the first human beings to take advantage of the rich fauna and flora along the river. Archaic peoples began to cultivate crops and create more permanent settlements. Poverty Point represented the apex of Archaic ceremonial and religious life with its mounds and concentric ridges. The impact of the Adena and

Hopewell cultures changed the religious culture of the people of the Mississippi Valley. Burial mounds became a common sight near every village, and the exchange of goods to develop kinship relations with neighbors flourished. Settled life reached another plateau with the emergence of Cahokia and other chiefdoms. Cahokia developed a social hierarchy and a sophisticated sacred landscape that supported a population of over ten thousand people. Mississippian culture spread through much of the southeastern North America. Cahokia's overexploitation of the natural resources of the Mississippi River Valley shows how fragile the relationship between human beings and the environment can be. Native American culture survived with the spread of Oneota culture, which effectively used the technologies of the past to mold a new world of village life. And then in 1541, the Spanish explorer Hernando De Soto and a small army of Europeans entered the Mississippi Valley. The world of Native Americans was about to change forever.

NOTES

1. Elizabeth S. Chilton, "Beyond 'Big': Gender, Age, and Subsistence Diversity in Paleoindian Societies," in *The Settlement of the American Continents: A Multidisciplinary Approach to Human Biogeography,* ed. C. Michael Barton, Geoffrey A. Clark, David R. Yesner, and Georges A. Pearson (Tuscon: University of Arizona Press, 2004), 172.

2. Lynda Norene Shaffer, *Native Americans Before 1492: The Moundbuilding Centers of the Eastern Woodlands* (Armonk, N.Y.: M. E. Sharpe, 1992), 24.

3. Edwin Alan Toth, *Early Marksville Phases in the Lower Mississippi Valley: A Study of Culture Contact Dynamics,* Archeological Report No. 21 (Jackson: Mississippi Department of Archives and History, 1988), 48, 53.

4. Jon Muller, *Mississippian Political Economy* (New York: Plenum Press, 1997), 192.

2

Native Americans, 1541–1881

The intrusion of Hernando De Soto and his army into the Central Mississippi Valley in 1541 brought a tide of change that dramatically altered the daily lives of Native Americans along the river. The natives encountered new technologies, new animals, and new diseases, and whether by choice or circumstances, natives adapted to the new realities in their interaction with Europeans. Their connection to the Atlantic market economy brought items that made some aspects of their lives easier, such as guns, copper kettles, metal knives, and axes. Yet, there were terrible costs. Alliances with the European powers generated tension within tribal societies between those who wanted to preserve the world that once was and those who embraced change. Tribes warred against each other to win the favor of a European power and access to new markets. Throughout the entire period of contact, diseases ravaged the native populations. Still, some native tribes managed to prosper even as others became extinct. With the victory of the United States in the War for Independence and the Louisiana Purchase in 1803, the geopolitical map changed fundamentally along the river. Native Americans faced a new peril to their existence from an aggressive United States and its land-hungry citizens. Within a century, nearly all Native Americans along the Mississippi had lost their land and only a few managed to hold on along the margins of American society.

Discovering the daily life of Native Americans at the moment of contact with European culture is problematic. The fog of time, the biases and inaccuracies of the Spanish explorers who reported on the natives, and the limits of archaeology warp our knowledge of this period. The 132 years between this first contact and subsequent European exploration is known as the protohistoric period. Almost nothing is known about the seemingly cataclysmic changes that swept the Native American world in the Mississippi Valley, following that first contact with Europeans. Not until the French period in the eighteenth century do the natives once again appear in the written record. Through eyewitness accounts, historians have been able to get a detailed, if also still skewed, picture of natives' lives. This chapter focuses on four tribes—the Tunicas, Quapaw, Natchez, and the Eastern Dakota—to suggest, by way of representative examples, the basic patterns of Native-American life along the Mississippi River. By the nineteenth century, the pressure of American migration into the region coupled with a U.S. policy that sought the removal of the natives raised havoc within these communities. Their daily lives resembled the ways of their forbearers less and less. Still, some members of tribes prospered as they adopted American agricultural practices and participated in the burgeoning market economy, but the majority became increasingly dependent on American products and government subsidies for their very survival. Eventually, they lost their ancestral lands and their freedom.

ORIGINS OF THE TUNICA

In what today is northwestern Mississippi, the ancestors of the Tunicas lived in Quizquiz, a chiefdom of several villages that paid tribute to the larger chiefdom of Pacaha from across the Mississippi River. The main village of the Tunica was organized around a central plaza and four mounds. One mound held a temple with a sacred fire that was never allowed to be extinguished. The dead were buried in nearby cemeteries. Unlike most tribes in the southeast where women worked in agriculture, the men of Quizquiz were the principal farmers, growing large surpluses of grain. Women gathered persimmons, pecans, and other fruits and nuts from the surrounding alluvial lands. The men supplemented their family's diet with fish and meat, especially deer, from the hunt. In case of war, the chief could call upon a fleet of 200 canoes, each carrying 80 men armed with bows and arrows and shields.

In the spring of 1541, De Soto and his army spent two months in the Central Mississippi Valley in search of wealthy native kingdoms to plunder. They raided Quizquiz and took its elderly men, women, and children hostage when the other adult men were working in the fields. De Soto freed his hostages as a gesture of good will, but the hostile act created tensions. Since the Quizquiz chief refused to submit to Spanish authority, De Soto was forced to withdraw to the chiefdom of Casqui across the Mississippi. There, the Spanish helped the Casqui attack and sack Pacaha, whose population had fled the town before the onslaught. Then, De Soto moved westward to continue his search for riches.

What occurred in the next 141 years is uncertain. When the French arrived in the area in 1673, the chiefdoms of what is today northwestern Arkansas and northeastern Mississippi were gone. Only the villages of the Quapaw at the mouth of the Arkansas River and the Tunica on the upper Yazoo River remained. Mound building stopped in northeast Arkansas, and burial sites no longer contained copper and shell ornamentation. De Soto's army very likely had cut into the food surplus of the natives. Such an act would have destabilized the political structures of the chiefdoms of the region whose leaders had been responsible for distributing surpluses of grain to the population in return for loyalty. Archaeologists are uncertain how much of a role disease played in the disruption. Smallpox spread among European children, but De Soto's expedition consisted of adults, none of whom were recorded to have smallpox nor any contact with European children for at least two years. Therefore, a smallpox epidemic was most unlikely at this time, and probably did not create catastrophic losses in the Native American population until the 1600s when more permanent European settlements appeared on the Atlantic coast. Other diseases, such as measles and typhus, may have spread to the locals from the De Soto expedition. Moreover, the natives adopted horses almost immediately after European contact, which may have exposed them to the diseases these animals carried. Or did the population simply migrate out of the region, as the Tunica had done when they moved from Quizquiz to the lower Yazoo River? We just don't know. Whereas the population of northeast Arkansas may have numbered in the tens of thousands or perhaps as many as 50,000 before the encounter with De Soto, when the French arrived a century later, there were only 2,500 to 4,000 Quapaw in the region, and there is evidence that they were recent migrants. Whatever the case, the Native American world that had existed in the Central Mississippi River Valley was no more by the late 1600s.

From 1673 to 1803, Native Americans along the Mississippi River became intrinsically linked to the European world. They were powerful enough, and the European powers, especially France and Spain, were sufficiently weak enough to forge a so-called middle ground where both cultures interacted with each other on a relatively equal footing. But this so-called middle ground could be dangerous for the Native Americans, as the Natchez learned when they were nearly exterminated by the French. And the situation was fragile—for as long as the Native Americans could play one European power against another, many tribes managed to remain autonomous. Still, during this entire period, Native Americans became increasingly dependent on European technologies, which they could not reproduce themselves. In these turbulent times, the daily life of four tribes irrevocably changed.

THE TUNICA

In 1699 the French encountered a Tunica world that still resembled that of the ancient Mississippians. The Tunica were one of the last native societies to continue to build mounds. Theirs were up to 10 meters high around a ceremonial plaza. On one of the mounds, they constructed a temple that contained a sacred fire and effigies of a woman and frog, which represented the sun and the earth. The Tunica worshipped nine deities: the sun; thunder; fire; the cardinal directions of east, west, north, and south; earth; and the heavens. Generally, they treated Christian missionaries with respect even when the missionaries entered the Tunica sacred temples to smash the statues of what by Christian standards were considered idols. Despite the pressure to convert to Christianity, the Tunica maintained their religious traditions into the nineteenth century.

The Tunica numbered about a thousand people. They were three separate villages, each made of round huts built from a frame of wooden poles interlaced with cane and plastered clay walls. There were no windows on the huts so the door provided the only source of ventilation. The women cooked outdoors in a hearth. Each family maintained a granary outside their hut. During the summer, men wore only a loin cloth and women wore a woven skirt, while their children remained naked until puberty. Both sexes wore their hair long. For cosmetic purposes, women displayed tattoos on their bodies, blackened their teeth, and wore earrings and other ornaments. On colder days, both sexes wore clothes made from animal skins or mulberry bark. They lived under the authority of a civil chief and a war chief. Warriors achieved status through their bravery in battle, which was recorded on their bodies with tattoos. Some men had more than one wife, and couples could easily end their marriages in divorce. The Tunica excelled at pottery, which they tempered with crushed live mussel shell. We know very little about their stone tools because the Tunica quickly adopted European metal tools and guns as early as 1700, only one year after they first came into contact with the French.

The Frenchman Jean-Bernard Bossu described the Tunica as "an Indian tribe which has always been very friendly to the French" and whose leaders "have always eagerly joined us in war."[1] The Tunica believed that the economic prosperity of their tribe depended on a close alliance with the French against the English. As Chief Perruquier told a French official in 1764, "the British have always corrupted the ways among all the tribes. They have given them liquor to drink which has killed them."[2] The Tunica had been active traders of salt before the Europeans came, and not surprisingly, they found a niche in the developing colonial market economy by supplying the French with food staples.

In 1706 military pressure from the English and the Chickasaw forced the Tunica to move to an abandoned Houma village near the mouth of the Red River on the east bank of the Mississippi at Portage de la Croix in order to be closer to the French. The location allowed them to continue to trade on the Mississippi River and gave them easy access to the Red River valley. Again, the Tunica built three villages, with the largest containing a square plaza with mounds upon which the temple and the house of the chief stood. Some of their huts were round while the ones that had been once used by the Houma were square. In 1721 Chief Cahura-Joligo dressed in the French fashion, practiced Catholicism, and encouraged his tribe to trade salt, horses, poultry, and maize with the French. Unlike other tribes in the region, the Tunica ignored the deerskin trade. The friendliness of the Tunica encouraged 48 French people in 1726 to settle near their villages. Although the Tunica could only provide 120 warriors by then, the French still relied on them as allies in their struggles with the English and the Chickasaw, and other hostile Indians. Although French missionaries had baptized dozens of Tunica children, Tunica religious customs remained strong.

During the Natchez War of 1729, the French attacked and destroyed Natchez villages in retaliation for the deaths of hundreds of its citizens after the Natchez had decided to drive Europeans from their land. The Tunica welcomed 150 Natchez refugees, who were fed and allowed to settle near the main Tunica village. After celebrations that first night, the Natchez attacked the Tunica, who had sided against them in past disputes, killing Chief Cahura-Joligo and dozens of others. Another war chief rallied the Tunica warriors and drove the Natchez out five days later, but their village had been torched, their food and ammunition stolen, and one-fifth of their population killed. Instead of rebuilding, the Tunica moved to the eastern side of the Mississippi near Tunica Bayou where they built only one village, which was known as Trudeau. Their population had decreased from 375 before the Natchez attack to only 150 people in 1737. Their village was still arranged around a central plaza, but they used a natural bluff to serve the function of a mound. Because Chief Cahura-Joligo had banned the eternal fire, a temple was no longer necessary.

Amazingly, the Tunica continued to prosper economically. Excavations in 1972, 1980, and 1981 at Trudeau reveal how thoroughly the Tunica had left the material world of their Stone Age ancestors. Metal tools of every type were in use, from the latest guns to nails and axes. While Tunica women and men still wore traditional shell ornamentations and used ochre to color their faces, they also cherished glass beads, metal balls, and medals. They cut damaged brass and copper kettles into strips and made ornaments out of them. In their daily dress, they mixed traditional and European fashions. Some Tunica used the heavier and more durable iron kettles that were being traded up and down the Mississippi River. Although native pottery continued to thrive, wooden chests and glass and ceramic containers were being used. The Tunica also enjoyed a varied and high protein diet that included deer, bear, bison, and domesticated chickens. They still supplemented corn with wild fruits and nuts. Unfortunately, many Tunica were acquiring a taste for European alcohol. The scarcity of Christian symbols in burials of this period show how marginal Christianity remained even though 27 children were baptized in 1740.

When the English acquired Louisiana, the Tunica fired upon an expedition of English troops in 1764. Consequently, they were forced to flee to Mobile, Alabama. The French officer in charge of the transition from French to British sovereignty allowed them to settle back on the Mississippi River, and eventually they established a village near Point Coupée on its east bank. Unfortunately for archeologists, the site has been destroyed by the Mississippi River. From historical accounts, we know that the traditional village pattern of the past was totally abandoned for two rows of 30 huts along the river. The Tunica numbered about 80 people in 1764 and only 60 people in 1783. They supplied meat to European colonists from the animals they hunted. Luckily, the English and the Spanish gave the Tunica presents to try to win their loyalty, which allowed the Tunica to remain economically prosperous. At the same time, the Europeanization of Tunica material life continued.

By the early 1790s, the Tunica had left the banks of the Mississippi River and established a village at Avoyelles, what is today Marksville, Louisiana, along the Red River. To survive, the tribe united or intermarried with other Indians as well as whites and blacks. Cultural assimilation continued to such a point that tribal recognition was taken away by the U.S. government in 1938. In 1981 the U.S. government recognized the Tunica-Biloxi tribe. Although their language is no longer spoken and they live in houses that resemble the homes of other rural Louisianans, as of 2006, the Tunica remain a vibrant community with 1,018 members.

THE QUAPAWS

In the 1600s, Dhegihan people had fled the Ohio River Valley because of Iroquois attacks and moved into the Mississippi River Valley where they split into two groups. The so-called upstream people moved north and then northwest along the Missouri River, eventually becoming known as the Omaha tribe. Another group migrated south and became known as the downstream people or Quapaw. The French had first encountered the Illini peoples, who referred to Quapaw as the Arkansas. When the French explorers Jacques Marquette and Louis Joliet reached the Mississippi River in 1673, they came into contact with the Quapaw, who were living on both banks of the Mississippi near the mouth of the Arkansas River.

The Quapaws greeted visitors with the calumet, a peace pipe often made out of a reed. By participating in a calumet ceremony, strangers became fictive relatives who were now bonded with the Quapaw in reciprocal obligations. The Quapaw carried their guests on their shoulders to the center of their town and placed them on a roofed platform, where the people of the village would feast and dance to music played with rattles, drums, bells, and reed flutes. For the Quapaw, every relationship was imbued with sacred meaning and the special bonds of kinship. A Quapaw traced his or her clan descent down the father's line. Each of the 21 clans possessed a guardian spirit, often a wild animal. The 21 clans were divided into two groups, each possessing different ceremonial functions: the Sky People performed rituals that assisted in maintaining relations with the spirit world, while the Earth People were in charge of rituals that insured the material prosperity of the community. Sky People could only marry members of the Earth People, and vice-versa.

The Quapaw lived in villages that were surrounded by cultivated fields. One of the villages may have had a palisade around it. Around a central plaza, they built long rectangular loghouses that were large enough for several families. The frames of the buildings were made of two rows of poles that had been driven into the ground and bent to be tied at a center point to bent poles from the opposite row. Pieces of bark covered the outer walls. Within the houses, family members would sit and sleep on raised wooden platforms around a hearth in the middle of the room. The chief had two structures: an open-sided building where the Quapaw council met and guests were entertained in warm weather and a loghouse not much different than that of the other members of the tribe.

André Pénicaut described Quapaw women as "[q]uite pretty and white-complexioned" who did "the work here [in the village] rather than the men."[3] In the summer, the women wore only deerskin skirts. Married women wore their hair loose, while unmarried women tied their hair into two braids that were rolled up behind their ears and decorated with ornaments. Although the animals that the men hunted were an important part of their diet, Quapaw women grew maize, beans, squash, gourds, melons, sunflowers, peaches, and grapes that provided the mainstay of the tribe's caloric intake. The women also gathered wild fruits, nuts, and roots, butchered animals, and prepared their hides for domestic use or to trade with the Europeans. They were responsible for managing the household, including cooking and taking care of the children. French visitors found the meals that the Quapaw women made to be delicious and creative. Women also wove baskets and mats, and made pottery. In other words, Quapaw women managed as well as produced nearly every aspect of the household economy. Intermarriages between Quapaw women and French traders were encouraged to foster kinship relationships, but sexual relations outside of marriage were discouraged.

Jean-Bernard Bossu observed that Quapaw men were "tall, well-built, brave Indians" who were "good swimmers and skillful hunters and fishermen."[4] Pénicaut described them as "very warlike, and they are great hunters," with most of them being "heavy and thickset."[5] Quapaw men wore buckskin loincloths, leggings, moccasins, shirts, and buffalo robes during the winter. They also decorated themselves with tattoos and strings of beads in their ears and noses. During ceremonies, the men painted their bodies red and black and wore headdresses decorated with feathers, buffalo horns, animal furs, or wooden masks. Although agriculture was within the women's sphere of daily duties, the men would assist in clearing land. As in all Native American societies along the Mississippi River, men held all the political power within the tribe. A council governed the Quapaw. The chief's authority rested on his ability to convince others in the council that his opinions were in the best interest of the tribe. He was in charge of ceremonial functions. The French tried to manipulate the chief by lavishing him with gifts of medals and gorgets.

The Quapaw believed in a life force, the *Wah-kon-tah,* which existed in every material object in the world. Before the sunrise on the day of a corn harvest ceremony, the tribe separated into three groups. As archaeologist Samuel D. Dickinson has explained, when light appeared over the horizon, "the warriors lifted up their weapons, the young men and women offered ears of corn and branches and women with babies" would show their children to the sun. Afterwards, the tribe prayed for "protection against their enemies, for sufficient food, and for an increase in population."[6] Holy men within the Quapaw village performed religious rites. Christian missionary activities were generally a failure until the nineteenth century.

Historian Morris S. Arnold described Quapaw warfare as a "potentially endless chain of reciprocated homicides, each of which was regarded as a just and required retaliation for ones that had preceded it."[7] Disputes with neighboring tribes usually involved control over hunting territories. The preparations for war began with a feast in which the main dish was dog, which the warriors considered brave. After the feast, the chief called a war council and explained the wrong committed against his people and what needed to be done about it. The warriors who wanted to participate in the raid would take a twig from a bundle held by the chief to symbolize their enlistment. After painting a war club red, one of the Quapaw warriors would slip into enemy territory and paint in red two crossed arrows to let the enemy know that the Quapaw would seek revenge. Then, the warriors participated in a war dance in which they were painted in red. Traveling light with only a few days' rations, the warriors left for battle. If they were successful, they brought back scalps of the enemy or prisoners. Quapaw women who had lost a husband or son could adopt one of the prisoners and make them a full member of the tribe. Otherwise, the prisoners were tortured and burned alive.

Before they had ever seen Europeans, the Quapaw had acquired European-made knives, hatchets, and beads by trading with other tribes, probably the Illini. Throughout their history, the Quapaw were eager to establish trade relationships with the Europeans, and at the same time, they tried to stymie any trade between the Europeans and their enemies further up the Arkansas River. Although friendly, the Quapaw were known as great warriors and hunters and were very interested in acquiring guns to defend themselves against the aggressive Chickasaw, who had already been armed by the English. By 1687, when the French visited Quapaw villages, the natives already possessed large quantities of guns and horses. With Quapaw permission, the French established a trading fort that they called the Arkansas Post. Items which the French kept on hand to trade with Quapaw included guns and related accessories such as powder and flint. Salt, flour, biscuits, and, illegally, rum and brandy were in demand. The Quapaw were also interested in lead, blankets, trade shirts, woolen cloth, breechcloths, and wool ribbons to supplement the animal skins that they wore. The Arkansas Post also kept tools such as metal awls, knives, and nails in stock. The French supplied white and blue paint that was used by the Quapaw in their ceremonies. In return for these European goods, the Quapaw supplied the French with meat and tallow from the buffalo they hunted in Arkansas. They also processed bear oil, which was used in cooking. Unlike the tribes of the upper Mississippi, the Quapaw did not trade much in deer and small mammal skins.

One of the main reasons why the Quapaw maintained their alliance with the Europeans was because they expected to receive annual presents of European goods. In 1769 the French spent four times more on the presents for the Quapaw than on any other tribe in Louisiana. During the short Spanish administration of Louisiana, the Spanish officials sent the Quapaw guns and gun-related accessories, knives, axes, kettles, and hoes. They also gave them gifts of clothing such as hats, handkerchiefs, coats, shirts, dresses, loincloths, and blankets. Everyday tools and accessories included scissors, awls, needles and thread for sewing, strike-a-lights, kettles, and pots. They also enjoyed luxury items such as mirrors, brass wire, tobacco, and brandy.

A look at the above products shows how deeply European goods had penetrated into the daily lives of the Quapaw. Before the Europeans came, the Quapaw had been a self-sufficient people who traded for chert and other raw materials, but made most of their tools in their own villages with their own hands for their own uses. The European goods could not be reproduced at home, so the material gains were offset by the loss of skill. Still, the Quapaw, like other natives, were rational people who realized that European items made life easier. Guns could kill prey and enemies at longer ranges. Steel hoes allowed a Quapaw woman to cultivate even the hardest soil. Copper pots and kettles were less fragile than clay pots and gave women the ability to cook directly over fires for extended periods. European clothes were lighter, thinner, and cooler than animal skins. Each generation of natives became more dependent on these goods as wants became needs. Unfortunately, when the buffalo were wiped out of Arkansas by the late eighteenth century and bears became less numerous, and the number of warriors that the Quapaw could field decreased, they had little to bargain with for these goods except their land. The U.S. government was not interested in continuing to give annual presents unless these annuities were tied to land cessions. This spelled doom for the tribe.

After European contact, the Quapaw suffered severe losses in population. Epidemics of smallpox and other diseases hit the Quapaw in 1690, 1699, 1721, 1748, 1752, 1777, and 1781. Whereas in 1699 the Quapaw numbered between three to ten thousand people, in 1806 their population was down to about nine hundred individuals. In 1818 and 1824, the U.S. government successfully pressured the Quapaw to cede their lands, and in 1839 the Federal Government established a Quapaw Reservation in the Indian Territory known today as Oklahoma. About five hundred Quapaw migrated there, and many of their descendents live there today.

THE NATCHEZ

Between 1000 and 1500 C.E., the Natchez moved to the region along the Mississippi River that today bears their name and set up one of the most sophisticated chiefdoms in the historic era. M. Le Page du Pratz said that the Natchez's "manners were more civilized, their manner of thinking more just and fuller of sentiment, their customs more reasonable, and their ceremonies more natural and serious; on all which accounts they were eminently distinguished above the other nations."[8] André Pénicaut believed that "of all the savages they are the most civilized nation."[9] The Europeans found a hierarchical society much like their own with a chief who had absolute power and a strict caste system that determined social relations. In 1700 the Natchez were a power in the Mississippi Valley. They numbered over 4,000 individuals and could amass an army of over 1,000 warriors. The Natchez had several subservient or allied tribes living near them that they could incorporate into their society to keep their population stable. The Natchez lived in five villages, but the most impressive was the Grand Village with its three mounds, palisade, and temple.

Natchez society was divided into four groupings: Suns, Nobles, Distinguished, and Commoners. The Suns held all the leadership positions in the society. The Natchez believed that the Grand Sun Chief was descended from the Sun deity, who had come down to earth and given their people a moral code and commanded them to obey his children, the Suns. Unlike any other tribe in the Mississippi Valley, the Grand Sun Chief of the Natchez ruled absolutely and possessed the highest respect from the rest of the tribe. Since the Natchez traced their lineage from the mother's family, the next Grand Sun chief would not be his son, but his sister's son. Each of the other Natchez villages had a subordinate Sun Chief. The families of the Suns lived in huts that were slightly elevated from those of the rest of Natchez society. A unique feature of their society involved marriage. Each member of the Suns had to marry a Commoner. When a Sun mother married a Commoner, their offspring would be a Sun. When a Sun male married a Commoner, their children would be Nobles. Noble females marrying a Commoner would produce Nobles, but a Noble male fathering a child with a Commoner would produce a Distinguished. In other words, a child would inherit the status of their higher ranking mother, but if their father was of higher rank than their mother, the children would be one class lower than the status of their father. The population of Commoners was replenished by admitting refugees and weaker tribes of the area into Natchez society.

The most sacred ceremony of the Natchez and the one that spurred both the curiosity and horror of Europeans was the funeral practices for the Grand Sun Chief and his sister. When the Grand Sun chief's sister died, her oldest son would strangle her husband. He would then select a dozen Commoner infants, who would be strangled by their parents and placed around the body of the sister of the Grand Sun Chief in her house. Her son could pick out as many other people as he desired to join his mother to the afterlife if he believed the number of volunteers already committed to accompany her was not enough. A person who volunteered brought honor to their families, and if they were Commoners, their families would be promoted to the rank of the Distinguished. On the day of the funeral procession, the parents of the strangled children would take their bodies and join the march, followed by the volunteers and the relatives of the Sun female, whose kin had cut their hair in mourning. The dead female Sun was carried out of her house by four men, and her house was immediately burned down. The fathers of the dead children would put their children down in front of the four men carrying the dead female so that the four men would step on them. Then, the fathers would pick up their trampled children and lay them before the procession again until they reached the temple. The volunteers who would accompany the female to her grave would undress, sit on the ground, and allow one person to sit on their knees and another behind them to place a deer skin over their head. A cord, which the volunteer had made, was wrapped around their neck. The volunteers swallowed three tobacco pills with some water, which caused them to lose consciousness. The relatives of the dead female Sun would pull the cord and strangle each of the volunteers. When the task was done, all the dead would be buried together. The death of the Grand Sun Chief could mean the death of 100 of his subjects, including his nurse maid.

Other social customs of the Natchez intrigued the Europeans. They were astonished to witness the sexual freedom practiced by unmarried Natchez women. Natchez society actually encouraged these women to engage in sex and keep track of the number of their sexual encounters. Their society saw nothing wrong that these young women received gifts or money for sexual favors from Natchez men or French traders. In fact, Natchez men wanted to marry women with extensive sexual experience. However, once a woman was married, she was to remain faithful to her husband. The Natchez ritual of marriage was common to many Native American tribes: the male gave presents to the parents of the young woman he intended to marry. The great-grandfathers of both families met and made sure that the couple was no closer than third cousins. Then, both sets of parents had to approve of the marriage. Males were usually not allowed to marry before they were 25 years old because they were seen as inexperienced and physically weak.

In 1704, Pénicaut visited the Grand Village and was impressed with its material wealth:

In this village one finds every amenity conducive to association with this nation, which does not at all have the fierce manner of the other savages. All the necessities of life are here, such as buffaloes, cows, hinds, harts, roes, chickens and turkeys, and an abundance of geese. There are also fish in abundance, all kinds of them; there are carp weighing more than twenty pounds, which are of an exquisite taste. As for fruit, there is more than in any other place in Louisiana. They have many cherries, which grow in bunches like our grapes in France; they are black and have a touch of bitterness, but are excellent in brandy, in which they put many of them. In their woods everywhere are many peach trees, plum trees, mulberries, and walnuts. They have three kinds of walnut trees: there are some that bear nuts as big as one's fist; from these they make bread for their soup. But the best are scarcely bigger than one's thumb; these they call *pacanes*.[10]

By all accounts, the Natchez lived in an environment of abundance where agriculture thrived and prey was numerous. Deer was by far the most common source of protein for them with alligator gar, a large fish, coming a distant second. Unfortunately for the Natchez, the French recognized the bounty of this land and wanted to procure some of it for themselves.

Still, the Natchez were interested in developing relations with the French to satisfy a growing taste for European goods. Archeologists have found the burial site of an important Natchez individual in the mortuary mound of the Grand Village. Some of the European items in this grave include a brass dutch oven, tinned brass pan, three-legged iron pot, flintlock pistol, iron hoe, brass dressing pins, four iron buckles, three iron and one brass coil springs, an iron hatchet, white glass beads, and brass buttons. The majority of items in the burial were of European origin. Although this burial was not representative of the rest of the people interred in the mound, whoever this Natchez male was, he had found meaning and status in accumulating European goods. Moreover, his family found it important to bury him with the objects that he could use in the afterlife. In other words, European goods were making their way not only into the daily lives of the Natchez in this world, but also in the afterlife.

The Grand Village was built around three mounds. On one of the mounds stood the Temple of the Natchez, which contained a sacred fire watched over by four guards whose duty it was to make sure it never went out. The Temple had two parts: an enclosed area 40 feet wide and 37 feet long that contained the main hearth in which the eternal fire burned and a roofed opened area or portico of 28 feet wide and 30 feet long where meetings were held. On a second mound stood the house of the Grand Sun Chief, a structure that was 25 feet wide and 45 feet long, and eight other huts, which held his relatives. Pierre F. X. Charlevoix left one of the few contemporary European descriptions of the Natchez houses. Within the house of the Grand Sun Chief, he only found "a bed of planks very narrow, and raised about two or three feet from the ground; probably when the chief lies down he spreads over it a matt, or the skin of some animal."[11] Charlevoix described the huts of the rest of the Natchez as having "the form of square pavilions, very low, and without windows. Their roofs are rounded pretty much in the same manner as an oven. Most of them are covered with the leaves and straw of maize. Some of them are built of a sort of mud, which seemed tolerably good, and is covered outside and inside with very thin mats."[12] He adds that the buildings "have no vent for the smoke, notwithstanding those into which I entered were tolerably white."[13]

Hostility between the Natchez and the French had surfaced on two occasions when the Natchez believed that the French had insulted them. Like most Native American tribes, the Natchez feuded among themselves over how to deal with the European intrusion onto their lands. In 1729 a French official with ambitions to create plantations on the rich agricultural soil around the Natchez ordered the people of one of the Natchez villages to move out. In a war council, the Natchez decided to launch a surprise attack on the French at Fort Rosalie, which had been built near the Grand Village. Secretly, they called on other native tribes to join them. One of the elders made a speech whose substance must have been repeated by Native American councils up and down the Mississippi River for decades to come:

> We have noticed for a long time that having the French as neighbors has done us more harm than good. We old men see it, but the young men do not. The supplies from Europe please them, but of what use are they? To seduce our women, to corrupt our nation, to lead our daughters astray, to make them proud and lazy. Our boys are the same. Young married men must work themselves to death to keep their wives in luxury. Before the French came into out lands, we were men, we were happy with what we had, we walked boldly upon all our paths, because then we were our own masters. But today we thread gropingly, fearing thorns. We walk like slaves which we will soon be, since they already treat us as though we were. When they are strong enough, they will no longer treat us with consideration. They will put us in chains. Has not their chief already threatened us with this affront? Is not death preferable to slavery?[14]

On the first day of the Natchez attack, 237 French were killed including 36 women and 56 children. About 300 slaves and 50 women and children were taken hostage. Unfortunately for the Natchez, other tribes did not join them against the French. The subsequent French response wiped out the Natchez as a tribe. The Natchez villages were burned down after a siege, and about five hundred Natchez men, women, and children were shipped to the Caribbean as slaves. Hundreds of others fled to neighboring tribes, such as the Creek and Chickasaw. Sporadic Natchez raids on

French settlements continued for at least another decade. Eventually, those Natchez who joined the Chickasaw or the Creek were moved with the rest of the tribes to Oklahoma. But the Natchez as a people with a unique world of their own were no more.

THE DAKOTA

About 800, C.E. ancestors of the Dakota arrived in central Minnesota and eventually became part of the Oneota culture that was flourishing around them. The Dakota spoke a language that was a member of the Siouan family. Around 1300 C.E., the Dakota organized into the loose federation called the People of the Seven Council Fires, which included the Mdewakanton, Wahpekute, Wahpeton, Sisseton, Yankton, Yanktonai, and Teton. They centralized the location of their permanent villages, built wooden palisades to protect themselves from attack, and placed a mound in a ceremonial center. After driving out other tribes from their territory, the Dakota staunchly defended their lands from any intruders. They and their neighbors maintained a buffer zone to the north where neither was allowed to settle. Unfortunately, warfare continued and eventually dissolved the Seven Council Fires. As a consequence, the Dakota became more mobile. Men and women had to adjust to a life of seasonal migration. The Yankton, Yanktonai, and Teton migrated westward and lost close contact with the other Dakota tribes that moved southward. At the same time, Siouan speakers such as the Iowa and Oto migrated into the Great Plains and competed with the Dakota. In the 1640s, when the Iroquois launched attacks on the tribes of the Great Lakes Region, tens of thousands of people fled before the onslaught. The Sauk, Mesquakie, Potowatomi, and Ottawa pushed into what is today Wisconsin. The Illinois and Cree migrated to Illinois. Over the next century, the Eastern Dakota successfully defended themselves against each of these invaders, but at the cost of abandoning their hunting lands in Wisconsin and Illinois.

In the face of these constant threats, the Dakota evolved into a warrior society that lived in semi-permanent settlements and adhered to strictly defined gender roles. Men gained status and economic goods though their achievements in war. Their weapons consisted of bows made out of hickory, ash, or black locust, and war clubs. Warriors would spend considerable time honing their skills in hand-to-hand combat that involved attacking their enemies from a crouching position and moving quickly from side to side to avoid being hit. Every summer, the men organized hunting expeditions to the western and southern prairies in search of buffalo. For the rest of the year, they hunted deer, elk, and small mammals. In contrast, women gathered wild rice, nuts, and fruits, learned to tap the maple trees for syrup, maintained the huts, and took care of the children. Women who accompanied their men on the hunt put up and took down the temporary shelters called tipis. It was also the task of women to clean the animal skins and cook the meals.

The lives of Dakota men and women changed when they came into contact with European goods. They first exchanged furs with the Huron for guns and powder. After 1670, the Dakota traded directly with the French. Kinship governed this frontier economy. In Dakota society, either a person was a kin or an enemy. The Dakota created fictive kin relations with strangers by the smoking of the calumet or peace pipe and a feast to celebrate the occasion. The military strength of the Dakota and their control of vast territories with fur-bearing animals forced French traders to accommodate the Dakota by developing and maintaining kinship ties with them. The Dakota encouraged the marriage between French traders and Dakota women in order to develop blood ties. Since the care of children was the responsibility of the woman and her family, French traders were not obligated to settle among the Dakota to raise a family. Although French officials and Christian missionaries looked down upon the practice, both the Dakota and the French traders realized the advantages of these marriages. The Dakota would get a ready supply of European goods, while the French traders got access to furs and the protection that the Dakota provided. In a kinship relationship, both sides had to meet their obligations and share their resources; otherwise, the relationship turned hostile. The French and English traders understood this, but after the Louisiana Purchase, the U.S. government wanted land cessions in return for annuities and debt repayment and were not at all interested in developing kinship relations with the Dakota. Increasingly, the American traders did not partake in the obligatory gift giving that had marked trade in the past. Instead, they kept account books that listed all the items purchased by the Dakota on credit and demanded repayment. Whereas the French had banned the trade of alcohol, the American traders openly sold it. For many Dakota, these changes in trade were a betrayal of kinship ties. Some advocated tolerance or movement west—others called for active resistance.

In 1650 the Eastern Dakota in the Upper Mississippi Valley may have numbered about 38,000 people. Conflict with tribes such as the Ojibwe in the north and the tribes who had fled from the Iroquis in the 1640s caused mounting losses in battle for the Dakota. European diseases also took their toll, especially the smallpox epidemics of the 1730s and 1780s which killed thousands of them. By 1805 the Eastern Sioux had been reduced to 25,000 people.

In 1819 the U.S. government built Fort Snelling at the confluence of the Mississippi and Minnesota Rivers. The fort had several purposes: to keep the Dakota and their neighbors the Ojibwe at peace, stop further intrusion of white settlers into Dakota territory, and prepare the Dakota for assimilation into American society. Assimilation meant getting the Dakota to learn how to read and write English as well as converting them into a nation of Christian farmers. Missionaries served as the instruments of this change.

In the 1830s, the artist George Catlin described the condition of the Dakota who still lived in the Mississippi Valley:

> The Sioux in these parts, who are out of reach of the beavers and buffaloes, are poor and very meanly clad, compared with those on the Missouri, where they are in the midst of those and other wild animals, whose skins supply them with picturesque and comfortable dresses. The same deterioration also is seen in the morals and constitutions of these, as amongst all other Indians, who live along the frontiers, in the vicinity of our settlements, where whisky is sold to them, and the small-pox and other diseases are introduced to shorten their lives.[15]

But Catlin also noted other changes as well that were a tribute to the adaptability of the Eastern Dakota. He observed that they "exhibit considerable industry in their agricultural pursuits, raising very handsome cornfields, laying up their food, thus procured, for their subsistence during the hard and tedious winters."[16]

The Dakota's connection to the fur trade for over a century had profound consequences for their environment. They killed beavers by the tens of thousands every year—the very beavers that created the dams that caused ponds to form that eventually turned into meadows that brought

Fort Snelling. Courtesy of the Library of Congress.

in the deer, elk and, other animals that the Dakota hunted for meat. By the 1800s, the beavers were nearly all gone, and the Dakota had to trade muskrat pelts, which were worth less. Salted pork that they bought from American merchants became the mainstay of their diet. Alcoholism was rampant. Continual waves of American immigrants to Minnesota and pressure from government officials and their Indian agents forced the Eastern Dakota to sign a series of treaties in 1837, 1851, and 1858 by which they ceded all their lands along the Mississippi to the U.S. government. In return, they received annual annuities and reservations along the Minnesota River in the western parts of the state. American merchants got the first cut of the annuity payments for outstanding loans every year, so not much of the payments actually got to the Dakota. Tension mounted between those Dakota who decried the exploitation by federal officials, the loss of land and traditional ways, and the migration of white settlers. The Eastern Dakota rose up in 1862, killing over 500 hundred American settlers before several thousand federal troops arrived and dispersed them. After executing dozens of Dakota in the largest mass execution in U.S. history and jailing many others, the federal government forced the rest of the tribe to move to reservations in the Dakota Territory.

CONCLUSION

Dozens of other tribes made the Mississippi Valley their home at some point in their history. On the upper Mississippi River, the Ojibwe migrated into northern Minnesota and pushed the Dakota south. By maintaining peaceful relations with the English and the Americans, they managed to stake out a life along the river. Today, they are one of the few Native American tribes to maintain a reservation there. The Mesquakie or Fox fled from the Iroquois onslaughts and established themselves near the headwaters of the Des Moines River. But war with the French and surrounding tribes forced them to join with the Sauk when their numbers reached less than a hundred. The Black Hawk War of 1832 was a disaster for the Sauk and the Mesquakie. It gave the federal government the excuse to force land cessions from the Sauk leadership, who were actually giving away the traditional lands of the Mesquakie. Both tribes were forced to move to western reservations.

The Ioway were descendents of the Oneota. As an agricultural people who supplemented their diet with hunting, they established villages along the Mississippi River in what is today Iowa and northern Arkansas. They maintained a strict social hierarchy of Chief, Noble Warriors, and Commoners in which members had to marry within their social class. The Ioway engaged in trade with the Europeans, but their numbers declined rapidly from disease and war. The great enemies of the Ioway were the Chickasaw, whose hunting and war parties patrolled a huge amount of territory that bordered on the Mississippi. By the 1830s, only 1,400 Ioway

Objibwe children and white settlers, ca. 1895 Courtesy of Pennington County Historical Society.

remained. They lost much of their autonomy when American Indian agents used annual annuity payments to control the tribe's chiefs, who were eventually compelled to sell their tribe's land and move to western states.

In Louisiana, refugees from the Choctaw tribe settled near New Orleans in the 1800s, but they were quickly absorbed by other tribes. Smaller tribes such as the Houma and the Bayogoula, and several others, carved out a living among the French. They found an economic niche by selling meat and wild fruits and nuts and later agricultural products in the open markets of New Orleans well into the nineteenth century. Most were absorbed into other tribes or became so mixed with European and American blood that they disappeared into American society.

The daily lives of Native Americans along the Mississippi River were dramatically altered when De Soto and his men arrived. In the next three centuries, they struggled to maintain their identity and their land in the face of European and American expansion. Trade with the invaders improved the material life of some natives, but it also bred a dependence that eventually led to the loss of their ancestral homes. Many of their descendants survive today in independent and autonomous regions far away from their ancestral homes. Some have left their reservations and moved to cities along the Mississippi River. Since the 1980s, the United

States government has actively sought to strengthen tribal identity by recognizing the special status of tribes, instead of trying to weaken them as they did in the 1890s and 1950s, but what federal policy will be in the future is uncertain. Economically, casinos have provided new sources of revenue for native tribes throughout the United States, generating 22 billion dollars in 2005. The Tunica-Biloxi, Ojibwe, Chickasaw, Ioway, Quapaw, and Dakota run successful gambling operations. But the age-old tensions within tribes remain between the need to preserve their heritage and the desire to assimilate and prosper in the American economy.

NOTES

1. Jean-Bernard Bossu, *Travels in the Interior of North America, 1751–1762,* trans. and ed. Seymour Feiler (Norman: University of Oklahoma Press, 1962), 30.
2. Carl D. Brasseaux, ed. and trans., *A Comparative View of French Louisiana, 1699 and 1762: The Journals of Pierre Le Moyne d'Iberville and Jean-Jacques-Balise d'Abbadie,* rev. ed. (Lafayette: Center of Louisiana Studies, University of Southwestern Louisiana, 1981), 123.
3. Richebourg Gaillard McWilliams, ed and trans., *Fleur de Lys and Calumet: Being the Pénicaut Narrative of French Adventure in Louisiana* (Baton Rouge: Louisiana State University Press, 1953), 35.
4. Jean-Bernard Bossu, *Travels in the Interior of North America,* 60.
5. André Pénicaut, *Fleur de Lys and Calumet,* 35.
6. Samuel D. Dickinson, "Shamans, Priests, Preachers, and Pilgrims at Arkansas Post," in *Arkansas Before the Americans,* ed. Hester A. Davis (Fayetteville: Arkansas Archeological Survey Research Series No. 40, 1991), 96–97.
7. Morris S. Arnold, *The Rumble of a Distant Drum: The Quapaws and the Old World Newcomers, 1673–1804* (Fayetteville: University of Arkansas Press, 2000), 23.
8. M. Le Page du Pratz, *The History of Louisiana: Translated from the French of M. Le Page du Pratz,* ed. Joseph G. Tregle, Jr. (Baton Rouge: Louisiana State University Press, 1975), 322.
9. Pénicaut, *Fleur de Lys and Calumet,* 28.
10. Ibid., 84.
11. Pierre F. X. Charlevoix, *Charlevoix's Louisiana: Selections from the History and the Journal,* ed. Charles E. O'Neill (Baton Rouge: Louisiana State University Press, 1977), 240.
12. Ibid., 239.
13. Ibid., 240.
14. Jean-Bernard Bossu, *Travels in the Interior of North America,* 39.
15. George Catlin, *Letters and Notes on the Manners, Customs, and Condition of the North American Indians,* vol. II, reprint (Minneapolis: Ross & Haines, Inc., 1965), 131.
16. Ibid., 132.

3

Life in the Colonial Era

In 1542 the tattered remnants of a Spanish force that once numbered 620 men placed the body of their dead leader, Hernando De Soto, into the waters of the Mississippi River for burial. Their dreams of conquest, gold treasures, and glory sunk with De Soto into the murky depths of the river. Although they had waged a campaign of terror that killed thousands of natives, spread diseases, and disrupted the political and social fabric of native tribes from Florida to Arkansas, they had failed to conquer North America. For the next 151 years, native societies along the Mississippi were left alone to recover with only a trickle of European goods making their way into their hands. Then in 1673, the French explorers Louis Joliet and Jacques Marquette rediscovered the Mississippi River, which they hoped would provide passage to the Pacific Ocean. When they reached the mouth of the Arkansas River, they realized that the Mississippi flowed south into the Gulf of Mexico and not west. Their fear of capture by the Spanish compelled them to return to Canada, but news of the Mississippi River Valley spread. Nine years later, another French explorer, Robert Cavelier de La Salle, and five other men canoed down the river. When they reached the mouth of the Arkansas, the Quapaw welcomed them in an elaborate ceremony, and La Salle took the opportunity to announce that the land of the tribe was now part of France. He continued south until he reached the mouth of the Mississippi. There he claimed the entire Mississippi Valley for Louis XIV and named it Louisiana. Within a few years, French traders established the first permanent settlement near the Quapaw in what was to be known as Arkansas Post. As the natives up the down the Mississippi would learn, the Europeans were here to stay.

The period from 1682 to 1803 in the Mississippi Valley was marked by a fierce competition between the European powers and later the United States over the control of the heartland of North America. They recognized the Mississippi River's strategic value as the main truck of a vast water system. Whoever controlled the river could exploit a seemingly endless territory that stretched from the Appalachian Mountains to the east to the Rocky Mountains in the west and the Great Lakes in the north. Since the goods coming into and out of this river system went past New Orleans, holding onto that city became the capstone of any grand plan of conquest.

Decisions made thousands of miles away in European capitals affected the daily life of the colonists and natives along the Mississippi. The Spanish sought to expand their North American empire beyond Florida into the Mississippi Valley so that it could serve as a barrier to prevent the English and the French from intruding onto Spain's more wealthy possessions in Mexico and Central America. The English wanted to break free from the bottleneck of the Appalachian Mountains and engage in trade with tribes in the Mississippi Valley and beyond. The French saw the Mississippi River as a way to connect their Canadian possessions with the Gulf of Mexico and allow it eventually to drive out the British and Spanish from the eastern continent.

By aligning with one European power or another, many Native Americans along the Mississippi River gained access to trade and maintained their independence through the colonial period. The historian Richard White has spoken of a "middle ground" that developed between Native Americans and Europeans in the Great Lakes region where neither side could impose its will on the other.[1] More often than not, Europeans had to accommodate to native customs in order to establish successful trade relations with them. Such a middle ground did occur in the Mississippi Valley, but in an abbreviated form. The French were never powerful enough to do as they pleased; nor were the British. Fur traders living in native villages had to respect native customs. However, if a native tribe or a coalition of tribes decided to wage war against the Europeans, the colonial powers responded with brutal force. By the mid-eighteenth century, the natives along the Mississippi River depended on European guns, copper or iron kettles, steel knives, and cotton clothing for hunting, trade, and their daily lives. As more and more Europeans settled in the Mississippi Valley, the middle ground eroded. Disease, warfare, and intermarriage with Europeans weakened traditional native societies. By sheer numbers, the people of the Old World overwhelmed the people of the New World and forced them to flee westward or face extermination.

France tried but failed to make Louisiana into a prosperous colony. After their defeat in the Seven Years War, the French eagerly gave away the colony to Spain because it had always been a drain on royal resources. French immigration policies had not succeeded in settling the New World with French migrants. Whereas the English colonies had 250,000 people in 1700, the French colonies had about 7,000 settlers. In 1754 two million people lived in the English colonies, but French colonial possessions had only 100,000 people. The historian Glenn R. Conrad has called the French "reluctant imperialists" for their lack of commitment to investing, populating, and developing their colonial possessions.[2] The fact that French settlements along the Mississippi survived 81 years was mostly due to the leadership of individual colonial leaders, the persistence of the few French colonists, the migration of Germans and Acadians, the forced labor of African slaves, and the assistance of neighboring native tribes who provided food, trade, and protection. French Louisiana never developed into a thriving plantation economy that exported more than it imported. Neither did it ever match the success of Canada in producing furs. Still, Louisiana had enormous potential that some were willing to risk everything to realize.

Of course, the Mississippi River placed its own mark on colonial history. Although flooding enriched the alluvial soils of the valley, it could and did sweep away entire settlements and agricultural enterprises. Navigation on the Mississippi was a perilous undertaking as well. The mouth of the river had several passes, all which were silted up with sandbars at one time or another, especially during low water. Sunken trees could rip a ship's hull apart in any season. Moreover, the waters of the Mississippi replenished the swamps and lakes along its banks to provide perfect breeding areas for mosquitoes that carried malaria and yellow fever. During the colonial era, infection with malaria became the price many settlers had to pay to live along the Mississippi and exploit its resources. The trade with the Caribbean exposed the people of New Orleans to yellow fever epidemics that killed thousands. The horrible reality of life in French New Orleans was that the majority of new immigrants to the city would die of some kind of disease within five years of their arrival. Children were also highly susceptible to diseases, and nearly half did not live to see adulthood. Despite these hardships, some Europeans clung to the hope that the Mississippi and its adjacent lands could yield the plentiful bounty that would make all the suffering worthwhile. This chapter is their story.

THE FRENCH COLONY OF LOUISIANA

The French monarchy appointed Pierre LeMoyne Sieur d'Iberville to lead the first colonizing effort along the Gulf of Mexico. In 1699 he had chosen Biloxi as the site of France's first fort on the coast. A year later, he called for the construction of Fort Boulaye on the Mississippi, 40 miles north of the mouth of the river. Consisting of a handful of cabins, it was abandoned five years later. When Iberville died in 1706, the 22-year-old

Jean-Baptiste Le Moyne Sieur de Bienville took over management of the struggling colony. Disease, the threat of an English invasion, and warfare with natives kept French people from migrating to Louisiana. In 1704 the colony had only a couple hundred inhabitants—the vast majority of them unmarried soldiers who knew very little about farming. Almost all their food had to be imported or bought from native tribes. To make matters worse, except for a small supply of furs, the colony had no marketable product to sell.

Nonetheless, the Mississippi River Valley looked promising for the future. In 1699 André Pénicaut had been a member of one of the first French expeditions to the lower Mississippi. Years later, he wrote about his first reaction on seeing the river and the valuable land around it:

> Coming out of this wood, we entered some tall reeds, or canes, which bear a grain very much like oats, from which the savages make a quite tasty bread and also a soup which they call *sagamité* [boiled corn and fat]. After crossing though these canes for a quarter of a league, we reached the bank of the Missicipy. This delighted us. We looked with admiration at the beauty of this river, which was at least a league wide at the spot where we saw it, which is forty leagues above its embouchure at the sea. Its water is light-colored, very good to drink, and quite clear. At this place its banks are covered with canes, about which we have just spoken. Everywhere else the area along the river appeared to us to be covered with all kinds of forest trees, as far as we were able to discover, such as oaks, ash, elms, and others whose names we did not know.[3]

Further to the north, the French from Canada were already establishing missions and trading posts in the Central Mississippi Valley. At Cahokia, the former site of the largest and most elaborate Native-American urban center in North America, French clergy built a mission south of the Cahokia Mounds in 1699. Natives who converted to Christianity and a few French farmers joined the missionaries to grow wheat and raise chickens. As more French arrived, the natives found it offensive that these new migrants built fences around their property to keep them out. In May 1733, one of the natives killed a Frenchman, and relations deteriorated rapidly afterwards. As the threat of war loomed, all the French fled to Fort de Chartres 30 miles down river. Negotiations and exchanges of gifts healed the relations between the French and the natives. French missionaries chose a new site for their mission within the Cahokia mound complex. On the first terrace of Monk's mound, the largest mound in North America, the missionaries built a chapel. On June 6, 1752, an attack by a force of 1,000 natives led by the Fox tribe wiped out the mission. For the rest of the colonial era, only natives lived in Cahokia. But other settlements in the region did succeed. Besides furs, the French were interested in developing lead mines, processing salt, and establishing farms on the rich alluvial lands of the river. Missionaries, fur traders, and native allies founded Kaskaskia in 1703 on the east bank of the Mississippi in Illinois country. By the 1730s, there were settlements at Prairie du Rocher and St. Phillipe as well.

After the abandonment of Fort Boulaye, the only French presence on the lower Mississippi River were its fur traders, most of whom had come down from Canada and were living in native villages. In 1708 there were at least sixty of them. The life of the fur traders infuriated French officials and the Catholic clergy who regarded the fur traders' adaptation to native ways as sinking into savagery and heathenism. In order to trade successfully with the natives and hunt on their lands, French fur traders lived in the middle ground between French and native society. They adopted many of the customs of the natives and often spoke their languages. Since most natives in the Mississippi Valley sought to expand their trade networks with real or fictive relatives, fur traders became members of the tribe. Usually this initiation into the tribe involved smoking a calumet pipe and exchanging gifts. The natives promised to protect the French fur traders, feed and clothe them in times of need, and most importantly to the French, trade with them. The French traders had their own set of obligations. They would be expected to keep the interest of the tribe in mind in any negotiations with European leaders, and they promised not to trade with the enemies of their fictive relatives.

Since French men outnumbered French women three-to-one in most settlements of Louisiana, fur traders sought out native women. In a few tribes like the Natchez, the French would be allowed to have causal sexual relations with unmarried women. Any offspring from this sexual union would be taken care of by the woman's family. More often, French traders married native women because marriage helped cement relations with the women's tribe and her immediate family and gave the fur trader a voice in village decision-making. It also provided sexual and emotional companionship for fur traders who spent most of the year far away from any French settlement. In the late colonial era, native wives often settled with their French husbands in French towns and cities along the Mississippi. The widespread practice of taking native women as wives and having children with them created a mixed population within Louisiana. Catholic missionaries preferred such marriages to sexual relations outside of matrimony, and they willingly baptized mixed children. Unfortunately, French leaders and other pure-blood colonists believed that these mixed children were naturally lazy, disobedient, and morally corrupt. In reality, many of these children would play crucial roles as intermediaries in the middle ground, and some would assume leadership positions in colonial society.

Throughout the colonial period, fur trading was based on a credit system. The native or French hunter borrowed needed supplies required for a seasonal hunt from trading posts. Upon returning, the hunter would bring his furs in, hoping he would have enough furs to pay off his debts and pocket a gain. The cycle began again the following year. Unfortunately, much could go wrong, and it often did. If the hunter was killed or injured or the supply of animals dried up, the owners of the trading post lost money. If a hunter sold his furs to someone else and avoided the traders who had loaned him money, then the fur traders were at a loss again. Not surprising, the French and later the Spanish government attempted to regulate the trade. Only licensed hunters were allowed to hunt in a given area, and they were allowed only to sell their furs to the trader who had outfitted them. Fur traders could only do their business in designated settlements to prevent one trader from taking the business of another. Alcohol was also tightly regulated to make sure the hunters did not trade their furs for liquor to unlicensed dealers before they had paid off their debts to their outfitter. Despite these precautions, abuses occurred. In the hinterland money was scarce, so furs or alcohol often served as currency for bartering. Tragically, as the numbers of fur-bearing animals decreased due to over-hunting, the French fur hunters became the poorest and most debt-ridden people in colonial society.

Fur trading was a dangerous way to make a living. In 1715 the Natchez killed four French fur traders after the new governor of Louisiana, Antonine de la Mothe-Cadillac, refused to smoke the calumet with their chief. Cadillac wanted to punish the Natchez, but he only gave his rival, Bienville, 45 men to deal with this crisis. After tense negotiations, Bienville convinced the Natchez to give up the men who had committed the murders, and they were promptly executed. To console the French, the Natchez agreed to the establishment of Fort Rosalie, which would allow the French to maintain a military force in the area to protect traders and settlers. The Natchez assisted the French in building the fort and supplied food to the soldiers stationed there.

The life of a French soldier in the colonial era was miserable. During the long summers on the lower Mississippi, the climate was unbearably hot and humid. Disease-carrying mosquitoes, questionable water supplies, and spoiled food added to the soldier's despair. They faced crude barracks and minimal health care and suffered from venereal diseases and other maladies. Reoccurring malarial fevers were every soldier's nightmare, and the majority of newly arrived recruits did not survive them. There were 180 troops in Louisiana in 1704; sickness and desertion reduced the number of troops to 60 in 1713.

Soldiers also were subject to harsh discipline and exploitation by their officers. Pre-Revolutionary France was a hierarchical feudal society where one's family's status determined future career prospects. The officers were mostly from the noble ranks, while the soldiers and non-commissioned officers were from subservient ones. The officers looked down upon the soldiers and considered them lazy and morally deficient so they believed strict discipline needed to be maintained. The officers in colonial France thought that it was in their right to supplement their meager wages with private money-making schemes, and many had no qualms about using the soldiers under their command to provide valuable labor.

When war did break out along the Mississippi River, the soldiers faced enormous challenges. Their army never outnumbered the natives. French prisoners could expect little mercy from the natives—scalping a victim while he was still alive was a common practice and so were other forms of torture. Not surprisingly, many French soldiers deserted when they believed the prospects of their survival looked grim. The French colonial government gave natives bounties to bring in deserters. When a deserter was captured, harsh punishment awaited him. But some deserters managed to survive by establishing relationships with natives and gaining their protection. Sometimes soldiers rebelled against their officers, but such insubordination was never tolerated. Nonetheless, mutinies occurred in 1716, 1717, 1719, and 1723.

About 15 percent of the troops in French colonial Louisiana were Swiss mercenaries, who maintained their own administrative structure and supply lines. To encourage the Swiss soldiers to stay in the colony after their enlistment, French colonial administrators promised them land concessions and three years worth of supplies. Unfortunately for the French colony, the vast majority of the Swiss soldiers chose to leave the colony when the opportunity arose.

In February 1718, Bienville had selected the site for New Orleans, which was a hundred miles upstream from the mouth of the Mississippi and next to Lake Pontchartrain. The strategic importance of the area was self-evident, so the colonial leaders of Louisiana moved the capital from Biloxi to New Orleans in 1722. Unfortunately, the city experienced problems that haunt it to this day. Natural levees protected the low lying area, but they could not stop a major flood. The first plans for the city called for artificial levees, but flooding in 1719 and 1724 forced the administration to build larger and longer levees. Levee building would remain a prominent feature of New Orleans history. In 1722 a hurricane devastated the region. New settlers flocked to the higher ground at Natchez. But the immense value of the New Orleans site precluded its abandonment, so building continued. In 1721 the population of the fledgling town was only 250, but by 1727 it had grown to 938. To increase migration to the city, boosters promoted the site as healthful and the location as one sure to bring prosperity to all migrants. Pierre F. X. de Charelvoix visited New Orleans in 1722, and he believed in its future:

> Your Grace will, perhaps, ask me upon what these hopes are founded? They are founded on the situation of this city on the banks of a navigable river, at the distance of thirty-three leagues from the sea, from which a vessel may come up in twenty-four hours; on the fertility of its soil; and the mildness and wholesomeness of the climate, in thirty degrees north latitude; on the industry of the inhabitants;

on its neighborhood to Mexico, the Havanna, the finest islands of America, and lastly, to the English colonies.[4]

Thirty years later, Jean-Bernard Bossu made a trip to New Orleans and wrote:

Negroes are brought over from Africa to clear the land, which is excellent for growing indigo, tobacco, rice, corn, and sugar cane; there are sugar plantations which are already doing very well. This country offers a delightful life to the merchant, artisan, and foreigners who inhabit it because of its healthful climate, its fertile soil, and its beautiful site. The city is situated on the banks of the Mississippi, one of biggest rivers in the world, which flows through eight hundred leagues of explored country. Its pure and delicious waters flow forty leagues among numerous plantations, which offer a delightful scene on both banks of the river, where there is a great deal of hunting, fishing, and other pleasures of life.... This water also has the power to increase fertility in women.[5]

Despite this optimism, the harsh reality was that New Orleans was a hot, humid, smelly, flood-prone, and disease-ridden city, and most of the colonists realized this quickly upon arrival. Several floods and hurricanes in the eighteenth century sent water into the streets. As late as 1802, a smallpox epidemic killed 1,500 children when the city's population numbered only ten thousand. Hurricanes and overflows of the Mississippi River destroyed crops in 1732, 1734, and 1740. The city was chronically short of coal, salt, clothing, candles for lighting, nails for building, and glass for windows. Meat supplies ran low in the summer, and wheat, which would not grow in lower Louisiana, had to be replaced with corn flour. Generally, the French back home stayed away. Merchants tried to make enough money to move out of the city and become planters. Except for its central plaza and a few hundred neighboring buildings, New Orleans remained more of a frontier town than a thriving city.

To make the colony profitable, the French monarchy allowed John Law, a Scottish financier, to take over the Company of the West in 1717 and then unite it with the Company of the Indies in 1719 with the hope that with proper promotion, organization, and funding, Louisiana could become something like the French colonies in the Caribbean and Canada. John Law conceived of a plan to sell stock of the company to the French public. The result was a speculative bubble that drove the stock price 2,000 percent higher than the initial offering. Law had personally received a large land concession near the lower Arkansas River, but he needed to populate the colony before it could actually make some money for himself and the company's investors.

In the first 17 years of its founding, Louisiana had been plagued by a shortage of people who were willing and able to work the land. The few colonists who did risk everything to leave for Louisiana were mostly fur traders, artisans, craftsmen, and other laborers who did not know how to grow food, let alone cash crops such as indigo, tobacco, and sugar. Chronic food shortages plagued the colony. Trade with native tribes like the Choctaw kept the French alive. No matter how bad the situation was in France for the poor, Louisiana appeared to promise only misery and premature death. To counter this perception, John Law launched a media blitz in which he called Louisiana the "El Dorado on the Mississippi." Deceitful advertising about the healthy climate and large land grants convinced almost 7,000 French and German immigrants, including 1,215 women and 502 children, to leave for Louisiana between 1717 and 1721. The French monarchy also decided to force unwanted and troublesome members of its society to migrate. Twelve hundred prostitutes, salt and tobacco smugglers, army deserters, and criminals from prisons were shipped to the colonies.

Since the immediate vicinity of New Orleans had experienced serious flooding in 1719, John Law decided to move many of these settlers further north. He hoped to send some of the German immigrants to work on his own track of land on the Arkansas River, but his disgrace after the stock price of his company crashed put an end to his plans. The fertile soil around Fort Rosalie near the Natchez tribe looked enticing for company officials. As early as 1700, the priest Paul du Ru, who had accompanied Iberville on an expedition up the Mississippi, noted that "[t]he plains of the Natchez which I observed a little more attentively to-day, are even more beautiful than I had realized. There are peach, plum, walnut and fig trees everywhere."[6] Each variety of those trees had been brought over by the Europeans. The Natchez had already been growing a small crop of tobacco for their own uses, so the Company of the Indies decided to make tobacco one of the cash crops that would transform Louisiana into a thriving and prosperous colony. They hired experienced growers of tobacco from the Caribbean and began clearing land.

A plantation economy required many laborers. In French Louisiana, as in the Caribbean and the English Chesapeake and Carolinas, slavery became the foundation of plantation systems growing staples for Atlantic markets. In any discussion of slavery in the Mississippi Valley it is important to understand the historical context from which this oppressive institution originated. European society was extremely hierarchical. Nobles and other higher ranking members had no qualms about exploiting the labor of those below them—in fact, they expected such subservience. They felt that God and the King of France had given them mastery over the land, and it was the duty of peasants, serfs, or slaves to work for them. Such was the natural order of things. As long as Christians were not enslaved, Church leaders sanctioned slavery. Before Columbus ever set sail for the New World, Europeans had been using slaves on plantations with great financial success on islands off the coast of Europe and Africa. The cold climate of Canada precluded the establishment of a plantation economy, but the islands of the Caribbean did not, and the sugar plantations that imported African slaves thrived. The leaders of Louisiana also needed laborers. In the early eighteenth century, hundreds of indentured servants were sent to Louisiana. Such people agreed to work for someone for a period of several years to pay for their passage. Unfortunately, the bad publicity in France about Louisiana gave poor French people second thoughts about moving there. The Company of the Indies turned to slavery as a solution to their labor needs.

Like many Europeans, the French did force some Native Americans into slavery. Even after 1763 when the Spanish took control of the area and prohibited the enslavement of natives, the French still used some native slaves as domestic servants. However, the wholesale use of Native Americans as a slave labor force was never attempted in Louisiana for several obvious reasons. First, Native Americans knew the landscape of the Mississippi Valley very well, so escape was easy and recapturing them difficult. Secondly, the natives could find support from their own tribes or other allied tribes who would be willing to provide shelter and protection from slave catchers. Thirdly and most importantly, until the middle of the eighteenth century, the French were dependent on the good will of the native tribes near their settlements for food and protection. A persistent policy of Indian enslavement would have encouraged hostility that would have endangered the very survival of the colony. By 1732 there were only 100 native slaves in Louisiana and their numbers would never grow larger than a few hundred.

Instead, the Company of the Indies turned to African slaves. In the sixteenth century, the Europeans tapped into the Islamic slave system in West Africa. For several hundred years, Africans were being traded in the Islamic world, but Islamic slavery was fundamentally different from that which would be practiced in the New World. Islamic slavery was not racial. A Muslim could purchase a blue-eyed European, an Asian, an Indian Hindu, or a black African in a slave market in Istanbul or Damascus. A Muslim was not allowed to enslave another Muslim, but everyone else was fair game. Most of these slaves served in some domestic capacity rather than on massive plantations. In the Ottoman Empire, the Janissaries, the elite warriors of the Sultan, were slaves and so were many of the bureaucrats administrating the empire. Throughout the Islamic world, the manumission of slaves was encouraged and often practiced as an act of charity. However, the most striking difference between Islamic slavery and the New World slavery had to do with Islamic Law. A child born of a union between a male Muslim and slave woman was free, and the mother was freed as well. Because of the nature of Islamic slavery, freed slaves and/or their children could become active members of the dominant society with little or no stigma attached. And since slavery was not racial, a former slave would walk down the street of Baghdad and not fear discrimination.

New World slavery was fundamentally different. Most slaves worked on plantations or farms that produced crops that were sold on the world market. Since the demand for sugar and tobacco became almost unquenchable in the seventeenth and eighteenth centuries, millions of slaves were needed to work the land. New World slavery became racial as Europeans moved away from enslaving Native Americans and began using Africans exclusively. There were many practical reasons for this change. The sickle-cell genetic trait allowed Africans to withstand malaria. Sub-Saharan Africans lived in a tropical climate so they could easily adapt to living and working in the hot climate of the Caribbean or Louisiana. Africans were also highly skilled agriculturalists. They knew how to grow rice and indigo, two staples that would become very important in Louisiana, but also a variety of other foods that kept French colonists from starving. But there were more sinister reasons as well. The slaves bought from West Africa were black. If they ran away in Louisiana, it was easy for the French or their Native-American allies to spot them from among the population and seize them. Europeans also believed that the sexual union of a free male and a slave woman produced a slave child. Although French authorities and the Church discouraged interracial sex, it did occur, and many European and later American men sold their own children on the slave market. The manumission of slaves created a free black population that was openly discriminated against because of their race. The dominant white culture put restrictions on free blacks to prevent them from uniting with the slaves in rebellion.

Unfortunately for French Louisianans, the demand for African slaves was almost never met. The Caribbean was far too profitable for France for it to divert valuable slaves to a colony that remained a drain on its treasury. In 1721 there were 514 slaves in Louisiana. By 1731 6,000 slaves had landed in Louisiana, but then the forced migration stopped and only 400 slaves would be sent over the next 30 years because the Company of the Indies refused to extend long-term credit to planters in Louisiana or exchange the slaves for goods at inflated prices. Still, in 1746 the 4,100 black slaves represented about half the population of Louisiana. At the end of the French colonial era in 1763, there were about 5,000 black slaves compared to 4,000 white colonists in Louisiana.

Keeping the black majority under control became imperative to the survival of the slave-owning class. The daily life of Africans changed the moment they were forced onto the slave ships heading for Louisiana. About a quarter to a third of them did not survive the horrific journey, which historians call the Middle Passage. Once the slaves reached Louisiana, they were sold on the market. By mid-century, about 30 percent of the rural households in Louisiana owned slaves. The French Black Code of 1724 legally defined their status. French slave owners were prohibited from arbitrarily abusing their slaves or overworking them. Slaves were only to work during daylight hours. There were minimum requirements for food and clothing. The Code forbade French men or women from having sex with their slaves. Recaptured slaves that had run away were to be branded and have their ears cropped. Slave owners were to take care of elderly and sick slaves. They were required to look after the spiritual development all their slaves. Slaves had a right to seek remedy in the courts if the slave owners failed in their obligations. Slave-owners were not allowed to break up slave families, and the children of slaves could not be sold until the age of 14. All that was the law, but the reality of slavery was that masters exercised almost unchecked power over their slaves.

Unlike the Protestant English colonies, the Catholic clergy in French Louisiana tried to baptize as many slave children as they could and give them some basic religious instruction. Slave-owners realized that keeping families together decreased the chances of individual members running away and it boosted morale and productivity. The end result was that the family became the central unit of slave society in colonial Louisiana. Since there were no schools or organized efforts to create black churches, the parents became the distillers of morality, the teachers of skills, and the authors of dreams for their children. The infrequency of new slave shipments to Louisiana during the eighteenth century only reinforced the family bonds. Many slaves knew and interacted with their grandparents.

Black slaves played a crucial role in the colonial life of Louisiana. They provided the physical labor and the agricultural skills, especially in the growing of rice that kept the entire colony fed. Slaves worked about nine to eleven hours a day with a half hour off for breakfast and lunch. As true with slaves throughout the antebellum South, more than three quarters of slaves worked on plantations and farms that possessed less than twenty slaves. About 23 percent of the slaves worked on farms with less than five slaves. As historian Gwendolyn Hall describes it, Africans "cleared, ditched, drained, and cultivated the lands of their masters, built their levees, buildings, and fences, cut trees and trimmed wood, and, in their copious spare time, engaged in public works projects in New Orleans and elsewhere."[7]

In towns and cities along the Mississippi, black slaves were apprenticed to artisans and craftsmen. On weekends, slave owners in New Orleans allowed their slaves to work for other whites in order to save on food costs. Unfortunately, slaves were often underfed, and the Superior Council of the city had to pass regulations to raise the minimum food requirements for slaves. Slaves were encouraged to have gardens and were allowed to sell or trade any surplus from their efforts. They interacted and traded with Native Americans, which helped supply both with needed goods.

There were many ways for slaves to resist oppression. Simple things like slowing down the pace of work, stealing food from the master, and secretly making money by trading goods could be acts of defiance. Violence perpetrated by slaves against whites occurred rarely because the government response was brutal. The most telling way that slaves maintained their dignity and expressed their yearning to be free was the act of running away. Sometimes running away was a sheer act of survival when food supplies ran low or there was physical abuse on the part of the master or the overseer. Even though the consequences of getting caught could range from whipping to maiming to execution, slaves continued to run away throughout the colonial period. On the lower Mississippi, a slave found it easier to run away because of the warm climate and the abundance of natural resources. Some runaway slaves would stay near the area they had lived so that they could keep in contact with loved ones, relatives, and friends. Runaway slaves could fish and hunt for their own needs and sell or trade any surplus to the slaves. In the cypress swamps of Louisiana, they cut and squared logs which they then sold to sawmill owners. For those who decided to flee the region, the Mississippi River and its tributaries provided the highway to freedom. A few managed to escape out of Louisiana altogether by catching a ship to Havana.

To better their chances of survival, runaway slaves formed communities in the hinterlands. If need be, they could more easily steal cattle or rob plantations to survive. Their actions became the stuff of legends in African-American history as songs, poems, and stories were told from generation to generation. During the era of Spanish colonization, runaways lived in the wetlands and swamps to the south of New Orleans. In 1784 St. Malo's famous runaway community had 38 members, including 12 women. French and Spanish colonists saw them as dangerous bandits who needed to be eliminated. Since there was no organized slave patrol during the French colonial period, a posse of armed men fought against them, and most of the runaway slaves met a tragic end.

The greatest fear among whites was of a slave uprising. In June of 1731, a plot was uncovered in Louisiana. Slaves from the Bambara, an ethnic group from West Africa, were about to unleash a rebellion which sought to kill all whites from Pointe Coupee to Balize [today's Pilotown] and establish a Bambara kingdom in Louisiana. The ring leaders of the revolt were not planning to liberate all African slaves, but only to overthrow the French landowners and allow Bambara Africans to become the new slave-owning elite. A slave gave the plot away before the rebellion could ever occur. The French colonial authorities sentenced the Bambara ringleaders to be broken on the wheel, a hideous form of death in which every joint in the body was crushed and the person left to die in a mangled form. French authorities left the broken body as a warning to discourage any further plots and rebellion.

In colonial Louisiana, a free black population emerged that was centered in New Orleans. Because free blacks left so few written records of themselves, their lives must be reconstructed from others' accounts of them. Such records relate their behavior, work, and basic information on their marital status, religion, and such but do not allow historians to go deep inside their private lives to discover their thoughts and emotions. The first free black person to appear in Louisiana records, in 1722, was sentenced to be flogged for stealing. In 1763 only 100 of the over 5,000 blacks in Louisiana were free. Some had been freed by their masters, while others had purchased their freedom. By the mid 1780s, the free black population increased to 1,000. Many free black women worked as seamstresses or laundresses, but almost as many engaged in business as shopkeepers and retail dealers. In the countryside, free black men worked as agricultural laborers or overseers and managers on plantations. In the city, many of them worked in housing construction or shipbuilding, and several were skilled shoemakers, coopers, and silversmiths.

The Spanish administration in Louisiana created a free black militia in which every free black male was obligated to serve. Within the militia, blacks interacted with each other and married their daughters to other free blacks. Black officers enjoyed some of the same privileges as white militia officers. They were tried in military courts, received medals, and were exempt from taxes and licensing fees. The family of a black militiaman killed while in the line of the duty would receive an invalid's salary for four years, which could be renewed. By 1801, 469 men were serving in the black militia. The militia provided a foundation for the development of free black community in Louisiana.

Hundreds of European women with valuable skills arrived to Louisiana during the migration of 1717–1721. They endured all the hardships of men and more. They worked as tailoresses, knitters, dressmakers, bakers, laundresses, menders of old clothes, linen drapers, cooks, and general laborers. According to French law, a woman had to live with her husband, so if he decided to move to Louisiana, she was forced to go. Because European men greatly outnumbered the women throughout the colonial era, families married off their daughters as soon as they reached physical maturity, which may have been as early as 14 or 15 years of age. The Chouteau family of St. Louis, for example, had their daughters marry at 16 and 17, a more common age for marriage. As head of the household, the husband managed the community property of the family. Yet, his wife did have a right to the property that was hers before the marriage and half the property acquired during the marriage. Her husband could not sell the share of property she brought into the marriage without her consent. If the husband squandered her portion of the estate, she had a right to sue him. Married French women could own and manage their businesses without interference from the husband. A widow could own all the family's property. If she remarried, the second husband would have no right to her property. Divorce was uncommon. Women could break the marriage if the husband failed to provide the necessities of life, openly professed heretical ideas, or abused her. Since the mortality rates were so high in Louisiana and few people lived into their fifties, women could expect to marry more than once. Widows ran plantations and businesses. Poor women could, and did, slip into destitution at the death of their husbands if they did not have family to support them. In New Orleans, prostitution thrived on the misfortunes of young women.

Despite the migration of 7,000 Europeans to the French colony between 1717 and 1721, the census of 1726 showed a total of only 2,228 Europeans in Louisiana. The vast majority of the immigrants had died or had fled back to France. When John Law's speculative bubble collapsed in 1719, the Company of the Indies continued managing the colony and hoped things would get better. Most of the new European colonists were granted land on the condition that they would improve it and bring it into production in one year. If they failed, administrators would take the land back and give it to someone else. Usually, farmers received about 200 acres with access to the Mississippi or some other navigable river. They were obligated to maintain levees and roads along the river in front of their property. About 200 Germans who were supposed to settle on the Arkansas River received land just north of New Orleans in what would be known as the German coast. Some of these farmers tried to make money on cash crops such as tobacco, but most concentrated on basic food staples such as corn and rice, which could feed their families and provide a surplus that the residents of New Orleans would eagerly purchase. Also, German settlers "provided cucumbers, salads, green peas and beans, artichokes, sweet-potato-greens, spinach, onions, pumpkins, dried peas and beans, French, Spanish, and English melons, sweet and white potatoes, and watermelon" to markets in New Orleans.[8] Colonists also grew oranges, lemons, figs, pears, plums, cherries, apples, and grapes in the Mississippi Valley.

Farmers and planters searched for products to sell on the world market. In the vicinity of New Orleans, some of the richer colonists formed large plantations to produce indigo, a plant that yielded a blue dye used in textile manufacturing. Indigo required large amounts of capital investment for machinery and a huge labor supply, but it was a profitable business through most the French colonial period. Competition from the English Carolinas and wars hurt the indigo business so that by the 1790s, Louisiana planters had to abandon the crop and turn to sugar production. At Point Coupee, which was north of New Orleans, tobacco became the staple crop with yields as much as 400 pounds per acre. Unfortunately, tobacco from English Virginia was not only cheaper, but usually of better quality than that from Louisiana, so French people generally preferred it. On the lower Mississippi, rice became the staple food and many plantations grew it alongside other crops. Pitch and tar were also processed for use by the French navy and merchant vessels.

Many planters invested in the cypress lumber industry. Cypress was naturally resistant to rot, insects, and worms, and easy to cut. The French found it a useful material for ships as well as the buildings in the hot and humid environment of lower Louisiana and the Caribbean. The problem was that cypress trees grew in swamps and marshes where carts pulled by horses or oxen could not get to them. Some French lumbermen took down the trees and cut them into planks in the swamps. Others waited until high water to move the cypress out. Since green cypress logs did not float, they tied the cypress to the logs of other trees to make a raft. In the 1720s, the French began to cut down the trees in autumn when the trees had lost their sap, which prevented the logs from floating. An even better technique was to cut the cypress during dry months and allow the logs to cure so they would float in the high water of the spring months. Water-powered saw mills processed the cypress. In the 1780s competition from the newly formed United States severely hurt the cypress industry, and it would not recover until the introduction of the steam engine in the 1820s.[9]

All colonists faced the danger from Native Americans. In 1729 a French official of the Fort Rosalie settlement had told one of the Natchez chiefs that his village would be moved in order to facilitate the arrival of more French colonists. The Natchez leadership met in council and decided to launch a surprise attack against the French settlers. They sent out messengers to recruit other neighboring tribes in a campaign to wipe the French colonial presence in the Mississippi River Valley. In the middle of the night the Natchez struck and caught the French at Fort Rosalie totally unprepared, killing 237 men, women, and children. Four pregnant women had their babies cut out of them and murdered. Two hundred other French settlers were taken prisoner. In a single night, 10 percent of the population of colonial Louisiana had been exterminated. The future of the French presence on the Mississippi was at stake. The attack sent a wave of panic throughout Louisiana. Some of the slaves of the murdered French had taken sides with the Natchez. What if their slaves rose up in rebellion at this moment? What if all the native tribes attacked at once?

The French authorities prepared for war. Bienville's excellent relationship with the Choctaw, Tunica, and other tribes paid off because none of them sided with the Natchez. A military expedition of French and native allied forces destroyed the Natchez as an organized tribe. Several hundred of them were captured and sent to the Caribbean as slaves. Hundreds of Natchez fled before the French attack to join the Chickasaw, the traditional enemies of the French and allies of the English. Three black slaves who had sided with the Natchez were burned alive as an example to other slaves.

Despite the victory, Fort Rosalie and the surrounding fertile lands were virtually abandoned by the French. In 1763 the land on the east side of the Mississippi became part of the English empire. Three years later, a few dozen English families founded the town of Natchez. Four merchants took advantage of the city's proximity to the Mississippi River to ply their trade. But it was the fertile land that once again lured planters and farmers to the area. During the American Revolution, the area became a refuge for hundreds of loyalists and developed into a thriving plantation society.

The first permanent French settlement on the west bank of the Mississippi River was Ste. Genevieve. Although some historians claim that the town existed as early as 1735, others push the date forward to the 1750s. What is clear is that by 1752 a census counted 23 individuals living in the town. As the children of the original nine families intermarried with each other, a close-knit community evolved. For the first few decades of the town's existence, the people of Ste. Genevieve lived in white-washed houses with picket fences along a mile-long road that ran parallel with the Mississippi River. After 1763 French colonists who had lived on the east bank of the Mississippi migrated to the town to flee from the English. As more and more people arrived, other roads were added. Outside the town was the common field, which had been divided into strips for the farmers. The town proudly possessed a church that served as the center of town activities. By 1772 the town had 691 people, but the founding of St. Louis to the north slowed its growth. Whereas St. Louis became a commercial center, Ste. Genevieve remained an agricultural community where farmers worked next to their slaves in the fields. During the Spanish colonial era, except for a Spanish garrison of nine soldiers renting a few houses, no Spanish settlers moved into the town. On May 26, 1780, 60 men from Ste. Genevieve's militia participated in the successful defense of St. Louis from a combined British and Native American force. Fear of attacks from the newly formed United States forced the Spanish to build a small fort in 1794, but by the time of the Louisiana Purchase it was falling apart.

Interestingly, no middle ground developed between the people of Ste. Genevieve and Native American tribes. As historian Carl J. Ekberg described it, "Indian-white relations in and around colonial Ste. Genevieve is largely a record of fear, distrust, tension and hostilities."[10] Self-sufficient farming communities did not need close ties with natives, but they did have horses and cattle that the natives desired. Indian raids on farms were a feature of life in rural communities on the Mississippi in the eighteenth century. Since the object of these attacks was to steal horses and livestock, the killing of colonists was rare. The people of Ste. Genevieve resented these attacks, and they made no attempts at establishing relations with the primary culprits, the Osages, who lived far to the west.

The farmers of Ste. Genevieve did not practice modern techniques such as crop rotation nor did they fertilize their fields. They plowed their fields with oxen, planted their crops, hoped that the Mississippi River would remain within its banks, and prayed that rain would water their fields. This was primarily wheat country, but corn and tobacco were also planted. This bountiful land had been part of the alluvial lands of the Mississippi, and in 1785, 1794, and 1797, its muddy waters flooded the common field. Over the course of several years, the residents of Ste. Genevieve moved their town to higher ground. Although as many as two out of five harvests were bad, Ste. Genevieve was a prosperous town that sold its surplus crops to the people of New Orleans and St. Louis.

Two industries did develop near Ste. Genevieve that helped diversify its economy. Beginning in the 1740s, miners found lead deposits near the town. In the 1790s, Moses Austin brought modern mining techniques and formed a mining community of 20 households at Mine á Breton. The mine's output rose from 60,000 pounds of lead in 1772 to 438,000 pounds of lead in 1800. The mining industry near Ste. Genevieve went into a decline in the decade after the Louisiana Purchase. In contrast, salt production was never a large business. Water was pumped out of nearby salt springs, and then boiled away to leave the salt and minerals. Laborers packed the salt and stored it.

Ste. Genevieve had wealthier families who dominated the political life of the town, but most of its people were yeoman farmers. There were artisans such as "blacksmiths, coopers, carpenters, masons, cartwrights, cabinetmakers, and even two goldsmiths" who provided needed services.[11] A few riverboat men, hunters, and trappers stayed temporarily in town. But the harsh realities of life in Louisiana reached this thriving community as well. About 50 percent of all children died before reaching adulthood. Only a few adults were lucky enough to reach the age of 60. Malaria was a constant problem, but the town did not suffer from smallpox epidemics. Since Ste. Genevieve was a tight-knit community with a respect for marriage, there were very few children born out of wedlock. The vast majority

Ste. Genevieve Hotel slave quarters. Courtesy of the Library of Congress.

of people in town did not know how to read. Since wheat was plentiful, bread was the main source of calories. The bountiful apples in the region and watermelon provided snacks and desert. Most of the people in Ste. Genevieve drank homemade beer and cedar, but wine, rum, coffee, and tea had to be imported. Billiard parlors provided some recreation.

During the French colonial period, the only permanent European settlement in what is today Arkansas was a fort called Arkansas Post near the Quapaw. Its origins go back to the earliest fur traders who had come down the Mississippi just after La Salle's expedition. The site was abandoned, reestablished, abandoned again before becoming a permanent settlement in 1731. In 1749 the English and their Chickasaw allies attacked Arkansas Post, but the French garrison repulsed the invasion. Soon afterwards, the fort was moved six miles inland on the Arkansas River nearer to the Quapaw for protection. In 1759 the fort was moved again onto a fertile flood plain, which, not surprisingly, flooded. The yearly inundations discouraged migration. Indeed, there were only 51 civilians at Arkansas Post in 1777. Two years later, the fort was moved again to higher ground upriver on the Arkansas. In the next two decades, the settlement expanded as 400 people made the area around the fort their home. Since most of the settlers were fur traders and trappers, the slave population of the Arkansas Post remained small.

The houses of Arkansas Post had the familiar French colonial architecture of upright logs, windows with shutters, French doors, and a covered porch surrounding the entire house. Most houses only had two rooms with a total of 400 square feet. Cooking was done outside in a kitchen, outdoor oven, and a smokehouse. The Arkansas Post was not able to maintain a Catholic parish with a permanent priest. Residents frequented a billiard parlor where alcohol and coffee was served, played card games, and danced on Sunday, a tradition that that offended Protestant preachers who came after the Louisiana Purchase.

One of the most dramatic immigrations to the Mississippi River Valley was the plight of the Acadians, who later became known as the Cajuns. The Acadians were originally French colonists of Nova Scotia who had been largely left alone by the French administration. In order to survive, they formed tight-knit communities based on kinship networks. In the 1750s, the English acquired Nova Scotia and kicked them out. Between 1757 and 1770, about 1,000 migrated to Louisiana. Another group of 1,598 came in 1785. They received land grants and supplies and promises that subsequent influxes of Acadians would be allowed to settle near them. Like immigrants before them, Acadians died from malaria and other diseases, but they were free to continue their traditional ways. Within 10 years of arrival, Acadians managed to obtain a standard of living they had achieved in Nova Scotia.

However, the Acadians had to adapt to survive. Instead of growing wheat, they grew corn and cotton. They put up cypress fences; kept of gardens with peas, turnips, various beans, and cabbage; planted fig, peach, and apricot trees; and participated in the building and maintenance of levees along the river. Some of them took up ranching in regions west of the Atchafalaya River with great success—on average, their ranches had 125 cattle and 23 horses. Acadians boiled their salted pork, wild game, and shellfish as well as vegetables such as turnips and cabbage. They only fried fish, eggs, and bacon. Baking was reserved for bread, particularly corn bread because wheat was in short supply. African influences on their diet included the addition of gumbo and okra. Most Acadians went barefoot during the summer and wore moccasins in the winter.

Except for the wealthiest members, Acadians were notorious for their frugality: they dressed simply and kept their homes and furniture sparse and practical. Most of them lived in one- or two-room cottages with an attic and small cellars for storage. At first, they built insulated walls as they had in Nova Scotia, but the oppressive heat changed their architecture. The Acadians began building buildings in a French style that cooled the house: raised floors on piers, parallel doors and windows, and front porches, cypress shingles, and storage buildings outside the house. The walls of the houses had horizontal beams with a mud-and-moss mixture stuck in-between.

Acadians were often in conflict with French planters born in Louisiana, who considered themselves an aristocracy and looked down upon new immigrants as an uncultured people who needed to be taught how to live properly. The egalitarian Acadians embraced slavery, a paradox that haunted the United States as well, and by 1785, 40 percent of the Acadians living along rivers owned slaves. Over time, an Acadian slaveholding elite emerged that sought to establish closer ties to the French slaveholding aristocracy while losing their connection to the greater Cajun community.

As a Catholic country, France forbade Protestants and Jews to settle in Louisiana. The Catholic clergy was always understaffed, and many priests assigned to Louisiana saw it as a punishment or exile. Not surprisingly, they did not have the best morale to deal with the difficult tasks at hand. Outside of New Orleans, there were few parishes along the river and mass was celebrated infrequently. Less than half the parishioners attended Easter mass, the most important holiday in the Catholic calendar. Generally, the French colonists were hostile to the clergy. In turn, the clergy bemoaned the lax morality among colonists. Although the Acadians were even more distrustful of the clergy, they led very spiritual lives that involved respecting the Catholic sacraments, especially baptism, marriage, and the last rites at funerals. Compared to other French colonists, Acadians more readily attended mass. Generally, they believed that the less a priest interfered in their lives, the better. Despite the protest of the clergy, Cajun women continued to ride their horses astride, men and women danced to music during Lent, and the community refused to support what they considered the extravagant lifestyles of the clergy.

Whatever criticism any visitor to New Orleans may have had of the city and its people, the lack of personality was not one of them. As historian John G. Clark observed, "a certain amount of opulence and splendor clothed New Orleans, evidenced by an increasing demand for luxury items, especially among the successful planters. Women dressed in high style; the consumption of wine and brandy, always large, became larger; more horses and carriages appeared on the streets; colonial officials complained of salaries inadequate to sustain a proper style of living; and consistently active markets greeted the arriving merchant vessels from France and the West Indies."[12]

New Orleans' merchants were the upper class in the city's society. For the entire colonial period, they maintained a strong French identity despite Spanish and later American rule. In the early years of the colony, merchants in New Orleans were agents of companies and individuals in France, but they had the right to trade on their own account as well. Merchants engaged in all opportunities presented to them. Insurance from French ports allowed them to endure the extreme risk of importing and exporting products. Whenever they could, they bought land and became planters, which gave them greater status in colonial society. Since hard currency was scarce, merchants and planters lived on credit, keeping accounts, and hoping the next shipment or the next crop would get them out of debt. Generally, Louisiana imported more than it exported.

In 1727 nine Ursuline nuns, two postulates, and one novice arrived in Louisiana with plans to open a school for children in New Orleans. It was the first free day school in North America, and its doors were open to white, Indian, and black children. After the Natchez Uprising in 1729, the Ursuline nuns took in orphaned children from the Fort Rosalie settlements and rescued young girls that had been held prisoners. Reading, writing, arithmetic, and the Catholic catechism were taught to the girls, but also skills useful in housework and manners. The Ursuline nun's commitment to education continues in New Orleans to this day.

By 1800, ten thousand people lived in New Orleans. Although the city had its rich and poor like any other urban center, social classes were not rigidly defined and economic success could propel a person higher. However, floods, hurricanes, fires, and diseases could destroy one's fortune just as quickly. Poverty was a fact of life in New Orleans. Historian John G. Clark has estimated that a working person in New Orleans would spend 31 percent of his daily income on a pound of bread and a pound of meat in 1797 and as much as 40 percent in 1798 and 50 percent in 1803.[13] A master carpenter would still spend 25 percent of his income on those two items. High rent ate away at the rest of the income. Still, as historian Jack

D. L. Holmes has put it, New Orleans was "[a] gay city, ready and eager at the first excuse to attend masked balls and operas."[14] Theater thrived during the Spanish period, despite censorship and strict regulations that stated that performances must begin at 5:30 P.M., and the audience was not allowed to stand up with their hats on or smoke during the performance. Mardi Gras was celebrated with zest. At the time of the American takeover, the people of the city frequented 15 ballrooms and as many as 500 people would attend a single dance. This resilience in the face of diversity made New Orleans, well, New Orleans.

SPANISH LOUISIANA

In 1763 the Seven Years War ended in defeat for France. For Louisiana, the war had devastated its economy. The English had prevented French shipping, so the Louisiana could neither export its goods nor import many of the necessities and luxuries that had made life in the colony bearable. Money was almost non-existent, and circulating treasury notes held little value. The fear of invasion only made matters worse. When the French gave Louisiana to Spain, French merchants in New Orleans worried about the consequences of breaking away from the French colonial system. In 1769 a few of them staged a revolt that was quickly crushed when the first Spanish garrison arrived and executed six of the ringleaders and imprisoned six others. To the surprise of the French colonists, however, the Spanish period was one of increasing prosperity. Spanish colonial policy protected the products of Louisiana from harsh competition with other more profitable Spanish colonies. More importantly, the treaty of 1763 allowed Great Britain the right to navigate the Mississippi. English goods from the colonies made their way to New Orleans and ended food shortages that had plagued the city throughout much of its history. Nonetheless, the Spanish worried that English influence on the city would be detrimental to their colonial plans, so, in 1769, they barred English merchants from taking residence in New Orleans. This only fueled the contraband trade as the English continued to meet demand.

Overall, the Spanish provided better leadership for the colony than the French. They brought law and order to New Orleans as never before. Spanish laws prohibited gambling or transportation on the Sabbath. To lessen crime and perhaps forestall rebellions, they forbade firearms and other weapons within the city of New Orleans. Taverns and billiard parlors had to open and close at specified times. The Spanish authorities regulated business by setting the price of goods and licensing merchants. Merchants were not allowed to sell alcohol to natives or blacks. The Spanish Cabildo, the administrative organ managing the colony, consisted mostly of merchants who knew where government regulation was most needed. The city government began to inspect meats and fish, establish prices, and make sure the weights used in the markets were accurate. The

Spanish tried to make New Orleans a healthier and cleaner city by paving sidewalks, working on draining the streets of water, burying dead horses, keeping dogs confined in houses and yards, and not allowing large supplies of gunpowder to be stored in people's houses. They created a system of public education, but most of the French stayed away and put their children in private schools with French teachers.

One of the success stories of the Spanish colonial period was the rise of St. Louis as an important settlement. In 1763 Pierre Laclede Ligueste had been awarded a monopoly on trade with tribes west of the Mississippi River. As he explored the central Mississippi River, he looked for an area that would give him the best access to native tribes and fur trappers to the west, but still allow him to maintain a connection with New Orleans. He sought an area of land that was not prone to flooding and was large enough for him to set up a settlement that could contain warehouses to store his goods. He stopped by Ste. Genevieve, but found the settlement too far south of the mouth of the Missouri River and its land too low to prevent inundation. He did find a prime location 10 miles south of the mouth of the Missouri with limestone shores and high elevation. The surrounding land had fertile soil, and the very tip of the Ozark Mountains with their rich mineral sources stood just a few miles to the southwest. He called the site St. Louis.

Laclede intended St. Louis to be a European settlement. When 400 desperate members of the Missouri tribe arrived to ask if they could live in the new city, Laclede denied their request and convinced them that what they really needed was to live further from the Mississippi River and nearer to the woods so that their enemies could not harm them. Although Native Americans would be a major part of daily life of colonial St. Louis, its founder intended the city to serve the economic interests of the white colonial population.

As a carefully planned community, St. Louis had three broad avenues where most of the business of the city was done. The farmers of St. Louis grew crops in a common field that belonged to the community as a whole, not the city government. The government allocated strips of land based on need the first time the common field was created, but it could not interfere thereafter. Individual farmers bought and sold the land from then on. The farmer could only use the land for farming, and he was responsible for maintaining his portion of the fence that kept out wild animals out of the fields. Another section of the commons was dedicated to grazing animals. By 1800, 1,200 people lived in St. Louis in 200 stone and wooden houses. During the colonial era, the city had to import food because of a shortage of dedicated farmers. St. Louis was foremost a large trading post that harnessed the fur trade in the Missouri River Valley and shipped the goods to New Orleans. After Laclede died, his son, August Chouteau, established a fur trading empire that thrived even though the fur trade declined in importance in the 1790s.

To spur the economy of Louisiana, the Spanish allowed slave ships from any country to ship their cargo to the colony. As a result, the number of black slaves in the colony increased from 5,000 to 20,000. Spanish laws gave slaves a few more rights than English and French laws did—including the right to own property, buy their own freedom, and appear in lawsuits. More importantly, the inflow of African-born slaves along the Mississippi River made the black slave community more African in their culture. By the 1790s, in Point Coupee just north of New Orleans on the Mississippi River, as many as 75 percent of the slaves in the region were African born. The African slaves formed communities that shared a common language and culture rooted in West African forms. As they mingled with the Creole blacks who were born in Louisiana, African folktales, proverbs, languages, and religious practices were reintroduced into black slave society. These Africans had known freedom and, not surprising, they were more inclined to resist the oppression forced upon them. Some fled and formed maroon communities in swamps. Since Point Coupee was far from the administrative control of officials in New Orleans, white violence against blacks was not punished, and whites could not control violence between blacks. To prevent an uprising, masters divided the slave community by placing mixed-race blacks in authority positions over Louisiana-born blacks. Both of them had power over African-born slaves.

The revolution in France shook Louisiana's slave-owning society to the core. In 1791 over one hundred thousand slaves rose up in rebellion against their French oppressors on the island of Saint Domingue. Over several weeks, they burnt plantations and killed many of their former slaveowners. Under François Dominique Toussaint L'Ouverture's leadership, the formers slaves managed to consolidate their gains, maintain their autonomy over large stretches of the island, and receive recognition from the National Assembly in Paris. In 1795, blacks in Pointe Coupee learned of the uprising at the same time that the revolutionary ideas about liberty and equality were spreading among them. Dozens of them began to organize a revolt, but the wife of one of the white leaders gave the plot away and slave owners crushed the rebellion before it actually occurred. Spanish authorities convicted 57 slaves. Twenty-three were first hung and then had their heads cut off and nailed to posts along the Mississippi River as a deterrent to other slaves. Thirty-one others were whipped and sent to hard labor in other Spanish colonies. Three whites were also convicted and were forced into hard labor in Havana. Throughout Louisiana, severe repression of slave and free blacks followed. The influx of Haitian refugees only reinforced the feeling that the black community needed to be controlled. The trading privileges and movement of slaves in New Orleans were curtailed and the free black community closely watched. The threat of a slave rebellion continued to haunt white Louisianans until the end of the Civil War, and it became an important tool of uniting various white constituencies in a common racist cause.

Although Louisiana began to realize its economic potential, it never became a prosperous colony for the Spanish. Like France, Spain failed to bring in its own colonists. Except for 2,000 Canary Islanders, many of whom died from disease once they arrived in Louisiana, no major wave of Spanish immigrants settled in the colony. Neither were the Spanish ever able to integrate Louisiana into the Spanish colonial system. When they tried, the priorities of more prosperous colonies took precedence over the needs of Louisiana. For example, in 1770, the Spanish colonial administration banned tobacco exports from Louisiana to protect the market for Cuban tobacco, which was of better quality. This devastated Louisiana's tobacco producers, but the ban was lifted in 1776 when Louisiana received the monopoly of tobacco trade with Mexico. For over a decade, Louisiana tobacco fetched good prices in Mexico, but overproduction and lack of quality control alienated Mexican consumers who convinced Spain in 1792 to ban all shipments of tobacco from Louisiana. The tobacco planters were ruined. Luckily, the steam-powered textile industry in England was in need of cotton, and the widespread use of cotton gins had finally solved the problem of separating cotton seed from the white fiber. Planters up and down the Mississippi River seemed to have finally found the cash crop that would make them wealthy. South of New Orleans, French refugees from Haiti assisted in establishing sugar plantations. Experiments in new varieties of sugar cane and more efficient distillation methods stimulated sugar production so that by 1803 Louisiana plantations produced between 4.5 and 6.2 million pounds of sugar.

But New Orleans did not seem so lucky. Although the city avoided major flooding from the Mississippi, a devastating hurricane hit the city in 1779. A fire in 1788 destroyed 800 homes, and another fire in 1794 left large portions of the city in ashes. Yellow fever epidemics in the summer months killed thousands. The closure of the port of New Orleans to American goods in 1784 hurt the city's merchants and angered American farmers and planters living on the east side of the Mississippi River and in the Ohio Valley. In 1787 James Wilkinson, an American commander who was also in the pay of the Spanish, arrived in New Orleans and proposed the secession of the western part of the United States to Spain and warned the Spanish that the western territories would likely secede from Spanish authority. Spain wisely reopened New Orleans to Americans in the trans-Appalachian region. By 1795 New Orleans was increasingly becoming dependent on trade with the United States as it also hitched American western fortunes to the river. Thereafter, the U.S. angled to get the right of navigation on the river and the deposit of goods in New Orleans. Failing to do so, as Thomas Jefferson noted, would force the fledging United States to align with the British to counter any French or Spanish ambitions in the Mississippi region. By 1801 about 19 percent of the entire production of cotton of the United States was reaching New Orleans. At the time of the Louisiana Purchase, more than 50 percent of the shipping in New Orleans was done on American vessels, and many of the ships flying the Spanish flag were owned by Americans.

Ironically, just as Louisiana was becoming profitable, Spain gave the colony to Napoleon Bonaparte of France, who had visions of a new French empire in the Americas. He sent thousands of troops to reestablish French control over Saint Domingue. Francois-Dominique Toussaint L'Ouverture was captured, but other black leaders continued the struggle. Disease and brutal warfare decimated the French forces. Napoleon gave up on Haiti and told an American delegation in Paris that he would sell the 828,000 square miles of the Louisiana to the United States for $15 million dollars. The American President Thomas Jefferson and the Senate quickly agreed. The Mississippi River would no longer serve as a border between two rival powers but would become the very heart of an expanding United States of America.

NOTES

1. See Richard White, *The Middle Ground: Indians, Empires, Republic in the Great Lakes Region, 1650–1815* (Cambridge: Cambridge University Press, 1991), 50–53.

2. Glenn R. Conrad, "Reluctant Imperialist: France in North America," *La Salle and His Legacy: Frenchmen and Indians in the Lower Mississippi Valley,* ed. Patricia K. Galloway (Jackson: University Press of Mississippi, 1982), 93.

3. André Pénicaut, *Fleur de Lys and Calumet: Being the Pénicaut Narrative of French Adventure in Louisiana,* trans. Richebourg Gaillard McWilliams (Baton Rouge: Louisiana State University Press, 1953), 14–15.

4. Pierre F. X. Charlevoix, *Charlevoix's Louisiana: Selections from the History and the Journal,* ed. Charles E. O'Neill (Baton Rouge: Louisiana State University Press, 1977), 258.

5. *Jean-Bernard Bossu, Travels in the Interior of North America, 1751–1762,* trans. Seymour Feiler (Norman: University of Oklahoma Press, 1962), 24.

6. Paul du Ru, *Journal of Paul du Ru [February 1 to May 8, 1700] Missionary Priest to Louisiana,* trans. Ruth Lapham Butler (Chicago: Printed for The Caxton Club, 1934), 38.

7. Gwendolyn Midlo Hall, *Africans in Colonial Louisiana: The Development of Afro-Creole Culture in the Eighteenth Century* (Baton Rouge: Louisiana State University Press, 1992), 126.

8. N. M. Miller, "Development of Industries in Louisiana," *The French Experience in Louisiana,* vol. I, ed. Glenn R. Conrad, The Louisiana Purchase Bicentennial Series in Louisiana History (Lafayette: Center for Louisiana Studies University of Southwestern Louisiana, 1995), 540.

9. John Hebron Moore, "The Cypress Lumber Industry of the Lower Mississippi Valley During the Colonial Period," *The French Experience in Louisiana,* vol. I, ed. Glenn R. Conrad,, The Louisiana Purchase Bicentennial Series in Louisiana History (Lafayette: Center for Louisiana Studies University of Southwestern Louisiana, 1995), 586–87.

10. Carl J. Ekberg, *Colonial Ste. Genevieve: An Adventure on the Mississippi Frontier* (Gerald, MO: The Patrice Press, 1985), 88.

11. Ibid., 184.
12. John G. Clark, *New Orleans 1718–1812: An Economic History* (Baton Rouge: Louisiana State University Press, 1970), 90.
13. Clark, *New Orleans 1718–1812*, 268.
14. Jack D. L. Holmes, "Spanish Laws on Sex and Marriage," *The Spanish Presence in Louisiana 1763–1803*, vol. II, ed. Gilbert C. Din, The Louisiana Purchase Bicentennial Series in Louisiana History (Lafayette: Center for Louisiana Studies University of Southwestern Louisiana, 1996), 99.

4

Rural Life during the Antebellum Era

In August 1831, Rebecca Burlend, her husband, and five of their seven children departed their rented property that had failed to provide a decent standard of living in Yorkshire, England, to immigrate to the Illinois country of the United States. After surviving a vicious Atlantic storm onboard the ship *Home,* the Burlend family arrived in New Orleans and proceeded to take a steamboat up the Mississippi River to St. Louis. On that journey, they were almost robbed one night by a black crew member, but their shouts scared the intruder away. They disembarked in St. Louis and took a small steamboat north up the Mississippi. Years later, Rebecca recounted what happened next:

> Already we had been on the vessel twenty-four hours, when just at nightfall the packet stopped: a little boat was lowered into the water, and we were invited to collect our luggage and descend into it, as we were at Phillip's Ferry; we were utterly confounded: there was no appearance of a landing place, no luggage yard, nor even a building of any kind within sight; we, however, attended to our directions, and in a few minutes saw ourselves standing by the brink of the river, bordered by a dark wood, with no one near to notice us or tell us where we might procure accommodation or find a harbour. This happened...as the evening shades were rapidly settling on the earth, and the stars through the clear blue atmosphere were beginning to twinkle. It was the middle of November, and already very frosty. My husband and I looked at each other till we burst into tears, and our children observing our disquietude began to cry bitterly. Is this America, thought I, is this the reception I meet with after my long, painfully anxious and bereaving voyage?[1]

The Burlend family spent their first three nights in a cabin with an unwelcoming couple who demanded immediate payment for their night's stay. Thankfully, Rebecca's husband John found Mr. B, the man whose letters to his brother in England had caught John's attention, and suggested to him that the Illinois country was where he would find prosperity for his family. When Rebecca arrived at Mr. B's cabin, she was not at all impressed by what she saw:

> In his letters sent to England, he had spoken of his situation as 'a land flowing with milk and honey'; but I assure you patient reader, his appearance would have led any one to suppose that he gathered his honey rather from thorns than flowers. He was verily as ragged as a sheep: too much so for decency to describe. And his house was more like the cell of a hermit who aims at super-excellence by enduring privations than the cottage of an industrious peasant. The bed on which he slept was only like a bolster which he had used on shipboard, and laid upon a kind of shelf of his own constructing. Then again the walls of his house were of hewn timber as others, but the joinings or interstices were left quite open.[2]

Not allowing discouragement to get the best of them, the Burlends bought 80 acres of improved land from a Mr. Oakes, who had cleared and plowed 12 acres of it to plant corn and oats and had also tapped 400 maple trees for syrup. Over time, the Burlends collected the syrup and traded it at a general store several miles away for food, goods, and farming implements. Slowly, year by year, the Burlends thrived in their new home, buying more land further inland, building a frame house, and having more children.

The story of the Burlend family is but one of the thousands of family histories of people who decided to make the land along the Mississippi their home in the antebellum era. Unfortunately, not all the stories had happy endings. Families were wiped out by diseases such as yellow fever, malaria, and typhoid. Health care was almost non-existent, so any accident could be life-threatening. Devastating floods or fluctuating market prices financially ruined many families. Still, for families like the Burlends, the lands adjacent to the Mississippi provided an opportunity to create a better life for themselves, and with luck, perseverance, and hard work, many families found what they had been looking for.

This chapter examines the rural life of people who made their home along the Mississippi River in the antebellum period. Agriculture was the foundation of the economy of the Mississippi Valley. Variations in climate and the character of the Mississippi River itself shaped the everyday lives of rural people. The Mississippi Valley north of Memphis was corn and wheat country where small family farms dominated the landscape, and still do. As long as a farmer could count on the labor of his wife, children, and the help of his neighbors and temporary laborers, slavery was never a necessity. Moreover, many European migrants as well as Americans from the Old Northwest generally looked down upon the institution of slavery even if they maintained a hostile attitude toward blacks and Native Americans. South of Memphis, where the growing season was longer and the danger of frosts minimal in the spring and fall, cotton was king. The rich alluvial soil of the lower Mississippi spread over the landscape. At its widest point, the alluvial plain stretched a 150 miles east to west from Memphis to Little Rock, Arkansas. From Vicksburg to the mouth of Red River, the Mississippi had deposited its silt over a width of 35 miles. Below the Red River to the Gulf, the alluvial plain could be as wide as 40 to 50 miles. Unfortunately, all of this land was subject to flooding. When farmers and planters worked together to build and properly maintain levees, the alluvial soil yielded some of the richest harvests of any land in the world. Since growing cotton required an extensive labor force in the delta region, planters used black slaves to help them claim the alluvial land and make it productive. On many levels, the story of the rural people who lived along Mississippi River is one of struggle—between humans and nature, but also among people themselves.

RURAL LIFE ON THE UPPER MISSISSIPPI

For most of the antebellum period, the upper Mississippi remained a frontier economy. In Minnesota, the Dakota were not expelled from the banks of the Mississippi until the 1850s and the Ojibwe were a presence throughout the period. In 1819 the U.S. military established a fort on an elevated site at the mouth of the Minnesota. They called it Fort St. Anthony, and later changed its name to Fort Snelling. Although there never was a battle fought here, the fort became the anchor for American settlement of the area. In 1823 the fort's soldiers were cultivating 200 acres to supplement their meager government-issued rations. Squatters moved into the area and sold their surplus food to the fort. In 1837 treaties with the Dakota and Ojibwe allowed American settlers to purchase land, and white migrants came by the thousands. During the winter months, ice prevented steamboats from reaching the upper Mississippi River, and this hampered the inflow of migrants. When in February of 1854 a railroad reached the river at Rock Island to unite the East Coast with the Mississippi Valley, migrants came by the tens of thousands. In 1859 there were 18,000 farms on half a million acres in what would become Minnesota, and they produced nearly three million bushels of corn, over two million bushels of wheat, and two million bushels of oats.

Frank G. O'Brien recounted how as a child he and his family came to Minnesota and built a house:

> It was a story-and-a-half structure with a roof so steep that the flies held "sliding bees" every Wednesday afternoon, coasting down the roof. The doors and windows would not be ready for some time; the mason was so busy in town, he could not get out to the farm for a week to put up the chimney; while the furniture was

> somewhere between Detroit and St. Paul. Fortunately with an ample supply of bedding, and an immense elevated oven cookstove, and with what tableware we have picked up in Anoka, we were ready for housekeeping. Quilts were hung for doors and windows; sheeting was tacked over the ceiling to prevent dust from sifting through the loose flooring in the rooms above; the stovepipe was temporarily run through the side of the house; and the bunks were constructed for beds. A crosslegged dining table large enough to accommodate all the family with space to spare for struggling claim-hunters, was made of matched flooring, while benches served as substitutes for chairs. With this outfit we began our pioneer experiences.[3]

Luckily for the O'Brien household, the mason came to put in their chimney and a carpenter installed doors and windows before the winter set in.

Life on Minnesota farms was isolated, and loneliness was a fact for many rural people, especially in the long and harsh winters. In the early decades of settlement, most of the meat and fish had to be hunted or caught. Even in the cold climate of Minnesota, measles, typhoid fever, diphtheria, mumps, scarlet fever, pneumonia, and tuberculosis were common. Passengers from steamboats that came from the South often infected Minnesota people with cholera. The lives of women were especially hard. They had to make basic necessities such as soap, candles, butter, and blankets as well as take care of the children, who had to help with the chores as soon as they were old enough.

Pioneering women lived in log cabins, dugouts, and sod houses with a few pieces of homemade furniture, a fire place, and maybe a wooden floor. Over time, families would build larger and sturdier homes. The women tended gardens, which were the main source of vegetables. Farm families used candlelight if they could afford to, but early settlers often turned to lard or other fat that they kept in a dish with a strip of rag for a wick. By 1859 kerosene lamps were sold in St. Paul, and prosperous farmers bought them.

In Iowa, the life of farmers was very similar. The population of the state had grown from 43,112 in 1840 to 192,214 in 1850 and over a half million by 1860. Most of the early settlers lived in counties that bordered on the Mississippi River, and the vast majority of them were farmers. They usually came by wagon with enough funds to purchase land and equipment. It was the male's role to build and maintain the wagon and his wife's job to make and maintain the fabric over it and prepare the provisions and clothing necessary for the journey. Since there was no bridge over the Mississippi during the antebellum era, migrants crossed the river by ferry or boats. In winter, many dared to cross the ice-covered river by wagon.

Once the migrants arrived at the site they wished to settle, they either found an abandoned cabin or they lived in their wagon until a hastily built cabin provided some shelter. At first, the cabins had dirt floors, but over time split logs or planks would provide flooring. The inhabitants of the cabin would then proceed to dig out a cellar to serve as a storehouse. Newspapers and then tarpaper would line the walls to provide some insulation from the cold until lime replaced it. Richer farmers plastered their walls. Even if glass covered the windows, there were no screens, so flies and mosquitoes invaded the house. The women of the house would keep a fire going throughout the winter in their fireplace or iron stove, which demanded cut wood. If a family had a son old enough to wield an axe, it would be his daily job to split wood. The farmer's wife and any able-bodied daughter would devote one entire day of every week to washing. Water had to be brought in and heated, and then the clothes run over a scrub board. Afterwards, the women hung the washed apparel out to dry on clothes lines. Another entire day was devoted to ironing, which demanded that the iron be heated on the fire. With families of 10 children common, the mother had a lot of work to do and older daughters had to contribute to the household chores. To supplement the diet of their families, women maintained gardens, and they would sell or trade any surplus to obtain goods that could not be made at home. Iowa resident Matilda Peitzke Paul remembered her childhood experiences:

> When the corn first came up we had to stay out in the field and chase the blackbirds to keep them from digging and eating the corn as fast as it came up. It was our work in spring to pull weeds for the hogs for feed. About the middle of June we used to pick wild strawberries.... We often had to watch our cattle to keep them out of other peoples as well as out of our own fields.... Before I was old enough to bind grain I helped carry bundles in piles, ready to be shocked up.... I often had to get water from a spring and carry it out to the field for drinking for the workers, before I was old enough to do other field work. Later on, I helped bind the grain.... We children had to go over the whole field and gather up the roots in piles and when they got dry we used them for fuel.... After harvest and haying was done we had to dig the potatoes and husk the corn ready for winter.[4]

As with farms all over the United States, U.S. land surveys had divided Iowa into townships that were six miles square. Each township was partitioned into 36 sections, of one square mile or 640 acres each. Each section was further divided into four equal parts of 160 acres, the most common lot of land sold to farmers or given as warrants to veterans of the Mexican War. To buy land, farmers sometimes had to borrow money and pay interest as high as 35 percent. Still, most farmers were easily able to reach a level of subsistence and produce enough surpluses to pay off their loans. If they could not, families just moved on and tried again elsewhere.

Although the Compromise of 1820 permitted slavery in Missouri, small farms were the norm in this state as well, and slaves never accounted for the majority of the population in any county, as in other southern states. In 1830 most of the slaves in the state were in St. Louis County, but they accounted for only 20 percent of the total population. By 1860 slaves represented only 1 percent of the population, and almost all of those were domestic workers. Slavery remained viable elsewhere in the rural counties. In Perry County along the Mississippi, farmers practiced a mixed agriculture—growing corn, wheat, oats, and barley as well as potatoes, peas, and beans, and keeping hogs, cattle, and sheep, which they allowed to graze on unimproved land. Slaves accounted for only 15.5 percent of the population in 1830 and 13 percent of the population in 1860. Generally, Perry County was not welcoming to free blacks, who were required to obtain a license to live in the county and that would be granted only if he or she could prove that they had a steady job and would not be burden on the government.

Like most Americans, Missouri farmers saw unimproved land as a symbol of ugliness, savagery, and violence. When a Missouri farmer purchased his land or squatted upon it, he began to improve the land by clearing it. Trees were cut down, and oxen were used to pull out the roots. Once the ground was no longer frozen, farmers began to plow their fields with oxen, horses, or mules. On virgin soil, iron plow blades dulled quickly so farmers would often keep two and switch them when one needed to be sent to the blacksmith for sharpening. In the early decades of the nineteenth century, farmers seeded their fields with hand-held seeders, but later switched to wheelbarrow feeders. A harrow would then be pulled over the ground to cover the seeds. By the 1840s, farmers widely used Seymour's Broadcast Seeder that was pulled by horses and spread the seeds evenly and quickly. With a team of animals, a farmer could have 50 acres plowed and seeded in about 30 days. If he could afford to hire laborers or owned slaves, the work could be done more quickly. Once the plants sprouted, the farmer would do the first weeding by having a horse or a mule pull a harrow with spikes down the row of plants to root out the weeds. Once the plants became taller, the farmer would have to weed with a hoe. Each corn and wheat season demanded at least four weedings. Planting grass for the farmer's livestock was also an important task. Once the grass was tall enough, early settlers used a cradle scythe to cut it. The cradle was made up of wooden fingers attached to the frame of the scythe that would leave the grass standing in upright sheaves for other family members to gather. By mid-nineteenth century, more and more farmers used horse-drawn mowers, such as the Hussey Reaper for hay. The hay needed to dry before farmers could place it in a barn or in a tight stack for later use.

Scythes could be used to harvest grain as well, but farmers switched as fast as they could to the horse-pulled McCormick Reaper. Once the wheat was cut, it needed to be threshed, which separated the grain from the rest of the straw. Most farmers used horse-powered threshers. Next, the shaft of the plant needed to be raked out and then the grain in the chaff picked up. Winnowing involved separating the grain from the chaff. By the 1840s, all these processes were accomplished in one machine, and four men and two horses could thresh 100 bushels of grain in a single day.

Corn was handled differently. It could be collected with a reaper, but since most of the corn was not eaten green, it was allowed to stay in the fields until all the other grains were harvested. Then, a farmer cut the stalk at the base with a corn knife, gathered the stalks into bundles called sheaves, and carefully placed them into a shock, which was a stack of these sheaves. Farmers used husking pegs or gloves with iron spikes to husk the corn. One worker could husk the harvest of one acre per a day. Then, the kernels would be separated from the cob in a process called shelling. Farmers used the Burrall Sheller, which was a tube with a blade that cut the kernels off when the ear of corn was pushed through. Dried corn husks were used as filler for the mattresses of slaves, and the stalks and cobs used as fodder or bedding for farm animals.

The wives of farmers grew vegetables to supplement their family's diet. As historian Pamela K. Sanfilippo has noted, a "typical Missouri garden might include cress, artichokes, eggplants, rhubarb, kale, lima and yellow beans, beets, cauliflower, cabbage, carrots, celery, corn, cucumbers, lettuce, melons, onion, parsnips, peas, potatoes (Irish and sweet), pumpkin, radishes, spinach, squash, tomatoes, and turnips."[5] Fruit would be eaten fresh and the rest dried and stored in cotton or linen bags, which had to be steamed twice in the winter to prevent worms. Another way to prevent infestation with worms was to sprinkle the dried fruit with whiskey before being stored. Fruit preserves involved boiling the fruit, adding sugar and sometimes honey, and then pouring the contents into jars that would be sealed with corks or just covered with paper.

RURAL LIFE ON THE LOWER MISSISSIPPI

In Arkansas, farmers and planters stayed away from the alluvial lands of the Mississippi in the first decades of the nineteenth century. Those who tried to farm the lowlands died from disease caused by the infestations of mosquitoes or were flooded out by the inundations of the Mississippi River. Levees would have provided security against the river, but most of the early settlers and local governments neither had the resources nor the will to build them. Instead, farmers preferred to move into the hill country further inland and farm inferior land than deal with the unhealthy environment of the lowlands. Only if the economic rewards of planting crops were sufficient enough would planters organize levee-building projects.

In Chicot, Arkansas's southernmost county that bordered on the Mississippi, the climate was warm enough to grow cotton and the rich alluvial soil ran several feet deep. The boom in cotton prices in the 1830s spurred migrant planters with capital and slaves to tackle the conquest of the lowlands. Whereas planters in Louisiana had organized themselves into levee-building communities since the colonial era, Arkansas's planters neglected constructing levees at first. Between 1834 and 1839, Chicot County experienced no major flooding so planters were lulled into complacency. During those years, the white population of the county increased by 24.4 percent and its slave population increased by 900 percent. The planter's ambivalence toward levees ended when a major flood in 1840 wrecked havoc in the county. In 1840 the Arkansas Legislature passed its first levee law, but it only granted counties the power to supervise levee construction with no promise of any money coming from the state. Still, the Chicot County Court forced landowners to build levees or it would confiscate their land if they failed to do so. Landowners who did not have riverfront property would be expected to contribute to the upkeep on the levees. Unfortunately, it was the riverfront landowners themselves who would have to collect the funds. Since the county forced them to put up levees at their own expense, the levee owners had no other recourse but to sue the landowners behind them if they failed to contribute. Not surprisingly, such a system failed. Modifications in 1841 created a paid position of levee commissioner who oversaw the building of levees. Forty-one landowners along the river were forced to build 70 miles of levees. Since the financial rewards were potentially so high, the planters constructed the levees with their own slaves. Although cotton prices crashed in 1841, Chicot's riverside planters continued to build Arkansas's first system of levees along the Mississippi. When the tax burden became overly heavy for planters, the county abolished the paid position of levee commissioner and replaced it with three volunteers from the planter class, who received prestige within the community rather than a salary. Although the flood of 1844 was one of the worst on record all along the Mississippi, the levees of Chicot County held and most of the plantations along the river remained dry even when the swamps behind them overflowed with water. The levee community had succeeded in protecting its investment.

Chicot's planters were never as educated nor were wealthy as those in Mississippi and Louisiana. In 1850 only 3 percent of the property in Chicot County paid taxes, which meant that most of the back swamps remained uninhabited. And since no other county in Arkansas that bordered on the Mississippi made any attempt to levee the river, most of the state's lowlands remained a wilderness with only a few planters and farmers attempting to farm them until the next flood wiped them out. In total, Arkansas's planter class, those who held 50 or more slaves, remained small compared to the counterparts in Mississippi or Louisiana. Throughout the antebellum period, Arkansas was the poorest and least developed southern state on the Mississippi and its population in 1860 was only one-third of that of Missouri.

The plantation economy developed most prominently in the state of Mississippi, especially in the counties near Natchez. The region had been largely abandoned during the French colonial era after the Natchez tribe massacred hundreds of French settlers in 1729. The British had acquired the area after the Peace of Paris in 1763, but it was not until the American Revolution that thousands of loyalists poured into the region. They were encouraged by a British land policy that gave 100 acres to a male head of the family and 50 additional acres for each member of the family and for every slave. Before 1800 the rich and poor settlers who migrated to Warren County lived as subsistent homesteaders. Although some failed, most homesteaders reached a subsistence level relatively easily, and in a few years had a surplus to sell. Farmers raised cattle to sell to New Orleans and planted cotton. As cotton prices rose, so did the income of these farmers who reinvested their earnings into more slaves and more land.

The cotton gin, the high demand from New England and Great Britain textile manufacturers, the switch to Mexican and then Petit Gulf cotton plants, and the availability of cheap labor in the form of slaves fostered the development one of the greatest plantation economies in U.S. history. By 1830 Mississippi produced more cotton than any other state. The opportunities afforded by cotton and the rich alluvial lands of Mississippi caused a wave of migrants to the state. The population of Mississippi doubled between 1830 and 1840 and almost doubled again between 1840 and 1850. Planters who owned 20 or more slaves made up 20 percent of the white rural population. When the cotton market crashed in 1837 and remained low into the 1840s, some plantations went bankrupt and moved on, but those who stayed and survived the initial crisis diversified their crops, improved their cotton production by fertilizing their fields with cotton seeds, adopted better strains of cotton, and used new technologies such as better seed planters, wheeled cultivators, double-shovels, and scrapers. When cotton prices rebounded in 1850, Mississippi planters were set to become some of the wealthiest people in the South.

Despite the patriarchal structure of southern society, women were not powerless and so dehumanized that they could not create a world filled with love, fulfillment, and friendship. Husbands and wives could be close or remain distant, but they did have clearly defined duties and responsibilities to each other and to their children. Women administered food production, purchase, and distribution not only in the planter's home but for the whole plantation. The mistress of the plantation was in charge of dairy production, the garden, and the smokehouse. She held the key to the storerooms, and she decided what and when the supplies would be distributed. She oversaw slaves who processed the carcass of a hog by cleaning its small intestines so they could be used for sausages, making the lard, and preparing the meat for smoking and salting. Southern women were also responsible for making soap and candles. They would be in charge of sewing and knitting and supplying the slaves with clothes and shoes. Women established kinship ties with relatives, neighbors, and church members to help them with daily tasks, assist in childbirth, and participate in the rituals of life. The men may have controlled planting and harvesting of the bounty of the fields, but it was the women who kept the household going and assured the survival of the family throughout the year. Such was her burden, but such was her reward.

The first cotton gin. Courtesy of the Library of Congress.

Unfortunately, a double standard was prevalent among slave-owning families in terms of sexuality. Within the planter class, it was not uncommon for unmarried young men to engage in sexual intercourse with slave women. Such sexual liaisons sometimes continued during marriage, and southern society grudgingly tolerated this behavior as long as the man was discrete about his adventures. In contrast, white women were to be faithful. The law rarely granted a woman a divorce, even if there was physical and psychological abuse. Still, most marriages were stable, with death rather than abandonment or divorce the cause of any breakup. Widowhood was a time of sorrow and a financial burden if the husband had accumulated large debts. Widows tended to remarry quickly because living in a family setting was the essential social and economic factor in building and maintaining a farming community.

A single woman's worth in antebellum society was based on her virtue, wealth, and education. To protect a woman's virtue, men attempted to control their movement. A so-called proper upper-class woman was supposed to appear in public with a chaperone to protect her, but such a male guardian was also there to keep her in line. A pregnant daughter who was not married would not only disgrace herself, but her family as well. Such a condition would almost certainly eliminate her marriage prospects to a respectable gentleman. Society also placed limits on women's educational opportunities. Upper-class planters sent their daughters to boarding schools, but opportunities in higher education were few. Academies were set up throughout the South to teach upper-class women skills such as reading, writing, arithmetic, and languages. In contrast, upper-class sons were sent off to college, often more for the social connections than interest in earning a degree. If the parents died, the maternal aunt usually took in the children. On average, women in the North married at 24 years of age, but their counterparts in the South married at 20 years of age. Most white women in the slave-owning families prospered. Since their livelihood rested on slavery, most of them wholeheartedly supported the institution.

For much of the year, daily life on a cotton plantation revolved around the successful planting, maintenance, and harvesting of the staple crop. The first settlers planted cotton by breaking the ground with hoes and planting the seed. By the 1830s, most used laborers to plow a furrow down a row in the field. A laborer trailing behind would throw the seeds into the trench and others used their hoes to cover them. Some plantations used horses to drag large blocks of wood to cover the seeds in the trenches. From April to the middle of May, gangs of slaves could plant 10 to 15 acres a day. The cotton grew in beds raised above ground about four to five apart. Once the plants germinated, slaves would thin them to one plant for every 18 inches within each row. Slaves would then get rid of the grass and weeds with a special plow that would scrape and pull out the weeds from the ground on either side of the cotton plants. This process did not damage the cotton roots because they grew straight down. When the cotton was high enough, no more weeding was necessary. A boll would develop where the cotton flowers had been. When the plant died, the cotton inside the boll dried, and the boll would burst and the cotton would be visible. The white balls announced the frenzy of cotton picking time, for the cotton had to be picked before rain and frost damaged the crop. Every able-bodied slave from six years old onward would take a sack and pick the cotton. On average, a person could pick 150 pounds of seed cotton a day, but some could pick as much as 400 pounds. The pickers brought the cotton bags to the gin house to be weighed.

Cotton growers used a gin to separate the seed from the fiber. On smaller plantations, gins were stored in a simple shed with just a roof to keep the rain out. Many large plantations constructed a building for the gin that was two stories high. Planters put the gin on the second floor, and its power was supplied by a horse on the first floor. The gin blew cotton lint into an adjacent room on the second floor where it would be stored. The cotton would be dropped to a room directly below to be pressed into bales of 400 pounds each. In the 1830s steam engines ran the gins on larger plantations. By then, the cotton seed that had once been discarded after

Day laborers picking cotton, near Clarksdale, Mississippi, ca. 1939. Courtesy of the Library of Congress.

the ginning process was used as a fertilizer. Farms and plantations along the Mississippi easily shipped their bales to market down the river to New Orleans. A well-managed large plantation of over a thousand acres could expect to yield a 7 percent profit on the owner's investment.

Food preparation was also a major task in the daily life of people on farms and plantations. For southerners, pork was the major source of meat. After slaughter, they would eat the backbone, ribs, liver, tongue, and brains fresh. Abdominal meat was used for bacon, and the pig's small intestines were made into chitterlings or cleaned to be used as casings for sausage. The rest of the meat on the hog was pickled or smoked. Southerners cured their meat with seasonings such as pepper, mustard, honey, and hundreds of secret combinations of spices. Women soaked the meat in brine, a mixture of salt, brown sugar or molasses, water and other ingredients, with a large rock on top of the meat to keep it submerged for 10 days to 12 weeks. Afterwards, the pork would be rinsed and soaked in water to remove the salt and then smoked for two to four weeks. The head, feet, tail, and ears were pickled and then boiled and then preserved in spicy vinegar in a jar or made into head cheese. Hog fat was boiled until it turned into clear liquid that hardened into lard, which became the oil used in frying. Generally, beef was eaten fresh. Women chopped the smaller cuts of beef and soaked them in molasses to make minced meat. Some cuts of beef were dried and smoked to make a jerky. Most plantations and farms kept chickens. The younger chickens were fried and older ones boiled or roasted. Southerners ate eggs when they were available in the summer. Hunting and fishing provided wild game and fish.

Generally, southerners ate well. With corn, cooks made cornbread, hoecakes, mush, hominy, and grits. The most popular vegetables were sweet potatoes, turnips, and peas, but rural people also ate collards, cabbage, okra, squash, onions, and pumpkins. When they were in season, southerners enjoyed apples, pears, peaches, and other fruits, and they ate dried fruits for the rest of year. Most white people drank coffee, tea, milk, buttermilk, and whiskey, but only rich planters could drink wine regularly. Slaves ate worse than their white counterparts. They received fat back, shoulders, joints, and received other parts of pig depending on what the needs of the planters and his family were. Slaves were given beef and mutton on special occasions and holidays. Slaves supplemented their diets with vegetables from their own gardens and protein from hunting and fishing.

The plantations just north and south of New Orleans were well established by the time of the Louisiana Purchase. To protect themselves from the overflows of the river, planters built a sophisticated levee system. In the French colonial era, a planter received a land grant with the stipulation that he would build and maintain a levee on his waterfront. If he did not, the French colonial government rescinded that grant and gave it to another. Neither death, sickness, nor any other excuse was permitted to interfere with levee building. After 1807 each Louisiana parish had a Police Jury whose members were first appointed and then elected. Their job was to make sure every planter along the Mississippi complied with his obligation to build and maintain levees of the prescribed width and height. All along the river, planters realized that a single break in the levee line could bring disaster upon them all. In 1858 Tryphena Blanche Holder Fox described in a letter to her mother the results of just such a break:

> The reason for his not getting his expected dues is the total loss of crop to all the planters on this side of the river, by the *crevasses*, which have completely submerged all the plantations in this vicinity. Messrs Stackhouse upon whom he depended for $170.00, the first of May is ruined. Their fields, sugar houses, quarters & dwelling are in under water—in some places four feet deep; We have the river very high one side & the overflowed land like a lake on the other. Fortunately our house is high off the ground—& our yard slants up to the river, so that our front yard is dry yet, but the lower end of the garden cow-lot are under water.... The levee which you know is like a raised railroad is the only terra firma visible for miles. In some places the backwater is so high that it runs over the levee from the fields into the river.... Many of the people have gone away, some to the city, others to the other side for a time. Most of the cattle have been sold and what few are left are in an almost starving condition—it is truly heart rendering to see the poor creatures standing upon the bare levee with hardly a blade of grass to appease their hunger.[6]

Although cotton plantations were the norm in Louisiana parishes across from the Natchez District, sugar was the main crop below New Orleans. The sugar plantations of southern Louisiana were among the richest enterprises in the entire South. Between 1824 and 1861, the number of sugar plantations increased from 193 to 1,308. Sugar plantations were generally larger than those that grew cotton, and by the 1850s they employed half the slaves in Louisiana. Sugar production grew from 75,000 hogsheads (barrels) of 1,000 pounds each in 1830 to 362,296 hogsheads in 1858.

With only a nine-month growing season, Louisiana's sugar plantations were always at a disadvantage to sugar producers from the Caribbean, who had tropical weather year round. Since sugar cane took more than a year before it could be harvested, Louisiana's sugar cane never could reach full maturity. The longer a planter waited to harvest the sugar, the higher his yield, but a frost could kill the entire crop in one night. To try to beat nature, Louisiana's sugar planters adopted Ribbon Cane, a plant that matured more quickly. Still, Louisiana's sugar plantations could not compete with those of the Caribbean without a protective tariff, which increased the price of foreign sugar coming into the United States.

The best sugar harvests came from newly planted cane. After the harvest, the fields would be plowed and the seed cane planted in rows at least six feet apart. During the growing season, slaves used a hoe to rid the fields of grass and weeds. Usually by the fourth of July, the sugar cane was large enough to shade the ground and prevent any weeds and grasses from developing. As the sugar plants matured, slaves worked on other crops or they did manual tasks around the plantation such as fixing fences, working on levees, or collecting wood. Slaves needed to cut the wood so it would be cured and ready to fuel the sugar processing. Since slaves were worth as much as a thousand dollars each, heavy labor such as fixing levees and digging ditches was often given to Irish laborers who earned a dollar a day and, if they got hurt or killed, it was no loss to the planter.

In October, the sugar would be harvested, which was called grinding. For most of the year, slaves had half of Saturday and all of Sunday off, but because of the threat of a frost, slaves worked seven days a week from sun up to sun down gathering and processing the cane. Slaves worked in gangs, with the strongest doing the most physically demanding task. Even slave children led by a slave woman were given assignments during grinding time. Slaves used special machetes with a hook at the end to cut the cane. In a continuous motion, they cut the top of the cane, peeled the blades away, and then cut the stalk near the ground. Other slaves would gather the cane and haul it to the sugar house, where the cane was crushed by two rollers and its juice collected. Before 1832 the juice would be boiled in one kettle and impurities skimmed and then boiled again in another kettle before it crystallized into brown sugar, and the molasses would be drained away. In 1832 Norbert Rillieux, a free black, created the vacuum-pan method in which one fire fueled the steam engine that ran the rollers and boiled the juice, and the steam from the syrup helped heat the pans as well, making the process more efficient. The wet sugar would be packed into hogheads. On average, a sugar plantation returned about 9 percent on investment.

SLAVERY ALONG THE LOWER MISSISSIPPI

There is no escaping the grim reality that the prosperity of the plantation economy was based on the enslavement of human beings. A plantation's goal was to grow a marketable crop for profit. Cotton and sugar were labor intensive so a compulsory labor supply was required. Native Americans had been nearly wiped out or pushed into the western territories. The compulsory labor of whites was impossible in a country that espoused equality and freedom for white men and where land for them was readily available. During the colonial era, planters tapped into the African slave trade as a solution. When the U.S. participation in the international slave trade ended in 1808, planters turned to the internal market and encouraged the development of slave families to propagate the slave population. Despite the brutality of slavery, the black population of the South reproduced itself and reached 4 million by 1860, of which 2.5 million were under the age of 15. In 1860 the United States was the largest slave-owning country in the world.

To keep so many slaves under control, planters used racist laws to keep the black population subjugated: with a few exceptions, a slave had no rights as a human being. Although some states did provide a few protections, legally slaves were chattel property completely at the mercy of their masters. Slaves resisted by feigning sickness, slowing work, running away, and even turning to violence. At the same time, slaves asserted control over their lives by cultivating an African-based slave community rooted in African-Caribbean folk life, religion, and sensibilities. Critical to that process was maintaining the black family, where values, pride, and traditions were fostered and their sense of humanity preserved.

In this atmosphere of violent oppression, black Americans made a life for themselves. Life expectancy for whites and blacks in the sugar parishes was lower than in cotton producing parishes largely because of disease. The slaves who worked the sugar plantations were mostly married men in their thirties and forties. About 73 percent of the slaves on sugar plantation lived in simple families and 49 percent lived in a household with both a husband and a wife. There were fewer single slave women on sugar plantations than elsewhere.

In the rest of Louisiana, 48.7 percent of slaves lived in a simple family household that consisted of both parents and children, and another 8.1 percent lived as husband and wife without children. Only 14.5 percent of slave households were headed by a single female with children and

18.3 percent of households consisted of single males or females. In other words, the simple family survived the brutal conditions of slavery and married life was the norm for most slaves. Three-quarters of slaves lived with their parents or some other relatives. Unfortunately, if a plantation was broken up because of the death of the master or sale, the slaves risked the dissolution of their families. The fragmentation of the black family into a majority of single-parent households, which occurred initially as a consequence of adapting to conditions of poverty and diminished opportunity in urban settings in the twentieth century did not have their origin in the antebellum era. As Ann Patton Malone has noted, "[b]ecause slaves lacked the autonomy to form separate formalized institutions, informal education, socialization, religious activity, occupational training, courtship, and even internal governance often took place within the framework of their domestic organizations—the family, household, kinship group, and community."[7] During periods of economic stagnation, masters bought and sold fewer slaves, which gave some stability to slave households, but in economically prosperous times like the 1830s and 1850s, the slave trade flourished, and slave family life suffered from the loss of its members. Consequently, the number of single slaves with no family ties on plantations increased.

Most slaves in Louisiana lived in wooden cabins with two rooms, a chimney, a covered front porch, and a roof made of shingles. Some lived in double cabins under one roof, and a hallway in the middle divided one cabin from the other. On average, a family would live in a 16-by-16 foot cabin. Each cabin had a larger room that held the fireplace and served as the general living area. The smaller room was usually reserved for sleeping. Slave cabins were lined up in a row along a road. The overseer lived nearby. Planters maintained the cabins, and a carpenter, almost invariably one of the slaves, would do repairs when the slaves were in the fields. Generally, the slave cabins were rather flimsy and needed to be repaired often. Slaves were responsible for cleaning their homes, but the planter would intervene if there was a serious outbreak of disease. Woodened boards sufficed as beds with a straw or Spanish-moss stuffed mattress. Children usually slept in one bed. Mosquitoes and bedbugs were a constant problem so some slaves bought mosquito-netting to protest themselves. Most of the slaves cooked breakfast communally, but the evening dinner was a family affair. Former slave Elizabeth Ross Hite explained that on the Trinity Plantation, in Louisiana,

> We slept on wooden beds wid fresh moss mattress. Our beds were kept clean, much cleaner den de beds of today. Dey was scrubbed every Saturday. Dere wasn't a chinch [bug] on a one of dem. Better not see a chinch on a bed. De master would sure fuss about it. . . . All de beds was made by carpenters on de plantation. Dere was four rows of houses for de quarters. Dere was no paint on dem. Also a house for children and a hospital.[8]

Masters supplied buckets, skillets, and pots for cooking. Sometimes the master provided cups and plates and utensils for eating, but often slaves made or bought these items themselves. The master issued clothes twice a year, and blankets annually, with skilled slaves and black foremen receiving better allotments. Domestic servants might also get hand-me-downs from the planter's household. Women almost always wore kerchiefs on their heads, which were a common present from the master for Christmas. Adults wore shoes that were purchased by the master, but children ran barefoot. Slaves dressed up for special occasions, such as weddings when some brides would wear white dresses and gloves. If the slaves were not allowed to buy and sell goods to merchants, they may only have had what the planter had given them and what they made from scraps and other items they gathered and collected.

No southern state legally acknowledged the marriage of slaves, yet masters and the slave community encouraged slaves to marry. For masters, Christian ideals may have contributed to their commitment to marriage, but economic factors also played a role. Married slaves produced children for the master and increased his wealth, were less prone to running away, and usually had a higher morale, which meant that they worked harder. Most masters attempted to keep families together, but slave marriages lasted as long as both partners survived the high mortality rates and as long as the master or his family did not have reason to break them up. The death of a master may have meant that the plantation was broken up among his children or the bank may have had to foreclose on it. If allowed, weddings were a time of celebration and joy for the slave community. Some masters allowed white ministers to preside over the wedding ceremony and some occurred in churches. Often marriages were recorded in church documents. Off-plantation marriages were not common in Louisiana, but they presented problems because couples were only allowed to see each other if their respective masters allowed them to do so. These couples often had to resort to secret meetings, but this could be dangerous if they were caught. Not all slave marriages were made in heaven, but unlike white couples, slaves had few resources that allowed them to break up their marriages. On smaller plantations and farms, masters sometimes named the babies of slaves, but most children were named by their parents and went by their given names within the slave community. From all indications, parental love was strong and the loss of a child was mourned not only by the parents, but by the entire slave community.

Slaves lived within a community, though the size and location of the plantation strongly influenced the extent to which a slave community was self-contained and able to minimize the master's intrusion into the slaves' private world. They had their closest ties with kin. If the grandparents were still alive, they were highly respected. It was considered taboo to marry within a kin group. As long as they were not sold off by their master, laves developed close relations with their brothers and sisters and cousins.

By the 1850s most slaves became Christian, but slave religion was infused with powerful African-Caribbean elements in much of the delta region and distinct ideas about blacks as a chosen people almost everywhere. In lower Louisiana and in the Mississippi Delta, many slaves were baptized as Catholics and practiced varieties of an African-Catholic faith. Elsewhere, slaves were mostly Protestant. Everywhere, slaves incorporated African elements such as dancing, spirit possession, and magic into their religious experience. Whatever their formal church affiliation, or lack of it, religion reaffirmed slaves' humanity as individuals, bonded them as a community, and reminded them that they had worth in the eyes of God. Almost half of the slaves attended biracial churches, where they participated in varying degrees in church life but often were relegated to the back of the church or the gallery during worship. If given a choice, slaves tended to gravitate toward Baptist and Methodists churches because they were more emotional in worship and fit more closely West African religious expressions such as cleansing by water and spirit possession. Masters emphasized obedience as much as salvation in their religious instruction, but slaves seized on themes of deliverance in crafting their own Christian message.

Slave societies had their own hierarchy. The house servants may have lived better in terms of material comforts than the slaves in the fields, but they often had less prestige within the larger slave community because they were viewed suspiciously. Their proximity to the master, always at the beck and call of the master's household, further separated them from the slave community. Similarly, the slave driver, who managed the daily work on the plantation and meted out rewards and punishments, lived in a better cabin and received more material goods than other slaves, but often at the cost of being regarded as the so-called master's man not to be trusted by the slaves. If he acted brutally, other slaves would seek revenge against him. In the slaves own ordering of status, conjurors such as voodoo practitioners, religious leaders, storytellers, midwives, and the slaves who were clever enough to outwit the master attained the highest regard.

Slaves did have some power over their labor. In the face of harsh punishment, they manipulated their productivity in order to convince the master of their need for more humane working and housing conditions. Slaves, especially the elderly, kept their own gardens and even kept chickens and hogs. Most were allowed to sell their produce and keep the money. Slaves were also given land called the "Negro grounds" where they were allowed to grow corn and other crops that they could eat or sell to the plantation, but they could work such land only on their days off. Slaves could also cut wood, which other plantations would buy.

The petit market economy slaves practiced ran against the law and logic of slavery, which regarded slaves only as property, but it made sense to planters who bought produce from slaves because it was cheaper than buying the same products on the open market. Planters also paid slaves to dig ditches on their days off. Slaves collected and dried Spanish moss that was used for stuffing in the furniture industry. Much of these goods were sold to traveling merchants along the Mississippi, on consignment to traders in towns, or among themselves. Slaves also sold stolen goods, which upset the planters. Overall, the slave economy gave participants self-worth, satisfaction, and material goods that improved the quality of their daily lives. With the money they earned, slaves bought so-called luxury items that made life bearable, if not a little enjoyable such as food, drink, clothes, and tobacco. More enterprising slaves bought a whole range of household items, tools, and livestock. A few managed to save enough to buy their own freedom.

White society had to keep slaves under control. Fear of slave insurrection and distrust of the free blacks caused Louisiana to pass laws to prevent contact between the two communities. In 1830 a law prohibited the writing, printing, publishing, or distributions of anything that could incite a rebellion. No one was allowed to teach slaves how to read or write. Restrictions were placed on selling liquor to free blacks. At all times, 1 white person needed to watch over every 30 slaves on a plantation. Restrictions were put on the ability of slaves to trade, though they were enforced irregularly. Racial laws further strengthened slavery—a person was mulatto if one grandparent was black. Neither a slave nor a mulatto could testify against a white person in court. Slaves were not allowed to practice medicine so as not to poison their masters. In 1808 a slave convicted of arson would receive the death penalty. A free person with one-quarter black blood could become a slave as a form of punishment for a crime. Former slave Robert St. Ann described the punishment allotted to one runaway slave on a farm that grew rice:

> I remember once a youngster run away, and dey put de bloodhounds behind him. When dey caught him, dey put a horse to him and drag him through de woods, drag him to de house, de breath plum out of him. Dey dig a hole and thrown him in it. After [later] you hear dat boy groan under de ground—he ain't dead.[9]

Slaves could not assemble off the plantation without permission of their master, and even then, a white person had to be in attendance. They were not allowed to bear arms. Louisiana's slave code did not allow the manumission of slaves under the age of 30. The master who did free his slave would have to get the permission of the parish police and post a bond to make sure the state would not have to take care of the freed slave. In 1852 no manumissions were allowed at all.

About 86 percent of Louisiana's slaveowners owned less than 20 slaves. If the master was kind and generous, the slave families would benefit, but if he was cruel, then the slaves had to bear the full brunt of his wrath. Because these planters were up-and-coming, they sought to exploit their slaves to the maximum advantage, and often their slaves were worked hard. The larger holdings of 50 to 100 slaves were growing in the 1850s. On the largest plantations, those with over 100 slaves, the slave family was more stable and the material life higher. As slave prices increased dramatically in the 1850s from about $900 to over $2,000 by 1859, planters held on to their slaves. Such stability contributed to the development of the slave community.

THE ACADIANS

The development of the plantation economy affected poor whites as well. The lands along the Mississippi not only required the construction of costly levees, but also became very expensive to purchase, especially when the cotton economy boomed in the 1830s and 1850s. In particular, the Acadian people suffered from the in-migration of Americans and their slaves to regions along the Mississippi that they had occupied since colonial times. During the early part of the nineteenth century, American cotton planters pushed the small-holding Acadian farmers off their lands along the Mississippi River. By subdividing their land among all their children, Acadian farmers had weakened their family holdings, which made them less profitable. Over time, Acadian owners of these small holdings sold out to the large planters. Some Acadians managed to become planters themselves, but in doing so they often abandoned their Acadian identity. Most of the Acadians left their land along the Mississippi and moved either to southwest Louisiana where they became subsistence farmers and ranchers, to the swamplands of central Louisiana where they worked as fishermen and trappers, or to the coast where they fished and trapped. Through isolation and their sense of family-oriented community life, the Acadians managed to preserve their culture if not their economic well-being. By the mid-century, they had become the Cajuns—a people who spoke a Louisiana/Acadian French that was different from the Creole French of the planter class; practiced Roman Catholicism that emphasized the sacraments of baptism, marriage, and funeral rites but remained distrustful of clerical authority that came under increasingly Irish and American control; and lived a lifestyle that emphasized simplicity in clothing, housing, and furnishings. They lived in close knit-communities, and they tended to marry within their ethnic group. When outsiders married Cajuns, they were usually absorbed into the larger Cajun community. Their cuisine reflected their self-reliance: they used rice, seafood, and other items which they either grew or could catch themselves. Although many Anglo-Americans would look down upon them as lazy, ignorant, and unmotivated, the Cajuns believed they were equal to anyone.

CONCLUSION

In antebellum times, rural people "Americanized" the Mississippi River. Whereas the French and Spanish colonial powers were never able to successfully integrate the Mississippi Valley into their larger economy, the United States quickly did so. As the cotton regions in Georgia and Alabama became depleted, southerners by the thousands brought their capital and slaves to the lower Mississippi. On the upper Mississippi, tens of thousands of yeomen farmers from the upper South, the Old Northwest, and Europe plowed up rich alluvial soil and created a corn and wheat empire. What made all this possible was the Mississippi River. Its annual flooding had deposited some of the richest alluvial soil for miles in either direction. On the lower Mississippi, planters and farmers built levees to reclaim the lowlands with mixed success. Moreover, rural people took advantage of the Mississippi as a water highway. The transportation revolution brought steamboats to the river and allowed goods and people to move quickly up and down it. As the next chapter will show, towns and cities along the river became transit points for the agricultural surplus of America's heartland.

NOTES

1. Rebecca Burlend and Edward Burlend, *A True Picture of Emigration*, ed. Milo Milton Quaife (Lincoln: University of Nebraska Press, 1987), 41–43.
2. Ibid., 51.
3. Frank G. O'Brien, *Minnesota Pioneer Sketches: From the Personal Recollections and Observations of a Pioneer Resident* (Minneapolis: H.H.S. Rowell, Publisher, Housekeeper Press, 1904), 21.
4. Quoted in Glenda Riley, *Frontierswomen: The Iowa Experience* (Ames: Iowa State University Press, 1981), 84.
5. Pamela K. Sanfilippo, *Agriculture in Antebellum St. Louis: A Special History Study* (St. Louis: Ulysses S. Grant Historic Site, 2000), 22.
6. Wilma King, ed., *A Northern Woman in the Plantation South: Letters of Tryphena Blanche Holder Fox 1856–1876* (Columbia: University of South Carolina Press, 1993), 70–73.
7. Ann Patton Malone, *Sweet Chariot: Slave Family and Household Structure in Nineteen-Century Louisiana* (Chapel Hill: University of North Carolina Press, 1992), 19.
8. Ronnie W. Clayton, *Mother Wit: The Ex-Slave Narratives of the Louisiana Writers' Project* (New York: Peter Lang, 1990), 99.
9. Ibid., 191.

5

Transportation and Urban Life in the Antebellum Era

For most of the antebellum era, the cities and towns along the Mississippi thrived as transit points for the produce and crops of America's heartland. Flatboats, keelboats, and steamboats picked up wheat, corn, pork, beef, and cotton from people who lived near the 14,000 miles of navigable streams that made up the Mississippi River system and brought them to New Orleans. They returned with manufactured and luxury goods and produce from New England, the Mid-Atlantic states, and foreign countries. Immigrants, slaves, merchants, missionaries, soldiers, runaways, gamblers, criminals, and prostitutes traversed these waters as well. The wharves of cities and towns up and down the Mississippi became a public space where goods and ideas were exchanged, and hopes and dreams fulfilled or dashed. City residents provided services for the countryside or for the people engaged in trade.

The river system connected north, south, east, and west, but it had its limits. The upper Mississippi was frozen in the winter, and the depth of its water was too low in the summer months for most boats to navigate. Many tributaries to the Mississippi suffered from the same problems. Sand bars obstructed the mouth of the Mississippi and stymied the progress of sea-going vessels for several months every year. All along the river, snags could rip the hull of even the largest steamboats. Boiler explosions and fires on steamboats killed thousands. As long as the river system remained the cheapest and most convenient artery for commercial and passenger traffic for the country, people were willing to put up with its risks, and most river towns and cities along it thrived. But by the late 1850s, as the east-west flow of goods became ever more important, railroads proved that they were a more economical and reliable form of transportation, and the first signs of the decline of river transportation were already becoming evident.

LIFE ON FLATBOATS AND KEELBOATS

For many Americans, the Mississippi River and its tributaries served as a highway for the transportation of goods that they wanted to buy or sell. During the antebellum era, tens of thousands of people made their daily living on keelboats, flatboats, and steamboats. Although downstream traffic had its perils, moving upstream tested the endurance of humans to the limits until steam power took over. The crew of a keelboat would have to push and pull their way upstream against the current of the Mississippi. The 1,350 mile journey from New Orleans to Louisville might take three to four months. In 1819 a steamboat could make that trip in 16 days, and by the 1850s, it could accomplish the task in six days. Whereas it cost $5 to move 100 pounds of freight from New Orleans to Louisville by keelboat, it only cost 33 cents to move it on a steamboat in the 1840s. Not surprisingly, keelboats quickly became obsolete. Moreover, the steamboats that conquered western waters actually increased all traffic on the Mississippi, as production and commerce grew apace. In fact, flatboat traffic downstream remained brisk into the 1840s, and it continued to survive into the late nineteenth century on the upper Mississippi and tributary streams.

Keelboats were made by expert boatmen in the shipyards of Pittsburgh and Louisville. The keel was a long timber that extended the whole length of the boat and supported a frame with wooden planks. Keelboats had a rounded bottom and a pointed front and back. A sturdy cabin sat in the middle of the boat, which was about 7 to 10 feet wide and 40 to 80 feet long. Generally, a keelboat carried around thirty tons of cargo. A few had sails, but the winding channel of the Mississippi made wind power a sporadic help for the crew. To travel downstream, the crew of the keelboat used the current, and a journey from Louisville to New Orleans took four weeks. To make their way upriver, a crew of at least 10 boatmen would have to use their muscles to overcome the power of the current. Most often, boatmen would take a long pole, sink one end into the bed of the river, place the other end into their padded shoulders, and then walk the length of the boat on a cleated pathway to push the boat forward. Once they reached to the back of the boat, they would run to the front and do it again. Sometimes the crew would use a technique called bushwacking, which meant grabbing hold of low-lying branches of trees and bushes along the river and pulling the boat forward. Warping involved sending a few crew members on a small boat forward to tie a rope to a tree or snag in the river and the rest of the crew would pull the keelboat along. Other times, the crew would walk along the riverbank and tow the boat. In every case, bringing a keelboat upriver was a time-consuming, backbreaking process that tried the health of every crew member.

Flatboats were easier to maneuver and cheaper to make. Basically, they were rectangular boxes from 20 to 100 feet long and 12 to 20 feet wide. With some tools, most farmers could construct one with a little help. The sole purpose of a flatboat was to float along with the current of the river, which did take some skill so as to avoid snags and other river perils. Historians estimate that 20 percent to 25 percent of flatboats never reached their destinations. Some sank while others faced mishaps that forced their crews to sell their cargoes to other boats or to people along the shore. Some boats became grounded, and the crew had to hire oxen to pull their boat out. Those who successfully reached their destination sold their cargo and then their flatboat as scrap timber. Once the crew received their pay, they would have to find their way back upriver. Some got hired on keelboats, but most either walked or went by horseback along a 200-mile wagon road from New Orleans to Natchez, and then on the Natchez Trace that took them to Nashville. The arrival of the steamboat actually helped the flatboat trade by providing a cheap passage for flatboat crews upriver, thus allowing them to increase the number of trips they could make in any given year. Often, the flatboat crews would work on the steamboats for their passage by collecting wood. The number of flatboats that reached the New Orleans actually increased from 1,287 in 1817 to 2,792 in 1846 to 1847, but fell to only 541 in 1856 to 1857. In terms of their share of freight, flatboating declined in importance. Whereas they carried 43 percent of all Mississippi River freight in 1826, their total volume of trade dropped to 20 percent in 1840 and was only 5 percent by 1860.

Mark Twain described the crews who worked these boats as:

> Hordes of rough and hardy men; rude, uneducated, brave, suffering terrific hardships with sailorlike stoicism; heavy drinkers, coarse frolickers in moral sties like the Natchez-under-the-hill of that day, heavy fighters, reckless fellows, every one, elephantinely jolly, foul witted, profane; prodigal of their money, bankrupt at the end of the trip, fond of barbaric finery, prodigious braggarts; yet, in the main, honest, trustworthy, faithful to promises and duty, and often picturesquely magnanimous.[1]

The life of these boatmen was hard. Keelboatmen were allowed to have a break every hour on the journey upriver. If a boat became grounded on a bar, the entire crew was obligated to jump into the water and try to push the boat, no matter how cold the water or what the temperature was like. To avoid the hazards of traveling at night, the crew of a keelboat tied their boat down and slept on blankets on board the boat. They ate simple meals of corn, potatoes, and salted meat. Nearly every boat carried a barrel of whiskey, which, as legends have it, they drank wholeheartedly. Boatmen were notorious for working drunk, but a few Christian boatmen forbade the use of alcohol. Crews entertained themselves with music from a fiddle, singing, and dancing. Gambling was endemic.

Unfortunately, sickness took its toll, especially when boatmen reached the lower Mississippi in the hot summer months when yellow fever and malaria were rampant. Since boatmen rarely bathed, lice, mites, and fleas were their constant companions. Dysentery, vomiting, and diarrhea were common maladies, and visits to brothels created a venereal disease epidemic. If a crew member died along the journey, he would be buried along the shore. Local governments and the federal government provided resources for hospitals in the major ports and rivermen had to pay special taxes to support them, but health care was minimal for most boatmen. The mortality rates on some boats reached 20 percent to 40 percent. The river itself was a constant source of danger. Many boatmen did not know how to swim, so any fall into the river could be fatal. Snags, whirlpools, and eddies on the river could prove disastrous for a crew. Indian attacks and later criminal activity made the journey hazardous as well.

Almost all the keelboatmen and flatboatmen were white. Only a few women ever served on these boats, mainly as cooks. Most of the men were native-born and illiterate. Despite risks and hardships, boatmen worked on the Mississippi for adventure and the high wages. They could make as much as 35 to 50 dollars on one journey. Each river town had temptations that lured them to spend their money: whorehouses, taverns, and gambling dens. Drunkenness and fighting were common occurrences. The unwary boatman could blow most of his wages before he every reached home. As steamboats made the return trip easier, more and more of the boatmen were married men with families who saved their hard-earned wages.

THE STEAMBOAT REVOLUTION

When the steamboat *New Orleans* left Pittsburgh and reached New Orleans in January 1812, a new era in transportation began on the Mississippi River. Within a decade, the river steamboat had superseded the keelboat. Steamboats became the dominant technology that shaped life on the people along the river during the antebellum era. Between 1820 and 1860, steamboats increased in numbers by 1,000 percent, their cargo capacity increased by 10,000 percent, and their time of travel fell by 75 percent. The steamboat decreased costs of transportation and created an economic boom for the Mississippi and Ohio valleys. Upriver traffic became economical, and goods from New England and foreign markets were now easily brought into the heartland of the United States. Unlike flatboats and keelboats, steamboats also could carry passengers. Between 1825 and 1855, the price of deck passage fell by two-thirds. Luxury accommodations on the upper levels of a steamboat brought middle-class and rich travelers to the Mississippi River. The steamboat allowed people to travel in relative safety and quickly over large distances. Many of the immigrants who poured into the Mississippi Valley made their journey by way of the steamboat.

The crew of a steamboat had a strict hierarchy. The officers were almost all white and native-born. At the top was the captain. George Byron Merrick, a former steamboat pilot, explained:

> The captain's official requirements are not altogether ornate. It is true that he must have sufficient polish to commend himself to his passengers. That is essential in popularizing his boat; but in addition he must thoroughly know a steamboat from stem to stern, and know what is essential to its safety, the comfort of his passengers, and the financial satisfaction of its owners. Nearly every old-time captain on the river could, in case of necessity, pilot his boat from St. Paul to Galena. Every captain could, and of necessity did, handle the deck crew, with the second mate as go-between, during the captain's watch on deck. Some few might have gone into the engine-room and taken charge of the machinery, but these were exceptional cases. All were supposed to know enough about the business of the office to enable them to determine between profit and loss in the running of the steamer.... He must be a man possessed of nerve and courage, quick to see what was required, and quick to give the necessary commands to his crew.[2]

As was true in ocean vessels, the captain of a steamboat had absolute power in terms of law on his vessel. He managed his crew and entertained the upper-class passengers. The best captains allowed their crew to work without much interference.

Although officially the mate was second in command, he was more of a general manager on a steamboat and the least skilled and lowest paid officer. His primary responsibility was to keep the deck crew in line, which often required more muscle than intelligence. He supervised the loading and unloading of cargo and made sure the weight of the cargo was evenly distributed on the boat. Mates were known for their profanity and harsh treatment of the deck crew, and they were not well-respected among passengers.

One of the most highly skilled jobs on the steamboat was that of the pilot, who was in sole charge of the navigation of the steamboat. Since the Mississippi constantly changed, he had to see those changes and interpret how best to get the steamboat to its destination safely. When banks caved in, trees and boulders plummeted into the water to create obstacles. Rock, gravel, or sand bars could obstruct the channel and ground a boat or tear up its bottom. Drifting logs could damage a hull or the boat's paddles. Snags, trees that implanted themselves in the river's bed, could impale the hull of a boat. A log became a sawyer when its upright end pointed downstream and moved back and forth with the current of the river. A pilot had to spot all these dangers above water or notice how the surface of the water moved to detect the ones that hid just below the surface. Since the federal government did not provide any navigation assistance such as lights, buoys, and weather forecasts until the 1870s, the pilot had to rely on his own skill. Not surprisingly, pilots on the Mississippi were highly paid, and the pilot was the most respected officer on the steamboat.

The engineer was in charge of the mechanical devices that propelled the steamboat. It was hard physical labor that got the engineer dirty and sweaty. He received neither the pay nor prestige of the pilot or captain. In fact, the engineer was the one who was most often blamed for disasters. Since there was no mass production of steam engines, every engine was unique, which meant that each engineer had to learn by experience what maintenance an engine and boiler required, and how much pressure could be asserted on each before catastrophic failure. The boiler had to be cleaned, sometimes every other day, to get rid of the accumulated mud. Engineers were responsible for fixing the machinery that made the steamboat work. The engineer had to make do with what he had, but if major repairs required parts, the steamboat would have to stop at a town and get help at a foundry. The first steamboats on the Mississippi River had low-pressure engines, but they could not compete in speed with high-pressure engines, which replaced them as early as 1815. Unfortunately, those high pressures put enormous strain on boilers, so it was the engineer's job to

Ferry on the Mississippi, ca. 1890. Courtesy of the Goodhue County Historical Society, R. J. Kosec collection, Red Wing, Minnesota.

keep the boiler from exploding. Boiler explosions were the most spectacular disasters on the Mississippi River. Between 1811 and 1851 there were 209 of them on western rivers, and they accounted for half the people killed in accidents on steamboats.

The cabin crew was made up of laborers who served wealthy cabin passengers—barbers, stewarts, waiters, porters, and chambermaids. During the antebellum era, African Americans made up about half the cabin crew. Since they earned as much as two to three times as much as the deck crew, they were considered elite workers in the free black community and formed a black middle class in the river towns and cities along the Mississippi River. Seventy-five percent of the chambermaids were African-American women, and about half of them were free. The black members of the cabin crew had the opportunity to travel up and down the Mississippi and meet other African Americans as few others were able to. They provided a vital link in information and news for the free black community along the river.

At the bottom of the steamboat hierarchy was the deck crew. Unskilled native-born and immigrant whites competed for jobs with blacks. The most physically demanding job was that of fireman, which was most often filled by African Americans. The immigrant Friedrich Gerstäcker worked as a fireman in 1838 and described his experiences years later:

> The work of a fireman is as hard as any in the world; though he has only four hours in the day and four in the night to keep up the fires, yet the heat of the boilers, the exposure to the cutting cold night air when in deep perspiration, and the quantity of brandy he drinks to prevent falling sick, the icy cold water poured into the burning throat, must, sooner or later, destroy the soundest and strongest constitution.... In addition, there was the dangerous work of carrying wood, particularly in the dark and wet nights. One has to carry logs four or five feet in length, six or seven at a time, down a steep, slippery bank, sometimes fifteen or twenty feet in height when the water is low, and then to cross a narrow, tottering plank frequently covered with ice, when a single false step would precipitate the unfortunate fireman into the deep stream, an accident which indeed happened to me another time in the Mississippi.[3]

Deckhands were primarily responsible for carrying cargo into and out of the hold, but they also assisted with the boat's watch, mopped the deck, and assisted the pilot with soundings of the river. Members of the deck crews who worked as roustabouts carried cargo on and off the steamboat at river ports on planks that connected the boat with the dock. Both deckhands and roustabouts engaged in hard physical labor, and they were on call at all hours of the day and night. They were provided with food, but generally slept wherever they could find a place on the deck. A few steamboats provide a row of bunks along the wall of the cargo hold. It would not be until 1898 that the federal government mandated that boats provided a heated space in the sleeping quarters of a deck crew. Popular accounts relate that deckhands drank heavily, gambled, and cursed often. The officers segregated black and white deck crews in their work responsibilities as well as in their sleeping arrangements on deck. The vast majority of deck crews were young men under the age of 35. Most of the native white laborers had families, while only 15 percent of the immigrant laborers did. Although the ethnicity of deck crews varied, by the 1850s, about half of them were Irish. Just as with the crews of flatboats, work on steamboats opened up a world of adventure to farm boys who had never been outside their county, and there was never a shortage of eager hands at port cities and towns.

Compared to the stagecoach, cabin quarters were the most elegant way to travel before the coming of the luxurious railroad cars. Rich white passengers purchased cabins on the second deck of the steamboat. By the 1820s, shared sleeping berths gave way to private sleeping rooms called staterooms. Cabin passengers enjoyed all the luxuries that the steamboat could afford. Each stateroom opened on one end to the gallery and the other end to the saloon. The sleeping quarters were segregated by gender, with women getting cabins that were the furthest from the engine and boiler room so as to limit their exposure to heat and noise. The cabin passengers enjoyed the saloon, which too was segregated by sex—the women's section was carpeted and the men's was not. Men could only cross into the women's part on invitation of a woman. Cabin passengers had access to washrooms and barbershops. A few of the largest steamboats in the 1850s also contained a bridal chamber and servant's quarters. The saloon usually had a decorative ceiling with chandeliers, fancy carpets, paintings on the walls, and mahogany or rosewood furniture. Lighting was provided by candles and whale-oil lamps, until gas lighting became popular in the 1840s. The food served in the saloon was plentiful and varied and generally of good quality on the larger vessels, but could be quite poor on the smaller ones. Liquor could be purchased at the bar. Cabin guests entertained themselves with music, dancing, card-playing, and gambling, even though the latter was generally forbidden by steamboat authorities.

Deck passengers enjoyed none of the luxuries of cabin passengers. Low fares only gave them passage on the ship, a stove to cook on, and a bucket of water. No food, sleeping quarters, or waste facilities were provided. These passengers tried to keep out of the way of the deck crew, which did not hesitate to curse them. The deck was primarily for freight, and the accommodations for deck passengers were not even an afterthought. Deck passengers sat on whatever bucket, barrel, or crate they could find. Since they were exposed to the weather, they could seek shelter near the engine room, but the noise and the danger from the boiler were a real concern, and if there was an accident, deck passengers suffered the greatest number of casualties. The deck crew sometimes committed crimes against them, including rape. Nonetheless, the cheap and quick passage enticed tens of thousands of people to travel on the deck every year.

TOWNS AND CITIES ON THE UPPER MISSISSIPPI

Forts and trading posts became gathering points for trade and social life and the foundation of town growth along the upper Mississippi. To pacify the Dakota and Ojibwe in lieu of future white settlement, the U.S. War Department called upon Colonel Josiah Snelling to build a fort at the confluence of the Minnesota and Mississippi Rivers. Snelling's men did so, putting up an imposing stone wall 10 feet high with towers in a diamond shaped pattern that protected buildings and blockhouses made of limestone and pine logs. Once the fort was finished, the soldier's life became "one of drills and routine from reveille to tattoo, roll calls, fatigue duties, parades, hard work on assigned jobs, care of horses and cattle, special errands, a cash income of six dollars a month, severe punishment for infraction of rules."[4] But there was also fun, even in the harsh winter. Soldiers and their families played card games, checkers, and chess, and attended balls and plays. In the summer, soldiers took their families to nearby lakes for picnics. The arrival of Native Americans gave Americans a chance to see their dances and ball games. Soldiers grew some of their own food in fields around the fort, but most of their supplies were brought in by steamboats. Soldiers supplemented their rations of salted pork with wild game that they received by trading with Native Americans. Thankfully for the soldiers, Fort Snelling was never attacked. Instead, it served as the first permanent American settlement in the region. Within the fort's walls, the soldiers built Minnesota's first hospital, its first school, and its first library.

Since Fort Snelling was the headquarters of the United States in the area, Native American tribes came to the fort to negotiate treaties and trade with the Indian agent assigned to Minnesota. The Indian agent's mission was to maintain peace among the Eastern Dakota and the Ojibwe and mitigate the hostility between Native Americans and the increasing number of Americans to the region. Lawrence Taliaferro, the agent from 1820 to 1839, had to deal with the constant tension and violence between the two tribes. On one occasion, the Dakota murdered two Ojibwe within the very walls of the fort after a feast that members of both tribes had shared. Taliaferro attempted to control the liquor trade to the natives, which totaled over 21,000 gallons a year, but his efforts largely failed because the Indians demanded alcohol and American traders were willing to supply it. Like many Americans, Taliaferro believed in the so-called civilization of natives; this goal was to be achieved by assimilating them into American culture by turning them into farmers. He encouraged the founding of a village called Eatonville, a small native agricultural community of 125 people. Unfortunately, the fighting between the Dakota and the Ojibwe only worsened. The Americans were forced to continue the French policy of gift-giving in order to establish relationships with the natives at Fort Snelling with the hope of securing peace.

Christian missionaries also came to save the Native Americans. Although they generally failed to convert the natives and change their culture so they could become more colonized, missionaries played an important role as intermediaries and cultural ambassadors to the natives. As historian Theodore C. Blegen noted, these men and women were not just preachers, they "were also farmers, teachers, recorders of Indian life, writers, scholars, linguists, compilers of dictionaries, and frontier travelers" who provided posterity with a record of nineteenth-century Indian life.[5] Many of these Protestant and Catholic missionaries received funding from American and European missionary organizations that sought to convert and improve the conditions of the natives as well as assistance from the U.S. government for their educational endeavors.

Although treaties in 1837 allowed white settlement on Indian lands, it was not until the 1850s that the U.S. government received major land concessions from the Eastern Dakota along the Mississippi. Whereas Minnesota's white population had been only just over 6,000 in 1850, it soared to 40,000 in 1855 and 150,000 just two years later. The Panic of 1857 closed down banks and businesses in Minnesota, but the future opportunities continued to beckon immigrants. By 1860 the state's population had reached 172,000 people, most of who lived on the nearly 18,000 farms that dotted the territory. Making their way to Minnesota by wagon and steamboat, most of the settlers were farmers seeking homesteads in the countryside or opportunities for trade along the Mississippi.

A Roman Catholic priest, Lucian Galtier, founded a community of Catholics near a steamboat landing along Mississippi River just south of Fort Snelling. In 1841 he built a chapel, which he called a basilica, and dedicated it to St. Paul. Merchants opened up stores nearby. By 1847 a steamboat line was regularly making stops at the village, and mail was being delivered to a post office in St. Paul. Two years later, a hand press turned out the territory's first newspaper the *Minnesota Pioneer,* in which boosters hailed the bountiful land to anyone who would listen. A hundred steamboat arrivals reached the town each year in the 1840s, but river traffic boomed in the 1850s when a thousand steamboats annually docked at St. Paul and nearly every one was loaded with immigrants seeking to establish a life in the new territory. St. Paul became the territorial capital in July of 1857.

In its early years, St. Paul had all the markings of a frontier town. Although there were legal bans on work, dancing, and profanity on Sundays, the reality was that disorder was a common site in its streets. Saloons and brothels thrived, especially when steamboats came to town, and there were fights and shootings during the night. Attempts to prohibit liquor sales failed. Slowly, St. Paul became a more settled community. By mid-century, its inhabitants went to lyceums to hear lectures by visiting intellectuals, took out books from the local library, attended theater performances, enjoyed touring circus troupes, and participated in religious services at the 15 Christian churches or with the one Jewish congregation. Gas lighting arrived in St. Paul on September 19, 1857, but it was expensive and most of the lamps were turned off to reduce cost. Through the harsh Minnesota winters, residents burned wood as a fuel—as much as 43 cords of wood per a household in a single year. The town had no sewage system before the Civil War, so the city suffered from sanitary problems. Rain water for laundry was collected in barrels under eaves, though wealthier people had the rainwater drain into underground cisterns. During the long winters, people got their ice for their ice boxes from the river.

In 1849 a Minnesota law stipulated that schools would be free to all between the ages of 4 and 21 years old. Between 1858 and 1861, the number of schools in the territory increased from 72 to 466. Students went to school for about three months in the winter, but the scarcity of good teachers hindered progress, so communities across the state chartered private academies. On February 9, 1851, the U.S. Congress gave 46,080 acres of land for the creation of a university in Minnesota, and a few weeks later the state legislature passed its charter that was signed by the governor, but classes would not begin until 1869. The first college in Minnesota to offer higher education courses was Hamline University, a private school founded in the town of Red Wing along the Mississippi River, but it closed its doors in 1869, and was reopened in St. Paul in 1880.

St. Paul and other towns along the Mississippi in Minnesota suffered from the fact that the river froze over for five months of every year. It became an annual event for residents of St. Paul to run to the levee along the Mississippi to greet the first steamboat that had made it to the town every spring. During the summer, low water on the Mississippi prevented most steamboats from reaching the city. The successful construction of the Rock Island railroad in 1854 signaled that a new era was dawning, but no railroads were built in Minnesota during the antebellum era, so steamboats remained the main source of transporting goods. Before 1865 Minnesota was still a frontier society, and the threat from Indians was real. In 1862 the Dakota Uprising killed 500 white settlers who lived along the Minnesota River to the west. It would not be until after the Civil War that the region blossomed as one of the most economically productive regions in the country.

NAUVOO: THE MORMON KINGDOM ON THE MISSISSIPPI

In 1839 Joseph Smith, the founding prophet of the Church of Jesus Christ of Latter-Day-Saints, personally picked a low-lying site along the Mississippi for a city that would serve as the foundation of a kingdom of God on

Earth. He and five thousand of his followers had just fled from persecution in Missouri, and thought that Illinois would offer them the sanctuary they needed. Nauvoo, which means "to be beautiful" in Sephardi Hebrew, was to be the gathering place of Mormons from around the world. The Illinois legislature had initially welcomed the hard-working Mormons and issued their city a charter that gave them much autonomy, including the organization of a militia and a municipal court.

But trouble came to Nauvoo. Joseph Smith created an aggressive theocracy that was at odds with an equally aggressive Jacksonian democracy that neighboring towns embraced. The Mormon leadership used Nauvoo courts to give virtual immunity for its members from crimes against non-Mormons. The creation of a Mormon militia of several thousand men under direct command of Joseph Smith sent ripples of concern throughout Illinois. The secretive nature of Mormon leadership, especially the Council of Fifty, was at odds with the open democratic process of nearby towns like Warsaw. Believing that he was receiving divine revelation from the angel Moroni, Joseph Smith introduced doctrines such as plural marriages that caused schism among the Mormons and invited the hostility of outsiders. Matters grew worse when Smith and other leaders

Nauvoo, IL. Courtesy of the Library of Congress.

crushed all dissent either by excommunication, social pressure, or actual violence.

The fact that Nauvoo grew from a marsh land to a growing community of 20,000 within six years attests to the success of Joseph Smith and his faithful followers. The town was a planned community from the start. The pride of the new city was the 165-foot high temple located on a bluff in the commons area. Every Mormon was to pay a special tithe for its construction, and only those who had paid up would be allowed to come in. For two years, Mormons practiced the baptism for the dead and other services within its walls. Also located on the bluff was the unfinished Nauvoo House, a hotel for special guests. The city was laid out in one-mile square that was divided in a grid pattern of four-acre blocks. Each block was subdivided into one-acre lots that were large enough for gardens, fruits trees, and domesticated animals. The Mormon leadership expected that the farmers within the community would work in fields outside the city.

Once Smith proclaimed that it was every Mormon's duty to move to Nauvoo, Mormons flocked into the city, including 4,733 converts from Great Britain. About a third of the residents of the city were farmers, and another third worked in the construction trade. The town teemed with people of various skills—including doctors, lawyers, school teachers, newspaper publishers, store owners, furniture-makes, and gunsmiths. Because Nauvoo was a cash poor economy, most people worked at more than one occupation to survive. Various trade associations were formed to pool the resources of the community. For instance, the Nauvoo Agriculture and Manufacturing Association built two dams to supply the water for a sawmill and a grist mill. Hundreds labored on building the temple, the Nauvoo House, and new homes for migrants to the city. Diseases common to all cities along the Mississippi—malaria, whooping cough, tuberculosis, measles, and mumps—plagued the new town. As elsewhere, crime was a problem. City officials arrested a gang of Mormons who preyed on the people of neighboring counties and expelled them from the church. Two brothers were executed for murder.

The political leadership had to deal with a host of urban problems and sought to manage public behavior in the common interest of the Mormon experiment. The council passed laws forcing owners to remove the carcasses of dead animals off the street, banned nude swimming, and imposed a curfew forbidding people to be on the streets between nine o'clock in the evening and sunrise. Gambling was prohibited, but Mormons eagerly played games and danced to music.

Nauvoo was different from other Mississippi towns in that religion played a dominating role in the lives of its residents. Smith's sermons were occasions of public meetings and also spectacle. By all accounts, he was a moving speaker. In the summer, he and other church leaders preached on platforms erected outside in a grove. In the winter, Smith held religious services in his home, with people gathered outside to listen to him through the windows. The Mormons also held religious meetings at home with their relatives to discuss and reflect on the Book of Mormon. Missionaries were invited to dinner, and the accounts of their experiences thrilled family members. The bond of religion and the memories of persecution in Missouri held the community together.

Conflict did exist within this community. Past experiences of persecution had convinced Joseph Smith that those who were not totally for him were against him. New revelations from the prophet were to be obeyed, no matter how unorthodox they seemed. Everyday life in Nauvoo teemed with tension. At first, the prophet kept his revelation of plural marriages from the general Mormon public, and only the elite could participate. Plural marriage meant that a man could take several wives, which he would have for all eternity. The members of the Council of Fifty had to conform or be expelled from the community. When Joseph Smith approached Lucy Walker, and as she later recalled, he said to her, "I have no flattering words to offer. It is a command of God to you. I will give you until to-morrow to decide this matter. If you reject this message the gates will be closed forever against you."[6] She had already rejected him twice, but the threat of expulsion from the community and burning in hell for eternity was too much for a young girl to bear. She agreed. She saw her submission as a sacrifice she had to bear for God. This disturbing compulsion enacted upon the women of Nauvoo caused many within the community to question their faith. Those women who rejected the advances of Joseph Smith and other leaders were slandered and expelled from the community. Some Mormons broke off from the main leadership of Mormons in protest to the practice. They were and still are labeled as apostates, damned to eternal fire. Even the prophet's widow, Emma Hale Smith, rejected plural marriage after the death of her husband, and Brigham Young and other leaders had her expelled.

The news of such troubling practices only reinforced the negative images of many Americans in the neighboring towns of Carthage and Warsaw, and made even those sympathetic to the Mormons look with fear at what Nauvoo represented. The fact that Joseph Smith decided to run for president in 1844 and that he called on Mormons to vote as one solid bloc caused many Americans to fear a Mormon coup against the constitutional government of this country. When the city of council of Nauvoo ordered the destruction of an opposition Mormon press using the Mormon Legion, an armed militia loyal to Smith, neighboring Americans and some Mormons were incensed. The editors of the opposition paper fled to Carthage and swore out a warrant for Smith's arrest. The governor of Illinois, Thomas Ford, came to Carthage to prevent a civil war, for the citizens of Hancock County had already organized a posse and Smith had mobilized the Legion in response. Ford organized a militia and arrested Smith, his brother, and 16 others, and forced the Mormon Legion to disarm. Tragically, a mob shot Smith and his brother dead in their cells before they were brought to trial. Those responsible were arrested, but never convicted.

For the next two years hostility toward the Mormons at Nauvoo continued. Brigham Young used the real threat of persecution to consolidate his power and expel those, like Smith's widow, who disagreed with him. In 1846 thousands of Mormons left Nauvoo to set up a new kingdom in Utah. Some of those who opposed Young set up the Reorganized Church of Jesus Christ of Latter Day Saints, which today is known as the Community of Christ. In 1860 they chose as their leader, the prophet's eldest son, Joseph Smith III, who disavowed the theocratic elements that some said plagued the church, and instead, focused on the spiritual community. Over time, Nauvoo declined in importance. Today, it exists as a pilgrimage site for the various denominations of Mormons.

LIFE IN ST. LOUIS

Founded in 1763 by a French fur trader, St. Louis was only 10 miles south of the confluence of the Missouri and Mississippi Rivers. Smaller boats from the Missouri and upper Mississippi rivers transferred their cargo to larger steamboats in St. Louis. So too did the larger steamboats coming from the lower Mississippi or the Ohio rivers which then sent their cargo north or west of St. Louis. By the 1850s, three thousand steamboats a year docked in the city. St. Louis was the staging area of the Sante Fe and Oregon trails for people moving out west. Residents manufactured goods to supply the tens of thousands of migrants every year. Moreover, farmers as far as 250 miles upriver from St. Louis shipped their crops directly to the city. Until the railroads through Duluth and La Crosse linked Chicago with the West, St. Louis was the region's gateway to the rest of the nation.

As with any growing city, St. Louis experienced problems. In 1832, 1848, and 1853, the city was ravaged by cholera epidemics. There were housing shortages. But city leaders responded with innovative programs, and migrants kept coming. In the 1820s, the city's mayor, William Carr Lane, "pioneered public health services, encouraged free schools, and worked for paved streets, a municipal water works, and improved wharf, public fountains, parks, and shade trees."[7] The city was home to the first university west of the Mississippi, St. Louis University, which was founded by Catholics in 1818 as St. Louis Academy. The city was home to Planter's House, one of the best hotels in the West, the second oldest symphony orchestra in the U.S., and a professional theater. By the 1830s, St. Louis had public schools and its first public high school opened 1853. That same year, Eliot Seminary was founded that would later became Washington University.

To protect their city, residents of St. Louis organized volunteer fire companies in which both rich and poor served. Into the 1840s, it was almost a necessity for a mayor of St. Louis to have served as a fireman if he wanted votes. The firehouse became a place for men to bond away from the home.

The first parochial school, St. Louis, ca. 1845. Courtesy of the Library of Congress.

Although members weren't paid a salary, they received social recognition and freedom from jury duty. Fire companies competed for status and resources, and fights often broke out between rivals. In 1849 public opinion in the city turned against the fire companies when firemen started a riot that led to $130,000 of property damage, and then failed to stop a fire that destroyed a square mile of St. Louis and most of its waterfront. Urban reformers in the East already had been viewing firehouses as places of drunkenness and corruption where single and married men did irresponsible things. Throughout the country, editors of newspapers and reformers believed that a modern city must have a professional fire department consisting of men who were paid and could be held responsible for doing their jobs. Steam engines and insurance did not make the heroic volunteer fireman as necessary to city life anymore. Skill and technology were replacing bravery as a treasured value among the elite and the emerging middle class, and responsible males in society held salaried jobs. Middle-class culture successfully eliminated volunteer firehouse most from American's large cities, including St. Louis, by the 1850s.

Although the majority of St. Louis's population was French at the time of the Louisiana Purchase, German and Irish immigrants were attracted to the opportunities the city had to offer. By 1850 a third of its 75,000 people were Germans, and they became very successful as skilled laborers, artisans, and business owners despite the hostility from native-born

Americans. They were instrumental in making St. Louis one of the major producers of beer in the country. As early as 1840 Adam Lemp had opened a brewery in St. Louis and made lager beer, which eventually became the most popular style of American beer. By the Civil War, 40 breweries were in the city, including one bankrupt brewery that had just been bought by Eberhard Anheuser and Adolphus Busch and would become the country's most dominant brewery.

Before the arrival of the so-called Famine Irish in the 1840s and 1850s, the Irish immigrants to St. Louis were skilled artisans and businessmen who established a small, but thriving ethnic community. When the potato famine hit the Irish countryside beginning in 1846, millions of rural Irish people fled their country. Several thousand of them entered the United States at New Orleans and traveled up the river to St. Louis looking for work. Most of these desperate people took hard physical jobs such working on the docks, constructing railroads, digging clay for the brick industry, or working on farms in the surrounding countryside. Irish women accepted positions as domestics. The flood of Irish immigrants caused many native Protestant Americans to look down upon them. The abolitionists Elijah P. Lovejoy used his newspaper the *St. Louis Observer* to viciously attack Catholic immigrants just as he did slaveowners. He believed that the Catholic Church was using the Irish immigrants and the Jesuits to infiltrate the United States and endanger the religious rights of Americans. Despite these attacks, immigrants continued to pour into the city

But not all immigrants found St. Louis so appealing. Salomon Koepfli, a Swiss immigrant to New Switzerland in Illinois, wrote:

> In Missouri, where slavery is permitted, we have witnessed incidents that would arouse the pity of the most hard-hearted. In St. Louis one can at all times see blacks being offered for sale. Prospective buyers poke and examine them before bidding on them at auction, ridiculing them the while. It is incomprehensible that such scene can be witnessed in a republic in which the inhabitants profess a love of freedom. We leave it to the prospective emigrant to decide whether to emigrate to a state which permits such appalling conditions to continue.[8]

Although Missouri was a slave state, St. Louis's connection to the slave trade weakened as the city developed into a commercial center with strong ties to the West and North. The slave population of the city fell from 20 percent in 1830 to only 1 percent by 1860. Because Missouri's legislature passed laws prohibiting free blacks from settling in the state, and those who did had to obtain a license, the free black community remained small at only 2 percent of the city's population, Even though it was also illegal to run a school for free black children, a few Catholic priests and Protestant ministers did so. Despite these obstacles, the small free black community thrived. In 1858 Cyrian Clamorgan published his book, *The Colored Aristocracy of St. Louis,* to show white America that although free blacks did not have the right to vote, they should get respect because they possessed economic power. Many free blacks held jobs as barbers or worked on steamboats as cabin crews. Black women ran boardinghouses or worked as washing women and chambermaids. Some of the richest free black women inherited their wealth. As he noted, "Wealth is power, and there is not a colored man in our midst who would not cheerfully part with his last dollar to effect the elevation of his race. They know who are their friends, and when the opportunity arrives they exhibit their gratitude in a manner most acceptable to the recipient."[9]

WILLIAM JOHNSON AND NATCHEZ, MISSISSIPPI

By the 1830s, Mississippi planters were growing more cotton than any other state. Not surprisingly, the two major towns in the state along the Mississippi, Vicksburg and Natchez, were foremost trade depots to load this production onto boats and send them to New Orleans. Businesses in town served either the passengers of steamboats and their crews or the neighboring planters and farmers who brought their produce into town. The economic dominance of New Orleans cast its veil over the growth of both towns. Yet, on the outskirts of Natchez were some of the most beautiful plantation homes on the lower Mississippi. As historian John Hebron Moore has noted, "[t]hese extremely wealthy planters in the suburbs of Natchez made the little community into the social capital of the planter class of Mississippi. Elsewhere in the state, slaveowning cotton growers tried to imitate Natchez fashions in architecture, carriages, dress, manners, and customs."[10]

The shipping of cotton was the most important economic transaction in Natchez. Before 1800 cotton was shipped in long cylindrical canvas bags. These bags were filled by getting the canvas wet, suspending it into the air, putting loose cotton in it, and having a man inside the bag trample the cotton. When the bag dried, the cotton canvas would shrink and bind tightly the cotton inside. A Natchez mechanic, David Greenleaf, invented the cotton press, which compressed cotton into a rectangular bale. Men would turn two horizontal screws that pressed the cotton into a hemp cloth covered wooden box. After pressing, the two wooden sides were removed and the bale was tied tightly with ropes. The cotton would expand once the press let go. William Dunbar designed a press that had more durable cast-iron screw, but this machine was expensive so it was not used widely until after 1840. Most planters continued to use a variety of wooden presses. Bales were usually 400 to 500 pounds each. Steamboats charged by the bale, so the more cotton that could be pressed into a standard size, the cheaper the transportation cost. During the height of economic prosperity for Natchez in the 1830s, the docks on its riverfront loaded 50,000 bales of cotton annually onto boats making their way to New Orleans. The bales would once again be pressed in New Orleans before being loaded onto ocean-going vessels. Steam presses would compact the bales to almost half of their original size to take up less room and give them better protection from fire or water.

Natchez was divided into two parts. Natchez-Under-the-Hill was the section of town along the riverfront with wharves, warehouses, and business establishments like brothels, taverns, and cheap hotels that catered to boatmen. In this section of town, petty crime was rampant and street fighting was almost a nightly occurrence. On the bluffs, the main part of the town showcased "the Adams County courthouse, the city hall; the county jail, three churches belonging to the Presbyterians, Methodists, and Episcopalians, respectively; a Masonic hall; a theater; a hospital; a Mechanics' hall; an orphan asylum; eleven hotels, a coffeehouse; and the Planters Bank, the Agricultural Bank, and the Commercial Bank."[11] The white residents on the bluff enjoyed lectures at the Natchez Institute, a city band, parades on Independence Day, and public balls, and frequented horse-races just outside town. Public education in Natchez during the antebellum period never caught on, and the population relied on four privately owned academies. The first college in the state of Mississippi, Jefferson College, was founded in the town in 1817 and except for its temporary closing during the Civil War, would serve the community until 1964. White men fraternized in four military companies, three divisions of a volunteer firemen company, two Masonic lodges, trade associations, and several other organizations. Protestant women attempted to remedy the ills troubling Natchez by creating the Female Charitable Society in 1816 to provide care and education for orphans and widows and the Ladies Charitable Mission Society in 1822. Before the abolitionist movement struck fear into the planter elite, planters and evangelicals worked together to found the Mississippi Colonization Society to ship free blacks to the colony of Liberia in West Africa, and encourage the manumission of slaves.

Natchez remained a small town throughout the antebellum era. Natchez reached its peak of prosperity in the 1830s, but the Panic of 1837 and the subsequent depression hurt the city. The railroad company that had promised to link the town with the rest of the expanding national network of railways went bankrupt. In 1838 and 1839, fires destroyed the business district and tornadoes from a hurricane in 1840 devastated much of what had survived. When cotton prices rose again in the mid-1850s, businesses and construction experienced a resurgence, but the population of Natchez in 1860 did not reach the numbers the town had achieved in the 1830s.

The diary of William Johnson, a successful free black businessman in Natchez, provides us a window into the social world of free blacks along the Mississippi. William Johnson's father was a white man and his mother a slave, whom his father freed. After his father successfully petitioned the legislature of Mississippi, William Johnson received his freedom at age 11. His mother established a retail store in Natchez, owned several slaves, and married a free black barber, who apprenticed the young William to his brother's barber shop. At 19 years old, William opened his first barbershop in Port Gibson, Mississippi, in 1828. Two years later, he bought the shop of his stepfather in Natchez. The barbershop was so successful that William Johnson purchased the building that he had been renting after three years and paid off a loan of $5,000 two years later. As a bachelor, Johnson went on trips to New Orleans, Philadelphia, and New York City, and thoroughly enjoyed himself. In 1835 he settled down to marry a twenty-year-old local girl, Ann Battles, and they had 10 children together.

Although prevented from participating in the white political and social world, Johnson was a well-respected citizen in the free black community. His barbershop was in the center of town amid the most important public buildings. Men frequented a barbershop not only to get groomed, but to meet friends, exchange news and gossip, and talk business. In the 1840s, reformers were trying to convince the public that bathing was necessary for health of the community. Johnson filled that need by providing bathing facilities even if it was not a big money maker. As any good businessman, Johnson understood he needed to cultivate his clientele and build a relationship of trust with them. Johnson charged 25 cents for a haircut, 12 1/2 cents for a shave, and 50 cents for a bath. He gave discounts for customers who paid a monthly subscription for his services. His barbershop was a model of cleanliness, and he made sure customers were more than satisfied with the service. The fine perfume smells that emanated from the barbershop contrasted with the odor from the unpaved, muddy streets of Natchez with their open sewers, dead animals, and garbage. His business was such a success that he opened two smaller barbershops in town.

When the Panic of 1837 hit and a depression lingered though the 1840s, Johnson managed to survive. He invested in 750 acres of farming and timber land, and set out to be a planter. With five slaves and hired laborers, he cleared the land. In his diary, Johnson admits to disciplining his slaves and whipping them when he thought they had done a serious misdeed. As a prominent citizen, he was a member of the volunteer fire department. One of his vices was gambling, and he actively bet on horses all his adult life, but never enough to threaten his financial position. He loaned people money, and made sure that his debtors paid him off. Like most Americans, Johnson was not too thrilled about paying taxes, "This is hard that a man has to pay so much for I may say Nothing."[12]

On the evening of June 16, 1851, someone shot and killed William Johnson as he was making his way from his farm back to the city. The murder of a prominent free black shocked the white and black community of Natchez. Baylor Winn, who had an ongoing property dispute with Johnson, was charged for the crime. The state designated Winn as a mulatto, but he claimed that he was a white man with Indian, not black blood. Winn's first trial ended in a mistrial. In the second trial, the state could not prove that he had black ancestry. The third trial ended without a conviction because of a lack of white witnesses to the crime. The only people who had been at the crime scene when the murder had been committed were black, but state law barred black or colored people from testifying against a white man. Johnson had hoped to forge a better life for himself and his family in Natchez by becoming a successful businessman. In the end, jealousy perhaps and race surely prevented Johnson's family and the free black community from receiving justice. Few free blacks had done so well as Johnson in making their own way. Restrictions on work, property, and basic civil rights kept them down.

NEW ORLEANS

In the antebellum era, New Orleans was the jewel of the Mississippi River. No other city on the river was as prosperous, heavily populated, ethnically and racially diverse, or culturally rich. New Orleans was a commercial hub rather than a manufacturing center. Most of the produce of America's heartland ended up here to be transferred to sea-going vessels. Goods coming from as far away as New England and foreign countries came through the city to be sent northward. In 1830, $22 million worth of goods arrived at New Orleans. By 1860 the trade had increased to $185 million. Docks and warehouses lined the city's riverfront, and white and black workers loaded and unloaded ships. Since two fires during the Spanish colonial era destroyed a good portion of the city, most of the buildings of New Orleans were built in a Spanish style. The city experienced phenomenal growth after the Louisiana Purchase. In 1800 the city had 10,000 residents, but just 10 years later the population had swelled to nearly 25,000, making it the largest city in the United States south of Baltimore. War and revolution in the French West Indies brought a wave of thousands of French immigrants to the city. In the spring of 1809 alone, 5,800 people arrived in the city; of these 4,000 were free people of color and blacks. Another 4,000 refugees came in the next few years. After the war of 1812, free blacks from other parts of the United States migrated to New Orleans and tens of thousands of Anglo-Americans, Irish, and Germans sought opportunities there. By 1860 the population of New Orleans had reached 168,000.

The city's location along a bend of the Mississippi River gave it its crescent shape. Since the natural levees provided the only land suitable for building, the Creole inhabitants built the Old Quarter of New Orleans on it. As new migrants made their way into the city, New Orleans expanded into what had been plantations north and south of it along the natural levee. The back swamps with their poor drainage were the least desirable lands because they were prone to flooding with every major rainfall. Americans moved just north of the French Quarter in Uptown—Canal Street divided the American and French portion of New Orleans. Uptown was divided into thin lots that touched the Mississippi River levee and moved inward toward the city, but since the Mississippi is not straight, this created a fan-like appearance. Canals were dug between the lots to drain water from Uptown into the back swamps. Later roads were placed along these canals, and they eventually became large boulevards. The new American elite built their houses in what would be know as the Garden District. In contrast to the Spanish who built their homes next to the street and had courtyards behind the buildings, American mansions were built with large front yards. South of the French Quarter, poorer Creoles and Irish and German immigrants settled in downtown, the poorest part of the city. African Americans lived either in the back streets behind the houses of the whites for whom they worked or in between the boulevards that were lined with the homes of wealthy whites. The poorest neighborhoods were the temporarily dwellings along the front of the levee known as the batture, which were washed away with every major flood. Poor neighborhoods expanded into the back swamps, but they also suffered from frequent inundations.

Creoles were a vital part of life in New Orleans. During the colonial era in Louisiana, the term *Creole* referred to any black, free, or slave born in the colony. After the American takeover of Louisiana in 1803, Creole referred to anyone, black or white, whose ancestors were born in Louisiana during the French or Spanish period. In the atmosphere of the racism of the nineteenth century, whites who considered themselves Creole believed that the term meant only whites who were born in Louisiana and had French or Spanish heritage. But Creole meant something else for the black community. For them, Creoles were free people of color with a mixture of French or Spanish and African blood, whose ancestors lived in colonial Louisiana. The largely Catholic free people of color saw themselves as better than pure-blood African and African-American slaves, whom they regarded as savage and heathen, and they believed that their Catholic religion and good character warranted respect from the white community. Many of the people of color were able to send their children to parochial schools, but the wealthiest sent their boys to France for an education and their girls to convent schools. French law made the children of a sexual union of a white male and his black or Indian female slave a slave because the status of the mother determined the status of the children. However, white fathers often freed the children and their mistresses, and these people became known as *gens de couleur libre,* or free people of color.

Free women of color had a unique place in Louisiana society. Some were known as quadroons, which literally meant mixed with one-quarter black blood, but in Louisiana society it meant seductress.[13] Many of these women were of lighter skin so they could pass in white society. These women often chose white men as their sexual partners to gain protection and some security. Also, the appalling death rates among free black men limited the chances for all-black unions during the colonial era. In the Spanish Louisiana, free women of color outnumbered free men of color by a factor of 6 to 1. Since white men outnumbered white women during the colonial period, some of them took black women as lovers. White society looked down upon these black women because it considered only white women as virtuous and honorable. In contrast, black women were seen as immoral temptresses. Spanish law prohibited these women from marrying pure-blooded blacks or free white men. To protect themselves, quadroons developed *plaçage*, a formal legal relationship of mistresses that protected the free woman of color and her children. Rich quadroon women organized themselves in the *Sociéte Cordon Bleu*. They would introduce their daughters to European men at elaborate balls called *Bal de Cordon Bleu* so *plaçage* could be established with rich white men who had been invited to attend. The daughters were guarded until a formal relationship had been established. The girls were allowed to dance with white men, but they could stop dancing with them if they did not find them attractive or amenable. If both parties agreed to a relationship, the white man would furnish her with a house and be obligated to take care of her and her children during their time together. If they wished to separate, he was obligated to provide a settlement. The children had legal status and could and did inherit property from their fathers. *Plaçage* continued informally into the American era. These arrangements created a class of women of color with wealth whose children went to the best schools and became important members of New Orleans society.

Free people of color did not fit in with the African-American community or with the ruling white community, but became a third powerful and influential group in the city—a mixed culture of African and French with its own language, foods, music, and social structure. Many men of color worked as skilled artisans in New Orleans and made up a middle class of free people of color. Free women of color worked as seamstresses, dressmakers, and hairdressers, washerwomen, street vendors, and domestic servants. Since they could inherit money and property from their white fathers, some men of color established their own businesses. Etienne Cordeviolle and François La Croix, for example, became tailors who established a successful clothier business in 1817. La Croix's brother, Julien Adophe, ran a grocery store, and when he died in 1868, his estate was worth $130,000. Other successful wealthy families of people of color families included names such as Colvis, Dumas, Aime, Legoaster, Mercier, Carriere, and Campanel. People of color owned plantations with slaves. Antoine Dubuclet's net worth in 1860 was $206,400, and his estate included a plantation and a house in New Orleans. The Dollioles, the Fouchés, and the Lamottes were successful contractors and builders in New Orleans. Free men of color were also architects, lithographers and engravers, physicians, engineers, ship brokers, ironworkers, and sculptors. In sum, free people of color were a vital part of everyday life in New Orleans.

New Orleans was a major slave market in the South. Solomon Northup, a northern black stolen into slavery in Louisiana, described what happened to him in the 1840s:

Next day many customers called to examine Freeman's "new lot." The latter gentleman was very loquacious, dwelling at much length upon our several good points and qualities. He would make us hold up our heads, walk briskly back and forth, while customers would feel of our hands and arms and bodies, turn us about, ask us what we could do, make us open our mouths and show our teeth, precisely as a jockey examines a horse which he is about to barter for or purchase. Sometimes a man or woman was taken back to the small house in the yard, stripped, and inspected more minutely. Scars upon a slave's back were considered evidence of a rebellious or unruly spirit, and hurt his sale.[14]

Competing firms ran a slave market where today the streets Chartres and Esplanade intersect. As many as a hundred slaves would be held in pens with high walls. They would be paraded in front of the building to attract potential customers. The examination of slaves by customers and their purchase would occur in a showroom. But slaves were not passive victims. They evaluated the person buying them and either tried to convince him to buy them or not. Slaves hoped to be sold to richer masters than poorer ones for a larger plantation promised life in a black community, and they explained their skills so as to avoid being sold as a field hand. Generally, they preferred to live in the city rather than be isolated in the country. They also tried to convince buyers to purchase family members. In the market, buyers learned to differentiate a so-called good slave from a so-called bad slave. Scars form whipping may indicate a slave with the propensity to run away. Muscles were touched to indicate any injuries. Teeth were examined to indicate age and general health. Buyers preferred light-skinned women for household work, and dark-skinned slaves were thought to be better workers in the fields.

CONCLUSION

The Americanization of the Mississippi River involved linking the Mississippi River system to the economy of the expanding United States. Hundreds of thousands of Americans and immigrants made the lands along the Mississippi River their home. Native American tribes were either eliminated or driven off further west. Cities and towns along the river became the centers of trade where the products of the heartland were shipped to New Orleans. As steamboats replaced keelboats and flatboats, the new technology employed tens of thousands and moved goods and people up and down the river. In the antebellum era, Minnesota was a frontier society that had just settled on Native-American lands. The lands along the Mississippi attracted Joseph Smith and the Mormons, who hoped to build a Kingdom of God on Earth. Cities like St. Louis and New Orleans offered hope, or at least work, for newly arrived immigrants. On the other hand, Natchez remained a town run by a planter aristocracy that never expanded beyond a trading center that served the local region.

Throughout the South, slaves and free people of color struggled under a system of racial oppression. But the coming of the railroad revealed that the prosperity along the Mississippi River system could be in jeopardy. Few could have predicted that a civil war would tear the country in two, and forever change the lives of the people living along the river.

NOTES

1. Mark Twain, *Life on the Mississippi* (New York: New American Library, 2001), 11.
2. George Byron Merrick, *Old Times on the Upper Mississippi: The Recollections of a Steamboat Pilot from 1854 to 1863* (St. Paul: Minnesota Historical Society Press, 1987), 71–72, 74.
3. Friedrich Gerstäcker, *Wild Sports in the Far West; The Narrative of a German Wanderer Beyond the Mississippi, 1837–1843,* Reprint (Durham: Duke University Press, 1968), 95–96.
4. Theodore C. Blegen, *Minnesota: A History of the State,* 2nd edition (Minneapolis: University of Minnesota Press, 1975), 103.
5. Ibid., 143.
6. Kathryn M. Daynes, "Mormon Polygomy: Belief and Practice in Nauvoo," *Kingdom on the Mississippi Revisted: Nauvoo in Mormon History,* eds. Roger D. Launius and John E. Hallwas (Urbana: University of Illinois Press, 1996), 136.
7. William E. Parrish, Charles T. Jones Jr., and Lawrence O. Christensen, eds., *Missouri: The Heart of the Nation* (St. Louis: Forum Press, 1980), 156.
8. Joseph Suppiger, Salomon Koepfli, and Kaspar Koepfli, *Travel Account of the Koepfli and Suppiger Family to St. Louis on the Mississippi and the Founding of New Switzerland in the State of Illinois,* trans. Raymond J. Spahn, ed. John C. Abbott (Carbondale: Southern Illinois University Press, 1987), 193.
9. Cyprian Clamorgan, *The Colored Aristocracy of St. Louis,* ed. Julie Winch (Columbia: University of Missouri Press, 1999), 47.
10. John Hebron Moore, *The Emergence of the Cotton Kingdom in the Old Southwest: Mississippi, 1770–1860* (Baton Rouge: Louisiana State University Press, 1988), 188.
11. Ibid., 191.
12. *William Johnson's Natchez: The Ante-Bellum Diary of a Free Negro,* William Ransom Hogan and Edwin Adams Davis, eds. (Baton Rouge: Louisiana State University Press, 1993), 359.
13. Joan M. Martin, "*Plaçage* and the Louisiana *Gen de Couleur Libre:* How Race and Sex Defined the Lifestyles of Free Women of Color," *Creole: The History and Legacy of Louisiana's Free People of Color,* ed. Sybil Kein (Baton Rouge: Louisiana State University Press, 2000), 57.
14. Solomon Northup, "Twelve Years a Slave. Narrative of Solomon Northup, A Citizen of New York, Kidnapped in Washington City in 1841, and Rescued in 1853, From a Cotton Plantation Near the Red River" *I Was Born a Slave: An Anthology of Classic Slave Narratives,* Vol. II, 1849–1866, ed. Yuval Taylor (Chicago: Lawrence Hill Books, 1999), 199.

6

Life during the Civil War

In May 1862, a Union sloop-of-war commanded by Captain Thomas T. Craven carefully made its way up the Mississippi River. Several months earlier, 11 southern States had seceded from the Union and had cut off river traffic from the north. Craven was a member of Admiral David Farragut's fleet that had just captured New Orleans and hoped to take the last Confederate stronghold at Vicksburg. Craven observed with fascination the southerners who gathered along the banks of the Mississippi as his ship sailed past:

> It was interesting and sometimes exciting as we steamed along inshore, to witness the dense crowds of spectators. In front of the large sugar plantations their white occupants were collected in groups, gazing askance at us, the ladies often turning their backs upon us, showing by their manner that they would give worlds, if they had them, to crush us from the face of the earth. Then as we passed the groups of darkies, particularly if they were hidden from their masters' view by intervening trees or houses, such demonstrations of joy, such jumping and bowing, and such antics and grins as could only be imagined by those who are familiar with the monkey traits of the negro character.[1]

Craven saw one white woman command her slaves to unfurl a Union flag to show where her sympathies lay. He was fortunate to buy supplies for his crew from a Creole landowner. Craven also noted that planters sympathetic to the Confederate cause obeyed orders from local authorities to burn their cotton bales to prevent them from falling into the hands of the invaders. However, Craven's comments about the slaves he encountered illustrates that negative views of blacks were common among white northerners.

Since the colonial era, the Mississippi River had served as a highway of goods, people, and culture. The Civil War changed this by cutting the river into two. The lifeblood of commerce that had sustained the people in the South deteriorated considerably. Tens of thousands of men went off to battle—some died, some were wounded, and most who made it back tried to rebuild shattered lives. In the meanwhile, thousands of women took over the management of farms and plantations, and not all succeeded. In cities along the river, upper-class women who could afford to pay for domestic help volunteered as nurses to take care of the wounded and organized fund-raisers for refugees. Confederate armies plundered the countryside just as readily as Union armies did. The vast majority of blacks eagerly awaited the arrival of Union armies, and thousands fled the plantation when they had the chance. Some black males joined Union armies, while others sought shelter in contraband camps. To their misfortune, they encountered unsanitary conditions and harassment by Confederate guerillas. In areas afflicted by war, uncertainty about how one was going to feed one's family reigned. Loyalty to the Union or to the Confederacy could save a southern family from advancing armies, but pillaging renegades showed little mercy. Death in battle or from sickness brought emotional and economic calamity to many residents along the Mississippi.

On the upper river in Union territory, the business of war further developed economic connections between the West and the East that from necessity had to bypass the American South. Wheat from Minnesota reached Chicago and then made its way east along railroad lines, and in turn the goods from the East reached an eager market in the Midwest. Businessmen in St. Louis made fortunes fulfilling government contracts to clothe, feed, and equip the Union armies. In contrast, the wharves of New Orleans were empty during the first year of the war. Southerners who so eagerly embraced secession slit their own economic throats by first severing their commercial ties with the North and then refusing to trade cotton with Great Britain in an attempt to get recognition of their independence. As the war dragged on, finding enough to eat became a daily struggle for city folk as well as those in the country. The Civil War pauperized the South, and the region never fully recovered.

Nearly every plantation, town and city along the Mississippi was in one way or another affected by the Civil War. Because the actual fighting occurred on the lower Mississippi, this chapter will focus on people in three cities of the South, St. Louis, New Orleans, and Vicksburg, and those who lived on the cotton and sugar plantations along the river. St. Louis provides us with a glimpse of a city torn between Union and Confederate sympathizers. In contrast, the majority of the white population of New

Orleans enthusiastically supported secession from the Union, but within a year they had to suffer the humiliation of being a conquered people. Vicksburg was the scene of a long siege in 1863 that led to near starvation and then surrender. At the same time that war disrupted cotton and sugar production, it also emboldened hundreds of thousands of slaves to risk moving near Union armies and camps with the hope that the day of freedom was near.

WARTIME ST. LOUIS

The results of the election of 1860 spurred passions throughout the country, but many people along the Mississippi looked on the possibility of secession with dread. In Vicksburg, St. Louis, and New Orleans the commercial ties between North and South had fueled the economy. Even with the secession of South Carolina in December of 1860, many civilians in these cities were uncertain of the future and hesitated to break their links with the North. In contrast, the majority of planters along the river embraced secession with vigor because they saw the Republican presidential victory as a direct threat on their way of life. The first shots that were fired at Fort Sumter and President Abraham Lincoln's subsequent call to arms in April 1861 convinced many urban white southerners to abandon their economic well-being and rush to join militia companies and other military units in the clamor for war.

Unfortunately, in border states such as Missouri, the choice between North and South was not so clear. Only a minority of people in Missouri had voted for the southern Democratic candidate John C. Breckenridge in the 1860 presidential election; rather, most had taken the middle ground and voted for candidates who sought compromise over the divisive issue of slavery in the territories. But when war broke out, people had to take sides in St. Louis. Missouri's governor Claiborne Jackson supported secession and so too did the planters of central Missouri. In contrast, the population of St. Louis was divided. Businessmen sold their goods to southern cities, but their capital and stock often came from the East by railroad. More importantly, many of the city's businessmen and industrialists had been born in New England. There were divisions among the immigrant ethnic groups as well. A third of the city's population was German-born, and they mostly supported the Union. But many Irish supported the South because they saw blacks as competitors in the free market and resented Republicans' seeming anti-Catholic, nativist stances on moral issues such as temperance.

Governor Jackson and the state legislature created the St. Louis Police Commission in order to place the city's police forces under the state control. This pro-Confederate police force tried to stymie any Union activity by closing down saloons and beer gardens on Sunday, preventing blacks from attending Sunday night services, ordering a curfew, and expelling the free black community from the city. The governor then ordered the state militia to seize the federal arsenal at St. Louis. In response, federal forces made up of German immigrant volunteers under the leadership of Captain Nathaniel Lyon surrounded the Confederate militia. As in the First Battle of Bull Run to the east, thousands of civilians wanted to witness the first battle in Missouri, but to their disappointment the Confederate militia surrendered without a fight. As the Union force marched back to St. Louis in triumph, bitter southern sympathizers taunted the soldiers and threw stones and brickbats at them. When a drunken man fired a gun and wounded a Union officer, the Union soldiers fired into the crowd. Once the scuffle was over, 28 people were dead and many others wounded. A mob of Confederate sympathizers sought revenge by destroying German property throughout the city and killing three German civilians. To restore order, federal forces took control of the city. All saloons and beer gardens were ordered shut down by the pro-Union mayor. Violent incidents between civilians and troops occurred again on June 17, 1861, when the gun of a soldier accidentally went off and his comrades opened fire on a crowd. Four people lay dead on the street.

Soon afterwards, the civilians of St. Louis felt the hard hand of military rule as their civil liberties deteriorated. Fear of a Confederate attack swept the civilian population after the defeat of Union forces at Wilson's Creek. John C. Frémont, the new military commander, ordered earthworks and gun emplacements to be built around the city. Every male resident was required to join the Home Guards. Just outside the city's fairgrounds, the army built the Benton Barracks to house 20,000 troops. Business people within St. Louis saw the economic opportunity and opened saloons, restaurants, and photograph galleries to accommodate the troops. Unionists within Missouri elected Hamilton R. Gamble as governor, and he placed Union sympathizers on the St. Louis Police Board. Unfortunately, the citizens of St. Louis had to endure unruly and criminal behavior of members of the Unionist Home Guard. To maintain order, Frémont thought that it was necessary to declare martial law at the end of August 1861. The military closed down newspapers sympathetic to the Confederate cause. Businesses serving the public were required to close by 10:30 P.M. and remain closed all day on Sundays. The carrying of firearms by citizens was prohibited. To prevent spying, citizens were required to obtain a pass if they wanted to leave the city. Even more shocking to Confederate sympathizers, the military threatened to confiscate the property and free the slaves of anyone who took up arms against the United States or actively supported the rebel armies in the field. When Frémont extended martial law to the rest of the state, he added that any person bearing arms against the Union "north of a line from Fort Leavenworth through Jefferson city to Cape Girardeau" would be court-martialed and shot. Editors of opposition newspapers such as the *St. Louis Evening News* were arrested. The Sisters of Mercy, a Catholic religious order, had been providing housing for orphans of both Union and Confederate soldiers and serving as intermediaries for Confederate prisoners and their families. Union leaders called for their exclusion from St. Louis hospitals and prisons because they dared to assist the enemy.

Frémont's replacement, Major General Henry W. Halleck, continued the crackdown on Confederate supporters. He ordered the arrest of anyone who by "word or deed" supported the Confederacy and assessed a fee on Confederate loyalists to pay for the support of refugees. Between December 1861 and March 1862, a board of assessors made a list of suspected Confederate sympathizers, examined their tax records, and levied a fine from $100 to $400 on 300 individuals. If these individuals took an oath of allegiance, the fines would rescinded, but if they refused to do so and failed to pay the fine, their property would be seized and sold at auction. Of the $16,340 assessed in fines, a little over $10,000 was collected, and another $6,000 came from auctioned property that included items such as pianos, buggies, tables, book cases, and candles. Assessments were levied in July 1862 to raise funds for the Missouri Militia and instituted again in 1864 during a Confederate invasion of the state.

As Missouri erupted into a chaotic battlefield, the citizens of St. Louis witnessed firsthand the horrors of war. Thousands of refugees who had lost everything flocked to St. Louis. Since existing charities were swamped, prominent women in St. Louis organized the Ladies' Union Refugee Aid Society, which housed the refugees in a shelter, supplied them with food and clothing, and then moved them to other states. After major battles, the military sent a flood of wounded to the city for medical care. Throughout the war, hospital ships brought wounded men to and from St. Louis. Compassionate citizens of St. Louis fed them, and women volunteers prepared bandages and donated supplies to the local military hospital. In 1861 the Western Sanitary Commission was formed to administer to the sick and wounded in six hospitals throughout St. Louis. Private donations funded its operation. Dorothea L. Dix, already organizing nurses in the East, came to St. Louis to recruit nurses. She required them to be between the ages of 25 and 50, maintain a serious yet cheerful personality, possess a good work ethic, and bring two recommendations from people who could verify the candidate's character. Since the government only provided the basic necessities for wounded soldiers, the women of St. Louis brought baskets of foods to the men and kept them company by reading to them or writing letters for them.

The first year of the war also brought economic hardship to many of St. Louis's citizens: property values plummeted as much as 75 percent, many buildings throughout the city remained vacant for lack of renters, and the commercial waterfront was converted into an army supply depot. Those merchants who could supply the army made fortunes, and the arrival of thousands of troops into the city was a boom for gamblers and prostitutes. As more and more troops poured into St. Louis, their spending fueled inflation for the civilian population as they competed with the soldiers for scarce goods. Many poorer women whose husbands went off to war had to seek employment to make ends meet. Some of them worked in the factories of St. Louis that provided supplies for the Union army. African-American women had been prominent in the laundry business, and now they washed clothes for soldiers as well.

When the Mississippi opened for trade in 1864 after the fall of Vicksburg and Port Gibson, St. Louis appeared on the road to recovery. A temporary setback occurred in the autumn of 1864 when Confederate General Sterling Price launched an invasion of Missouri. Although his army was defeated before it reached St. Louis, a sense of panic pervaded the city and thousands of refugees once again flocked into the city. The assessments on Confederate loyalists were reinstated to offset the cost of taking care of these poor souls. Fundraisers organized by women provided further funds. By 1865, St. Louis was thriving once again. A new elite of industrialists and merchants who had benefited from government contracts and the war economy emerged to lead St. Louis into the industrial age.

THE PLIGHT OF NEW ORLEANS

The white citizens of New Orleans overwhelmingly supported secession, and those that did not were quickly silenced by the New Orleans police or mobs in the streets. Even the free black community was swept in the euphoria of war, and three regiments of free black volunteers were created as part of the state militia. The white elites soon had second thoughts about arming blacks and disbanded the regiments when early Confederate victories suggested that the war would be over soon. However, it only took a few months of war to make it clear to the people of New Orleans how dependent their city was on the trade with the North. With the Mississippi River cut off, the produce of the Midwest no longer flowed down to New Orleans. To make matters worse, only a few ships from the city were able to break through the Union blockade off the coast of the Gulf of Mexico. Flour, coffee, and soap became scarce. In the first months of 1862, the city government provided relief for 2,000 families. Fear of a slave rebellion caused plantation owners and the local government to be vigilant, and the free black community suffered repression. Disenchantment with the war among the city's citizens became more visible when in April of 1862 the Confederate government began conscription, a forced draft. Poorer whites were horrified to learn that the government allowed wealthy men to pay for a substitute, and an amendment to the conscription law in October provided exemptions for those who owned more than 20 slaves.

Disaster struck the Confederate sympathizers in New Orleans when Admiral Farragut quickly subdued the forts guarding the mouth of the Mississippi and sailed into New Orleans. Confederate forces withdrew from the city, and the most populous city of the South fell without a fight. For the next three years the city had to endure military occupation.

The first Union military commander in charge, Benjamin Butler, came to represent the oppressive nature of the occupation, at least in the eyes of white southerners. Butler was a balding, overweight man who did not strike southerners as what a gentleman would look like, nor did he act the part. Butler was determined to break the so-called secessionist spirit in New Orleans. Moreover, he was sympathetic to black aspirations for freedom. He got rid of the whipping posts in the city and disallowed segregation on the street cars of New Orleans and freed slaves who had suffered extraordinary cruelty from their masters. Butler put free blacks into military uniforms under the command of black officers. When a white southerner tore down a U.S. flag, Butler had the man hanged at that very spot. Butler and his subordinates eagerly enforced the Confiscation Act, which allowed the Union military commanders to seize the property of the supporters of the Confederacy. As a result, many New Orleans businessmen were ruined when their mansions and all their furniture were auctioned off. Butler ordered the seizure of all firearms and paid a bounty to informants who were willing to tattletale on their neighbors. The cherished American freedom of assembly was taken away—a meeting of three or more people on the streets was forbidden. Any citizen who wanted to deal with the U.S. government in any way had to take an oath of allegiance first. Butler jailed clergymen who refused to pray for Lincoln. Perhaps no act of Butler's so outraged southerners as his treatment of southern ladies. After Union troops repeatedly received insults from the women of New Orleans, Butler issued an edict on May 28, 1862, which stated that the city government would treat the women who shouted negative remarks toward Union soldiers as prostitutes. News of the edict swept the South and received condemnation as far as England.

The citizens of New Orleans did have Butler to thank for making their city the cleanest it had ever been and would be in the nineteenth century. Many citizens prayed that yellow fever would visit the city as it had in the past and wipe out the Union forces unused to the scourge, but Butler was well aware of the danger and launched a campaign to cleanse the city of filth, which people at the time believed caused the disease. Laborers scrubbed the streets and then allowed water to flow over the pavement and sweep the residue away. Putrid standing water in the canals was drained, and levees repaired. Butler initiated regular garbage pickup throughout the city. Residents were required to put their garbage in containers out on a certain days, and the containers would be washed out with lime afterwards. Yards throughout the city were to be kept clean of trash or the owner would suffer stiff penalties. Littering in the streets was not allowed. Butler also had every ship inspected at a quarantine station before arriving at New Orleans to keep sick passengers out. Butler made the mistake of allowing one ship to come through without undergoing inspection because its captain had promised that everyone onboard was healthy. Unfortunately, yellow fever was present on the ship. Butler did not hesitate to take the initiative and correct his error. Union troops quickly surrounded the building where the sick men had died, quarantined the area, and had the furniture and other articles in the interior of the house burned. For all his efforts, Butler succeeded in preventing yellow fever in New Orleans during the war.

Although Butler and the Union army cleaned up New Orleans, they could not revive its prosperity. In 1863 a quarter of the population of New Orleans was on relief. With much of the Louisiana countryside still in the hands of the Confederacy, food supplies to the city were strained. It would not be until the fall of Vicksburg and the reopening of the Mississippi River for trade that the city's residents witnessed once again hundreds of steamboats unloading goods along the riverfront. Material conditions quickly improved and the glory of the Crescent City was at least marginally restored.

SOLDIERS AND CIVILIANS AT VICKSBURG

By late 1862, Union forces controlled most the lower Mississippi as far south as Port Hudson, Louisiana, and north from New Orleans to Vicksburg, Mississippi. But a small stretch remained in Confederate hands to provide a vital link with the resources and men west of the river. Jefferson Davis and other Confederate leaders had decided that Vicksburg must be held at all cost to keep the Union armies from controlling the Mississippi River and splitting the Confederacy in two.

In 1860 Vicksburg had 4,500 residents, making it the largest city in Mississippi. Although a thriving commercial center, Vicksburg did have its problems: unpaved streets turned to mud in the rain, hogs and homeless dogs competed with each other to pilfer garbage, and nearly every house suffered from a roach infestation. Although city residents had literally run gamblers and prostitutes out of town in the 1830s, criminal elements still catered to the needs of boatmen along the city's wharves. Like New Orleans and St. Louis, Vicksburg's population was cosmopolitan; indeed, only a third of its residents were born in the South. Since the city sat on bluffs overlooking the Mississippi river and an imposing courthouse dominated its skyline, the city was more picturesque than its rivals. However, the leading citizens of Vicksburg had failed to divert the steamboat and ocean traffic from New Orleans so the town never became a great inland port, and principally served as a depot for the surrounding countryside. The majority of the residents of Vicksburg were not immediately for secession in 1860 or early 1861, but when war did break out, they endorsed the Confederacy.

During the first months of the war, life for the citizens of Vicksburg went on as before. News of Confederate victories in the East fostered hope that the war would end soon. But the fall of New Orleans to Union forces, the burning of the town of Grand Gulf just to the south of the city, and Confederate losses in Missouri and Tennessee cast a feeling of dread over the people of Vicksburg.

The appearance of Farragut's fleet on May 18, 1862, brought the war to the city's doorstep. Confederate artillery units in Vicksburg exchanged fire with Union vessels. Confederate troops and slave labor constructed earthworks around the city and dug artillery onto mudflats and terraces along the bluffs. Hundreds of citizens fled the city, but most of the population stayed. On June 25, thirty-five Union vessels bombarded the city, but only one female civilian was killed and all the Confederate batteries remained unharmed.

As the battle continued, civilians were beginning to see the normal rhythms of life change. Railroad service from the east stopped before it reached the city, and passengers and freight had to be brought the rest of the way by wagon or foot. Fearing that Union sympathizers might act as spies, Confederate authorities ordered that anyone leaving the city had to be issued a pass. To protect lines of communication, the post office and telegraph station were moved out of the city. Civilians were thrilled to see Confederate reinforcements arrive to defend their town, but over time, the relationship between military and civilians became strained. As food supplies dwindled, soldiers were inclined to believe that private property

U.S. Gunboat *Fort Hindman*, ca. 1861–1865. Courtesy of the Library of Congress.

was really community property, and they raided the gardens of civilians and stole whatever was edible. In response to the tension, Confederate commander General Earl Van Dorn ordered his troops to respect private property, and if they did not, their units would be charged for any damage done. Shortages of food and supplies led to wide-spread speculation. Although there was food in the countryside, planters feared injury to their slaves if they allowed them to haul the produce into markets within the city. In response to the crisis within Vicksburg, on July 4, 1862, Van Dorn declared martial law in the town and several other river counties. Those who gave information to the enemy, criticized military commanders, or charged outrageous prices were to be fined, jailed, and have their property confiscated. The order was so unpopular that the Confederate leadership in Richmond, Virginia, made Van Dorn rescind it and apologize.

The civilians at Vicksburg briefly cheered when the Confederate ironclad *Arkansas* fought its way past the Farragut's entire fleet and docked at Vicksburg. Yet, after the initial exultation, the citizens of Vicksburg realized that the *Arkansas* was just as trapped and isolated as they were.

Since Farragut did not have the means to conquer the city, he and his other commanders decided to build a canal which would allow his fleet and other ships on the Mississippi River to bypass Vicksburg. The Union units assigned to the task had not brought any tents along. Fifteen hundred African-Americans were brought in to help in the excavation and shared in the misery. One Union soldier described the living conditions:

> There was nothing to eat for weeks but pork and hard-tack; no water to drink but the muddy water of the Mississippi. The swamp reeked with malaria, and the men slept upon the mud. The supply of quinine, that panacea for all the soldiers' aches and ills, was exhausted; there was little medicine of any sort.... Almost the whole of the Ninth regiment was at one time on the sick list with fever caused by exposure and privation. The poor fellows died sometimes at the fearful rate of a score a week.[2]

The canal proved a lot harder to build than initially anticipated. Union commanders abandoned the project when the Union fleet was forced to retreat from Vicksburg.

With Union supply lines tenuous and without the land forces necessary to surround Vicksburg and starve it out, Farragut faced a dilemma. Almost half of the men on his gunboats were sick and many of his gunboats were damaged because they were particularly vulnerable to Confederate artillery. The armored sides of the gunboats were sloped to make enemy projectiles fired from a horizontal plane bounce off them, but Confederate artillery at Vicksburg were located up on the bluffs of the town and their projectiles were coming from a height down upon the boats, thus hitting the sides of the gunboats at nearly right angles, with devastating consequences for the boats and their crew. Moreover, the top decks were unarmored and could be easily penetrated by such fire. As losses mounted,

Farragut retreated grudgingly from Vicksburg, and Union commanders pondered the lessons learned.

For now Vicksburg was saved. The Union retreat had come none too soon since 40 percent of the Confederate soldiers were sick and supplies had been running short. Strategically, holding on to Vicksburg allowed the western states of the Confederacy to continue to supply the eastern states with shipments of flour, cornmeal, beef, sugar, salt, and munitions and weapons that came from Europe via Mexico. But the Union forces had destroyed the railroad links east of Vicksburg so now all the supplies would have to be shipped by water between Shreveport and Vicksburg along the Red and Mississippi rivers. Because this route was vulnerable to Union gunboats, the supplies from the west arrived erratically. For the citizens of Vicksburg, the end of the siege did not alleviate high food prices. Some of the civilians who had fled the city before the battle returned, but they were greeted with hostility from those who had endured the siege. Many women of Vicksburg continued to work in hospitals to tend the sick or sew blankets for the soldiers.

As most people in Vicksburg expected, the Union forces, this time under the command of Ulysses Grant, returned in 1863. When the bombardment of the town resumed, most of the civilians retreated once again into caves dug into the bluffs. Some resourceful men made digging out caves a successful business with prices for caves ranging from $20 for a one-room cave to $50 dollars for one with several chambers that were reinforced with timbers. Since the caves were damp and dark, civilians tried to stay out of them unless it was absolutely necessary.

Tragically for civilians, this time the battle for Vicksburg took a more savage turn. On orders from Washington, Grant issued commands that the Union force begin punishing disloyal southerners in the countryside by confiscating their property. The town of Napoleon was burned down as retribution from guerilla raids. It was along the banks of the Mississippi that Union commanders learned that their armies could live off the land instead of totally depending on supplies from the North. The result was the pauperization of the southern population. Food supplies in Vicksburg dwindled once again.

After Grant's army was beaten back north of the city, the Union commander proposed a bold maneuver: float transports full of his men past Vicksburg and attack the city from the south. The strategy worked brilliantly. Confederate forces from the city tried to slow Grant's advance in several battles, but they were soundly defeated. On May 17, Vicksburg resident Emma Balfour wrote:

> I hope never to witness against such a scene as the return of our routed army! From twelve o'clock until late in the night the streets and roads were *jammed* with wagons, cannons, horses, men, mules, stock, sheep, everything you can imagine that appertains to an army—being brought hurriedly within the intrechment [sic].

Nothing like order prevailed, of course, as divisions, brigades, and regiments were broken and separated. As the poor fellows passed, every house poured forth all it had to refresh them. I have every one on the lot and there were some visitors carrying buckets of water to the corner for the men. Then on the back gallery I had everything that was eatable put out—and fed as many as I could.[3]

The Union army subsequently surrounded the city and cut it off from supplies. Grant thought the town could not hold out for more than several days, but the Confederates fought for 10 weeks. Citizens within the town still hoped that a Confederate army would break the siege, but the Confederate army under General Joseph Johnston had been defeated and fled east of Jackson, the state's capital. The soldiers and civilians of Vicksburg were alone. Daily life in the city took on heroic dimensions. People learned how to walk safely through the city during a bombardment. At night, they watched the trail of an enemy shell flying through the sky and were able to predict where it was going to explode. If it exploded overhead, they knew that they would not be hurt because the shell fragments would scatter in front of them. Finding enough to eat was another challenge. Rice and milk became the mainstay of most people's diet, and those who could afford it bought mule meat and corn bread. Cooking was done outside of the caves, which exposed people to artillery fire. Soldiers and civilians waited in hunger for the fighting to end, and the heat of the summer made that wait unbearable. Since all of the streams that supplied Vicksburg with water came from the eastern part of the state, Union soldiers contaminated them by throwing carcasses of dead animals into the water. Within the city, water was rationed to one cup a day. Soldiers suffered from malaria, dysentery, and diarrhea. One Confederate officer confided in his diary that "the mortality here at this time is very great; hardly a day passes but I see dozens of men carried to their last homes. They are buried in a trench with a blanket for their shroud. Coffins can not be had for all of them. Graves are dug today for use tomorrow."[4]

On July 4, 1863, the Confederate force in Vicksburg surrendered. The city was in ruins. Mortar shells had damaged houses and left craters in the streets. Civilians had to keep away from the scores of drunken Union and Confederate soldiers that wandered through the city. Some soldiers resorted to looting. Carcasses of dead animals and humans lay in the trenches, and the Union army had to bury them in shallow graves to make sure disease did not spread. The Union commander of the occupying forces, James McPherson, set up programs to distribute aid to the survivors of the siege, who now had to battle with inflation and high unemployment rates. With the business district devastated and southern sources for capital investment nonexistent, local merchants lost much of their control of the regional cotton trade to northern businessmen who were eager to reap the benefits of high prices for the staple. Many cotton planters in neighboring counties had to abandon their Confederate patriotism and sell their bales to despised Yankee merchants to make ends meet. For the vast majority of the white population of Vicksburg, daily life was a struggle.

THE WAR IN THE SUGAR PARISHES OF LOUISIANA

In 1860 sugar planters in lower Louisiana could not foresee how their plantations could survive without slaves. For over a century, the growing and processing of sugar entailed long and intensive gang labor in hot and humid conditions under the close scrutiny of overseers. Planters believed that no one would work under such conditions unless they were coerced. Not surprisingly, when the Republicans won the White House on a platform of free labor, sugar planters became the dominant group in Louisiana's secession convention. Sugar planting went on in 1861 as it had before, and the crop was the best ever. Unfortunately, the Union blockade successfully thwarted the planters' access to markets, which meant that hundreds of thousands of hogheads of sugar just sat in warehouses while the price of corn, pork, and other foodstuffs on which the plantations depended rose. Planters tried to sell sugar to other Confederate states, but the fall of New Orleans cut their link to the Mississippi River system. Some planters sold some of their crop to boats that plied the Red and Ouachita rivers into the interior of Louisiana or to merchants who moved the sugar by rail to Texas. Still, the high cost of transportation and the dangers of war allowed only a small fraction of the sugar crop to be sold.

Since sugar planting was a labor intensive operation that depended on overseers, sugar planters faced another crisis when many of their white laborers volunteered for the military and, as a consequence, their plantations were becoming more dependent on blacks overseeing other blacks. Fear of a slave rebellion caused sugar parishes to strictly control their black population. Every slave that was traveling had to have a pass or they would receive 20 lashes and be held in a cell until they were picked up by their masters. Vigilantes had their own brand of justice and were not afraid to use violence to punish any black who appeared to threaten white control.

Sugar planters faced other problems as well. With the war draining state and local government funds, levee repair along the Mississippi stopped. Slave owners preferred to risk flooding than send their own slaves to work on the levees. The levee system that protected the alluvial lands of the Mississippi River was in shambles by the end of the war, and flooding added to the misery on the sugar plantations. The war brought other mishaps. Confederate and Union forces did not hesitate to confiscate horses and mules that were so vital to the operation of the sugar plantations, and they took livestock and tore up wood fences for their camp fires. Those sugar planters who fled to Texas with their slaves when the Union forces captured New Orleans risked having their abandoned plantations looted.

Sugar planters took another hit in November of 1862 when General Butler ordered that the property of disloyal citizens who had borne arms against the United States be seized in Louisiana west of the Mississippi River. To keep their land, planters would have to take a loyalty oath. Luckily for many planters, Butler was replaced a few months later and only a million dollars of property was seized.

Union occupation brought an end to the slave labor system in the sugar parishes of Louisiana. Union commanders imposed a wage labor system with a set amount that planters had to pay their black laborers: $10 for males minus the cost of clothing. Planters would provide food, shelter, and medical care for the laborers and their families. Black laborers were expected to work 10 hours a day for 26 days every month. Most importantly, the Union army allowed blacks the freedom to reject a contract with a planter and go elsewhere to sign with someone else. Once a contract was signed, Union forces prevented laborers from leaving the plantations.

The combination of these factors led to a terrible harvest of only 87,000 hogheads of sugar in 1862 compared to the crop of 460,000 hogheads in 1861. Planters' attempts to diversify into other crops such as corn failed because of the hot and humid conditions of lower Louisiana. Overall, the planters were in deep financial trouble. Planters blamed the disruptions of labor as the principal reason of the disaster, and they were probably correct. The black slaves sensed that their oppression was at an end. Since planters under Union control were prohibited from whipping them, black workers did not work at the pace they did before. Many fled for freedom. Others went from plantation to plantation seeking better wages. But the reality was that if blacks were paid a decent wage and given good working conditions, they were willing to work for a better life. The planters would have none of that. They used whatever influence they had to get the next commander of New Orleans, General Nathaniel Banks, to change the labor arrangements to their benefit. They were helped by the worries Union commanders had over the expense of caring for the tens of thousands of black refugees who were showing up at military camps in wretched condition. Banks responded by creating new labor laws; all the laborers of a particular plantation would receive one-twentieth of the money received from the sale of the sugar crop. If the laborers wanted wages, they would only receive $2 per month for men and $1 per month for women. Still, labor problems persisted because black laborers refused to be treated as slaves. Since sugar production required great skill, black laborers realized their market value and demanded better wages and treatment. Fear of losing valuable laborers forced planters to negotiate. Unfortunately in the long run, what seemed like victories for black laborers only intensified the determination of planters to one way or another control their laborers.

In 1864 Banks effectively ended slavery in Louisiana. Black laborers had two options: either they could receive wages of $8 a month or get one-fourteenth of the crop. If laborers chose the share-crop arrangement, they and their family were to receive a one-acre plot for a garden. Generally, black laborers preferred wages. However, once a laborer signed a contract with a plantation, he or she was not free to leave the plantation during the term of the agreement. Since half of the wages would not be paid until the end of the year, if a laborer did leave, the planter could withhold that amount. Moreover, those caught fleeing the plantation could be arrested and forced to work on public road projects. Despite these regulations, the laborers still held a lot of power in their negotiations with planters. Sugar planting required intense skilled work during the processing of the sugar cane, and it was at those times that laborers learned they had the best leverage to negotiate with the planters. On many plantations, blacks bargained to have either part or the entire Saturday off. Others made sure their wives received less work.

Despite the changes, planters faced another disastrous harvest: in 1864 only 10,387 hogheads were produced. Historian John C. Rodrigue has estimated that losses in capital not including slaves on sugar plantations amounted to $190 million of the total of $200 million investment before the war.[5] Since sugar production was the most technologically advanced and capital intensive agricultural operation in the South, it took years for it to recover after the war. Of the over 1,200 sugar plantations that had thrived in Louisiana before the war, only 200 were still in operation in 1865.

WAR AND THE COTTON PLANTATIONS

Along sections of the Mississippi River from northern Louisiana to southern Arkansas, planters created a society based on the production of cotton. The Mississippi Delta, the region between the Yazoo and Mississippi Rivers, was still underdeveloped and, except for Chicot County, most of Arkansas that bordered on the Mississippi remained swampland. The most productive area in antebellum times was called the Natchez district—a region that included three parishes in Louisiana and five counties in Mississippi that surrounded the town of Natchez. On the eve of the Civil War, cotton plantations in this region produced 400,000 bales of cotton or about 10 percent of the entire cotton output of the South. Large plantations were the rule in the Natchez district, and its elite were some of the wealthiest people in the South, only eclipsed by the sugar plantations of Louisiana and the rice and cotton plantations of the sea islands in South Carolina.

Generally, cotton planters supported the secession of the South from the Union. A northern threat to slavery challenged the very economic foundation of the cotton society along the Mississippi River. But the war did not go well for the planters of the Delta. There were mostly Union victories in the Mississippi theater of operations, and the fall of New Orleans signaled the beginning of the end for cotton planters along the river. Natchez surrendered without a shot being fired. During the Vicksburg campaign, the federal armies adopted a "hard war" strategy that sought to bring the war to disloyal citizens through confiscation of their livestock and crops. Union troops responded to Confederate guerilla actions with the burning of mansions, ginhouses, and stables. Those planters who fled the region with their slaves in tow were considered traitors by Union officials, and Union troops and ex-slaves readily looted their property. Those planters who decided to stay and ride out the war were sometimes considered Union sympatheizers by Confederate guerillas, and became prime targets for pillaging by southern forces and guerillas. On other plantations where the males had gone off to war, women had to manage the plantation and suffered deprivations by Union and Confederate armies. Planters were also adversely affected by the Confederate government policy that called for the burning of cotton bales so they would not fall into enemy hands. Those planters who refused often found that Union military commanders either burned or confiscated their bales of cotton.

With almost no cotton crop to sell, the debt that had accumulated before and during the war was now becoming onerous for planters. Northern investors came pouring into the region and leased or bought confiscated, foreclosed, or debt-ridden lands at rock bottom prices. Black laborers quickly learned that conditions on these northern-owned plantations were often worse than the southern plantations they had run from because the northerners saw these plantations as an investment that needed to maximize profits as quickly as possible. As a result, black laborers were worked harder and paid less than on plantations owned by southerners. To make matters worse, northerners did not hesitate to use the Union army to enforce their will on the laborers if they acted up.

Throughout the cotton-growing region, planters turned to a sustenance economy just to survive. In the countryside, planters and farmers hunted wild hogs to augment their meat supply. Planters learned to make do with what they had. Women used looms and spinning wheels to make clothes. As historian John K. Bettersworth has described, "[t]hrown largely on the labor of their own hands and the inventiveness of their own minds, the people learned to make 'coffee' out of parched corn and okra or dried sweet potatoes; tea from dried raspberry leaves; the equivalent of soda from sour milk, vinegar, or another acid mixed with lye burnt out of corn cobs; wax candles by adding quicklime to mutton suet from a few prickly pear leaves to harden the mixture; ink and dyes from berries and tree barks; and horse collars out of plaited cornshucks."[6] Planters who decided to grow more corn faced a severe drought in central and southern Mississippi that devastated the crop. Although many planters found trading with Union merchants repulsive, sheer economic survival forced many to do so. With northerners willing to pay high prices for cotton, planters moved back to cotton planting, but the cotton crop in southern Louisiana was hit with heavy rains and an infestation of army worms.

To make matters worse, former slaves no longer wanted to work for cotton planters under the conditions that existed before the war. As Union armies moved through the Natchez district, slaves abandoned plantations by the tens of thousands. Some of the slaves went in search of relatives and loved ones. Others just wanted to get away from the oppressive plantations and seek opportunities elsewhere. Getting to regions controlled by the Union army meant freedom, and thousands of slaves up and down the Mississippi River were willing to risk everything to obtain it. Those who fled were in great danger from Confederate guerilla forces that had no tolerance for what they considered to be runaway slaves. If the slaves did reach Union camps, they were labeled as contraband and put into special camps that were often overcrowded and a breeding ground for disease. Union officers forced these blacks to work for the army in return for rations. Thousands of black men volunteered to join the Union army with the hope of getting a wage and contributing to the liberation of their people. Unfortunately, they encountered northern racism and had to prove to their white officers that they were fully capable of fighting bravely.

In the Mississippi Delta in 1862, those blacks who stayed on the plantations used the disruptions caused by the war to forge a new world. On some abandoned plantations along the Mississippi River, black families settled on the land and started farming it with the hope that the federal government would grant them title someday in the future. On plantations where the white planter still held control, blacks negotiated with the owners of the land for a share of the crop and the ability to sell their cotton in the market, which during the war was paying high prices. With their new-found freedom, black families set to work. As historian Nancy Bercaw has noted, "[m]en ginned, pressed, dug ditches, and wove baskets for the picked cotton, while women and children shelled corn, repaired fences, and cut down the cornstalks after harvesting. Together, men and women plowed, chopped, and picked the cotton."[7] Once the cotton was put into bales, the black community on the plantation selected a few of the men to go into town to sell the crop, and when they returned the profits would be distributed among families. For several months, African Americans in the Mississippi Delta showed that they could function and thrive without white supervision. In August 1862, their fortunes turned for the worse when the U.S. government decided that the property rights of the white community must be preserved, and Union commanders declared that the former slaves did not own property. The land of Confederate loyalists was actually U.S. government property. As the Union army moved through the Mississippi Delta plantations, it forced young black men to join the military while the rest of the black population had to sign leases with northern whites who were allowed to rent the land from the government. During the war, 45,000 blacks, of whom 69 percent were women, worked under this lease system in the region. The government determined the wages and terms of labor, and punished those who fled. Still, black family members worked in gardens to supply themselves with food and sell their surplus on the market. In negotiations with their new landlords, blacks often won the right to claim corn and livestock. When conditions on these plantations became oppressive, many blacks fled to other plantations or nearby towns and cities.

CONCLUSION

The Civil War brought devastation, misery, and pain to some, but partial freedom, opportunity, and hope to others who lived along the Mississippi River. The Civil War did end slavery, but it also initiated an era of hatred, mistrust, and broken dreams. It was a revolution and it wasn't. The freed slaves never really had a chance to achieve the rights granted in U.S. Constitution during the Civil War and its immediate aftermath. With their sugar and cotton plantations in ruins, southern whites who supported the Confederate cause were bitter in defeat, and they were not going to sit idle and accept their former slaves as political, social, and economic equals. In a more ominous sign for the future of the freed slaves, most northerners who liberated them never wanted equality for them either. Over and over along the Mississippi, former slaves tried to forge a life for themselves among the ashes of war, but planters, Confederate guerillas, Union troops, and U.S. army commanders refused to give blacks full freedom. Racism, greed, and political expediency blinded white America. The war was about slavery, but for most northern whites it was not about integrating blacks fully into American society. The decades following the war would sadly show how true that was.

NOTES

1. Quoted in Edwin C. Bearss, *Rebel Victory at Vicksburg,* reprint (Wilmington: Broadfoot Publishing Company, 1989), 3. From *Official Records of the Union and Confederate Navies in the War of the Rebellion,* Series 1, Vol. 18 (Washington, DC), 529.

2. Ibid., 199.

3. Emma Balfour, *Vicksburg, A City Under Siege: Diary of Emma Balfour May 16, 1863–June 2, 1863* (Phillip C. Weinberger, 1983), entry May 17, 1863.

4. Quoted in William L. Shea and Terrence J. Winschel, *Vicksburg is the Key: The Struggle for the Mississippi River,* Great Campaigns of the Civil War Series (Lincoln: University of Nebraska Press, 2003), 162.

5. John C. Rodrigue, *Reconstruction in the Cane Fields: From Slavery to Free Labor in Louisiana's Sugar Parishes 1862–1880* (Baton Rouge: Louisiana State University Press, 2001), 57.

6. John K. Bettersworth, "The Home Front 1861–1865" *A History of Mississippi,* vol. I, ed. Richard Aubrey McLemore (Hattiesburg: University & College Press of Mississippi, 1973), 507.

7. Nancy Bercaw, *Gendered Freedoms: Race, Rights, and the Politics of Household in the Delta, 1861–1875* (Gainesville: University Press of Florida, 2003), 29.

7

Life during Reconstruction, 1865–1900

In the four decades after the Civil War, the people along the Mississippi River witnessed fundamental changes in their lives. Blacks in the South appeared to be on the verge of sharing in the American ideals of liberty and equality, but new forms of political oppression and economic and social peonage shattered that dream. By 1900, in custom and law, African Americans in the southern states were segregated from the white community in nearly every aspect of life and denied the right to vote. Freed slaves had hoped to acquire land from the former confederates, but the federal government steadfastly preserved property rights, refusing to turn over confiscated lands to former slaves after the war. Whites simply opposed any sale of land to blacks. Although sharecropping appeared as a viable alternative to actual land ownership, the sharp decline of cotton prices created a spiral of debt and poverty that entrapped poor blacks and whites and impoverished many planters as well.

In contrast, most people in the states along the upper Mississippi prospered. Temporary setbacks such as the Panic of 1873 and the depression that followed caused wheat prices to fall, but the majority of farmers responded by diversifying their crops and introducing new technology that increased yields per an acre. Even though their indebtedness increased, a large number of farmers in Minnesota, Iowa, and Illinois succeeded in making a better life for themselves and were beginning to share in the consumer culture of the cities. While the cities and towns of the Deep South along the river stagnated, Minneapolis became the flour capital of the world, and despite competition from Chicago, St. Louis continued to grow. River cities in Iowa, Illinois, and Minnesota prospered in transshipment, agricultural product processing, and manufacturing. Industrialization reshaped workers' lives by increasing their productivity, but it also reduced workers' control over their labor. Railroads, not the steamboat, carried most of the freight and passengers into and out of the states along the upper Mississippi. Because steamboat traffic had been hampered by low water during the summer months, the U.S. Army Corps of Engineers began building dams to achieve a year-round 4.5 foot channel. Despite these improvements, by 1900 it appeared clear that the steamboat, the most famous symbol of the Mississippi River, had become almost obsolete.

THE POSTWAR SOUTH

The various attempts of the federal government to remake the South after the Civil War offered African Americans hope that a more equitable political, social, and economic system would replace slavery. Simply, they wanted to be treated as white Americans were treated in law, civil rights, and economic opportunity. In the first months after the war, southern white elites admitted that slavery was dead, but they were not about to acknowledge their former slaves as equals. To assure themselves a subservient labor supply, white legislators passed the Black Codes of 1865 and 1866 that abridged the civil rights of blacks and relegated them in law to manual or menial labor. Republicans in Congress responded to southern whites' refusal to concede basic rights to the freed slaves with the Civil Rights Act of 1866, the Freedmen's Bureau Act of 1866, the Fourteenth Amendment, and the Reconstruction Acts of 1867. The latter imposed a military regime on the southern states that attempted to force white southerners to accept blacks as American citizens and to respect the law. Although Reconstruction had some initial success, it only fostered greater hatred toward blacks and northerners among many southern whites and created disenchantment with the federal government as the guardian of freedom among blacks whose hopes were dashed by southern whites' violence and, in, time, northern whites' indifference.

In the first months after the Civil War, southern whites were a defeated people. Nearly 70 percent of the adult white males between 18 and 35 years old had been casualties during the war, and Union and Confederate armies had cut a path of destruction along the lower Mississippi River. Union forces had waged a so-called hard war to punish Confederate civilians for their disloyalty and destroy the south's productive resources. What Union forces did not confiscate, use up, or obliterate, Confederate guerillas, foragers, and hungry deserters and refugees often did. Although New Orleans and Natchez got through the war physically largely unscathed, Vicksburg and Baton Rouge were in ruins, and many plantations along the Mississippi were devastated.

For the former slaves, the end of the Civil War offered them hope that they would participate fully in the promise of America. Above all, freedmen wanted land. For centuries their ancestors had labored under the burden of slavery, and now they felt that their disloyal former confederate masters and the United States owed them a piece of property so they could become productive citizens and establish their economic autonomy. If they did have to work for someone else, they wanted to have some control over who they worked for, for how much, and for how long. Specifically, black men wanted to get their wives out of the fields and their children into schools, and black leaders demanded to be part of the democratic process. Hopefully, as blacks became integrated into white society, white violence against them would diminish.

Southern planters along the Mississippi refused to give up their control over their land and their labor supply. They were appalled that their former slaves were now moving around freely and negotiating contracts with them. They wanted to reinstate gang labor, but workers wanted none of that. Since President Andrew Johnson's Reconstruction plan only called for the South to accept the abolishment of slavery and apologize for secession, white elites felt empowered to reestablish their control of their former slaves with Black Codes. The legislature of Mississippi did grant blacks some basic legal rights—they could sue and be sued, purchase personal property, and be witnesses in court cases. Only a few years earlier, a slave could not do any of those things. The Mississippi legislature also granted blacks the right to marry, and they recognized marriages that had existed outside the law during slavery. Nonetheless, the code also set boundaries—a black person could not marry a white person. If they did, they would be guilty of a felony and could serve a life sentence upon conviction. Mississippi's legislature forbade blacks from renting or leasing land in the countryside. Moreover, every black person had to get a license so that they could prove that they had a place of residence and employment. Labor contracts between blacks and whites had to be in writing. If a black person broke the contract, he or she would forfeit their wages and could be subject to arrest by any white person. Black orphans would be contracted out to whites as indentured servants. The Mississippi Black Code disarmed the black population by making it illegal for them to possess a firearm, ammunition, or a large knife. All kinds of vagrancy stipulations gave whites the authority to break up a public assembly of blacks for just about any reason. To control the black leadership, all black ministers had to be registered with the state, and they could be arrested if they did not comply. Since drinking liquor led to disorderly conduct according to the white elite, blacks were not allowed to sell it.

In New Orleans, the white population went further and asserted its control over the black community through violence. A state constitutional convention promised to give blacks the right to vote and, at the same time, disenfranchise former Confederates. On July 30, 1866, delegates to the state constitutional convention met at the Mechanic's Institute, but not enough delegates had yet arrived to create a quorum. Outside the meeting, a rowdy crowd of whites gathered, and white firemen and police joined them. As a procession of about hundred black men arrived to attend the convention, fights broke out between them and the white crowd. A white police officer fired at the black men, and they fired back. The fighting caused hundreds of white people to rush to the scene and attack. Once the blacks fled, the white mob broke into the Mechanic's Institute and targeted the delegates, who were beaten, stabbed, and shot. Those delegates who tried to surrender were attacked, and those who managed to escape through the windows were beset by the crowd outside. By the time federal troops arrived in mid-afternoon, 38 people were dead, most of them black, and another several hundred people were wounded. To the horror of northerners, no one was ever convicted of murder for the atrocity.

Radical and moderate Republicans were furious at the ex-Confederates. Had not the Union won the war? Had not the slaves been emancipated? In 1867 Congress passed a series of acts over the veto of President Andrew Johnson that placed the former Confederate states under military control. Ex-Confederates were banned from the state convention drawing up the new constitutions. Voter registration drives extended suffrage not only to all black males, but to many poor whites who had been excluded from politics because of high property qualifications. A southern Republican party consisting of a coalition of blacks, northerners, and southern white farmers and businessmen emerged. White farmers wanted to get back at the planters for years of political and economic domination. Southern businessmen saw a chance to attract northern capital to fund their ventures. Seeking opportunities, thousands of northerners made their way to the South. Some bought plantations bankrupted during the war or started new businesses in order to make their fortunes. Other northerners came for more altruistic purposes such as to teach at schools for blacks and poor whites that had sprung up throughout the South.

In the countryside, African Americans refused to work in gangs on plantations. Since the cotton plantations along the Mississippi were cash poor, sharecropping emerged as a viable alternative to wage labor. The male head of a family would agree to give a percentage of his cotton crop, usually 50 percent, in exchange for use of the landlord's land. There were benefits to this arrangement for both parties. By giving laborers a stake in the crop, the planters were assured that they would work hard and try to produce as much cotton as possible. In return, sharecroppers won the right to control their own labor because there was no overseer telling them when and how to work. Pregnant women and young children no longer had to toil in the fields. Another benefit was that black families did not have to live in close proximity to the landlord as they had under slavery. Their house would now be near the fields where they worked. Since black households lived in isolated cabins rather than adjacent slave quarters, black community life increasingly focused on meeting places such as churches.

Reconstruction allowed black elites in New Orleans to lead their community into a new era of social and political equality. Before the Civil War, New Orleans had the largest and most diverse free black community in the South. Former slaves, French Creoles, Caribbean migrants, and mulattoes interacted with each other on the streets of the city. A few owned plantations with slaves, and some kept household slaves. More than half of them worked as skilled laborers in occupations such as cigar makers, carpenters, shoemakers, printers, masons, bakers, clothiers, brokers, and barbers. Many owned their own businesses. When Union troops took over the city, the free black community sought suffrage for themselves, but over time they embraced the cause of political rights for the entire black community. Black newspapers served as important instruments for political debate. Unfortunately, most of the newspapers were short lived because a majority of the black population was illiterate and advertising revenues were low. The black community suffered another economic loss when the Freedmen's Savings and Trust Company went bankrupt in 1874 and lost 2 million dollars that thousands of black depositors had worked hard to save.

In the cities and the countryside, black churches were the center of community life. Before the Civil War, when slaveowners had taken slaves to their own white churches, they often made them sit in the back or in the gallery. Sermons by white preachers emphasized obedience to God and their masters and acceptance of their inferior status in society. Not surprisingly, blacks left white churches after the war to form their own. In rural areas, blacks flocked to Methodist and Baptist churches where emotion and music were emphasized over theological debates. The more charismatic the preacher, the bigger the congregation he could attract. As in antebellum times, black ministers were important spokespersons for the community. Preachers had mixed reactions toward public education: some saw it as a threat to their own power and the stability of the community while others saw it as a way to solidify the gains made by blacks and as springboard for greater civil rights. Black ministers often tried to establish private schools, but they usually lasted only a few years because of a lack of funding. Nonetheless, black churches provided the forum for blacks to discuss politics, organize against the threats of white supremacists, and assist each other in the struggles of everyday life.

The black family in New Orleans was also a strong institution within the African-American community. In 1880, 78.5 percent of black families had a male as a head of household, and only 30 percent of married women had to work outside the home. Black families experienced a low divorce rate and low illegitimacy rates. Families living near the levee and the wharves were more prone to be disrupted by the transient male population that worked the steamboats. The central districts near the river held most of the city's brothels, saloons, dance halls, and gambling dens, and the people who lived there experienced the highest levels of criminal activity, unwed motherhood, and divorces. The most common reason for the breakdown of the black family was the high mortality rate of black males. In families headed by widows, 81.5 percent were females whose husbands had passed away. In the city, life expectancy of a black male was only 36 years, compared to 46 years for a white male. Many black families lived in crowded conditions with bad water. Black mutual aid societies and benevolent organizations came to the aid of poor blacks by providing assistance in cases of sickness, relief from poverty, and the support of black orphanages. At the end of the nineteenth century, the black family provided comfort and security in the face of increasing racial oppression.

Despite hardships, Congressional Reconstruction did bring about changes in education to the people along the lower Mississippi River. In New Orleans, for example, General Nathaniel Banks had opened the first public schools for blacks in 1864. Funded by a tax on personal and real property, the schools served nearly 10,000 students. A year later, the Freedmen's Bureau oversaw the public school system that had grown to 19,000 students in 126 schools with 230 teachers. Whites protested against the taxes, and the schools were always short of funds. To solve the problem, students were made to pay tuition, but the move resulted in a dramatic drop in enrollment. In the fall of 1867, the New Orleans School Board took control, and three years later the numbers of students increased to 17,000 in 404 schools. Overall, illiteracy among blacks in Louisiana decreased 23 percent. Still, three-quarters of the black population of the state remained illiterate. To tackle this legacy of slavery, Republican politicians called upon every parish to have a public school system and levy a tax to support it. By 1874, of the 280,000 children that were of education age, 74,000 were enrolled in public schools in the state, and another 26,000 children were enrolled in parochial schools.

Radical Republicans and many black elites wanted to integrate white and black schools. Whites refused to put their children in the same classrooms as blacks, and a struggle ensued. Some schools were integrated in New Orleans, but almost none elsewhere. In 1874 white high school boys drove blacks out of Central Boy's High School in the city. Black girls were frightened out of the Lower Girl's High School, but they returned. Many parents took their children to black schools to avoid confrontation. The end of Reconstruction in 1877 resulted in the immediate segregation of schools, and financial support for black schools fell. In the 1880s, twenty thousand black children in the city attended five overcrowded and poorly funded schools. About 60 percent of black children were not attending schools at all.

In 1867 the New Orleans police department was desegregated, and blacks were well represented on the force until the end of Reconstruction in 1877. When the Democrats won the mayor's race in 1868, the Republicans in the state legislature united the police forces of the parishes of Orleans, Jefferson, and St. Bernard into one Metropolitan police force. About half the leadership of this police force was black and they made up 65 percent of the officers, but their numbers declined to 28.1 percent two years later. To the horror of whites, black officers had the power to arrest them. The Metropolitan police force introduced several innovations to the city: police surgeons cared for the health needs of the force, officers were given pensions, and the city was divided into precincts for more efficient administration. Most importantly for the daily life of the citizens of New Orleans, the police became involved in poverty relief. Among their many projects, they provided shelters for the homeless and food for the hungry in a soup house.

For many whites in the city, the Metropolitan police force was an aberration that only reinforced their notions that they were living in a military occupied city. Local governments withheld taxes that supported the police. Since many of the civilians in New Orleans carried guns, the Metropolitan police were engaged in frequent firefights. On average every year during Reconstruction, 22 officers were shot and another 20 were injured while on duty. Whites sought to overthrow the Republican government by organizing themselves into paramilitary organizations, such as the White League, which attacked the members of Metropolitan police. The culmination of this struggle occurred on September 14, 1874, when the White League planned a military attack on the Republican state government. Five thousand whites took to the streets to support the White League. When Metropolitan police tried to stop them, a fire fight ensued. The White League retreated and eventually its men laid down their arms, but the white population of Louisiana saw it as a victory even though losses on both sides were heavy—the White League lost 16 dead and 45 wounded and the Metropolitans lost 11 dead and 60 wounded. After the Compromise of 1877, the Louisiana's state legislature restored the New Orleans Police force. In the next three decades, the Democratic leaders of New Orleans cut down the police force to save money and decreased black employment. By 1900 only 5.1 percent of the police force was black, even though African Americans made up 27 percent of the population of the city.

A culture of violence had been part of southern history before the Civil War, but the war only reinforced the idea that solving problems with guns was an acceptable practice. During Reconstruction, whites did not hesitate to use guns to reassert their control over the black population. The Ku Klux Klan was an organization of former Confederate veterans that sought to reverse what it considered grievous changes to southern society. In Louisiana, thousands of whites joined a similar organization called the White League. The preferred method of coercion for both groups was terror—white supremacists did not have to kill all the blacks, just some of them in a cruel and public way as a warning to other African Americans. While northern troops occupied southern states, this violence could sometimes be checked. After 1877, whites could kill blacks at will because no white jury would convict a white man of killing a black man. White mobs further terrorized the black population with lynchings. If the white community did not believe that justice was served, they took the matter into their own hands. Blacks did fight back against this increasingly oppressive atmosphere, and a black person could retaliate against whites with arson or the African-American community itself could organize into armed militias. Nonetheless, the last two decades of the nineteenth century were the worst years in the number of lynchings as the white community sought to enforce racial segregation and black disempowerment by law and by violence.

The Mardi Gras festivals reflected what was happening to the people of New Orleans in the late nineteenth century. Although there were no organized parades during the Union occupation, the people of New Orleans celebrated Mardi Gras as they had in the early years of the celebration with drinking, dancing, masked balls, and theater performances. In 1866 The Mystic Krewe of Comus, an organization of white elites, made a comeback, and they once again organized parades. Comus used the parade as an opportunity to openly criticize Republican politicians and the idea of black equality. In one parade, one masked marcher dressed as the Missing Link—a half-man, half-gorilla creature who played a banjo. In 1872 the Mardi Gras festivities sported their first king, Rex, who arrived at the celebrations with an escort of attendants and music and 300 masked men. Among the masked men were white people impersonating and making fun of black politicians. The emergence of Rex was an attempt by white elites to give the parades and New Orleans a sense of hierarchy and order. Rex dictated who was allowed to walk in the parade, while relegating the rest of the population to the status of spectators. In the 1870s, Rex exuded his power over the parades by banning obscene displays and behavior and forcing maskers to remain in their assigned formations. After the Riot of 1875, Union leader General Philip Sheridan banned parades because he believed the Mardi Gras incited the white population to violence. Even though the Compromise of 1877 ended Reconstruction, some marchers in the Mardi Gras parade lashed out one more time at the Republican legacy by making fun of President Ulysses Grant and Frederick Douglas. Rex openly criticized them because the white supremacists had already emerged politically victorious, and there was no need to bring bad publicity to the festivities.

In the late nineteenth century, yellow fever did not spare Republicans, Democrats, whites, or blacks when it descended upon the residents of New Orleans. Thankfully, yellow fever did not devastate the city's population as it had in antebellum times. During the Union occupation of New Orleans, General Butler had cleaned the city and applied quarantine measures to keep the disease out. When Democrats gained control of the city government in 1866, they were not concerned about the cleanliness—garbage once again lay on the streets, dead animals rotted for days in the open air, and the gutters were filthy. Not surprisingly, yellow fever made a comeback. In 1867 an epidemic killed 3,320 out of the 41,000 people who had contracted the disease. As in prewar times, the Howard Association, a volunteer organization of doctors, gave free care to over 4,000 patients and provided relief to 6,000 family members of the people they were treating.

The most deadly yellow fever epidemic of the postwar period occurred in 1878. The disease entered the city through a sick sailor onboard a ship that had come in from Havana, Cuba. This time the disease struck middle- and upper-class neighborhoods and infected many children. About 20,000 people caught the disease in the city, and 4,000 died, over half of them children under the age of 16. The vector of the disease was different than in antebellum times, when most of the victims of yellow fever had been recent immigrants of the city. Since the disease was visiting New Orleans less frequently, native New Orleanians did not build up immunity. The economic impact of the yellow fever outbreak of 1878 on New Orleans was striking. Cities and towns along the Mississippi refused to do business with the city. About 12 million dollars of business was lost to New Orleans in that summer of 1878. Food shortages hit the city. Private charity distributed over 900,000 rations to impoverished people in the city, and the U.S. Army handed out another 250,000 rations.

Yellow fever flared up in other southern states killing another 20,000 people and making 120,000 people sick. Between 1878 and 1879, 20,000 residents of Memphis contracted yellow fever, and 6,000 of them died. Thousands of survivors fled the city. Memphis was so depopulated, that the city gave up its charter for lack of a tax base. It would take decades for the city to recover. Thereafter, yellow fever only rarely hit the Lower Mississippi Valley. By the end of the century, the connection between mosquitoes and yellow fever had been made. Disinfection of fruits coming from the Caribbean and quarantine of sick passengers on ships kept yellow fever from ravaging the people of New Orleans as it had in the past.

By 1900 Mississippi had become one of the poorest states in the country, and it remains so today. The legacy of poverty and economic stagnation had its origins in the late nineteenth century. The alluvial lands along the Mississippi River had been and would remain in the hands of a white planter elite. Just east of these plantations was a low country of woods and swamps between the Mississippi and Yazoo rivers known as the Mississippi Delta. In 1865, 90 percent of the Delta was wilderness. The clearing of this land offered hope for poor blacks and whites that they too could share in the wealth generated by the cotton kingdom. Blacks rented the land from white property owners at cheap prices, cleared and drained it, and set up small cotton farms. But this clearing took time and enormous effort. As late as 1883, 75 percent of the Delta was still wilderness. Nonetheless, white landowners speculated in land in the Delta and bought enormous plantations for themselves. Edmund Richardson, the largest plantation owner in the region, owned 10 square miles of land. To keep wages low, planters encouraged Chinese immigrants into the area. The Chinese did not approve of the low wages and most left the region after only a few years, so to secure a cheap labor supply, some plantation owners resorted to the use of convict labor, which consisted mostly of blacks. Death rates for these convicts reached 12 percent a year. Other planters turned to using orphaned black children, and if they fled, they could be arrested and hauled back to the plantation. Slowly, white planters were asserting their control over the land in the Delta just as they had along the Mississippi River.

In Mississippi, poor whites and blacks also suffered from an abysmal state public education system. In 1878 only 41 percent of school-aged whites and 38 percent of school-aged blacks attended public schools on any given day. By 1890 the number of school children attending school only increased slightly for whites to 47 percent, while the black percentage dropped to 37 percent. Some of the richer white children and a few black students attended private schools, but most poor whites and blacks could not afford to pay to support such education. Generally, blacks received three or four years of education and rural whites about eight years. Few ever got a chance at a higher education.

For poor white and black agricultural workers in the cotton regions along the Mississippi, sharecropping became the dominant form of contract

Home of a sharecropper, Mississippi, ca. 1938. Courtesy of the Library of Congress.

labor by the 1880s. Over time, however, sharecroppers became dependent on merchants in town for daily goods and supplies and, since they only got paid when they had to a crop to sell, they had to establish a line of credit. When the cotton crop could not cover what had been bought on credit, the sharecropper would have to negotiate with the merchant for more credit. Legally, the merchant received a lien on the sharecropper's crop the following year. If that crop did not pay off the loan, further credit was necessary. Thus, debt became a fact of life on the alluvial lands of the Mississippi as elsewhere in the South.

Further north in Arkansas in the 1890s, the owners of Sunnyside Plantation searched for an alternative labor supply. After contacting an Italian immigrant agency and getting support from an Italian government official, they decided to encourage Italian immigrants to settle on it. The Sunnyside Company divided the plantation into 250 plots of twelve-and-a-half acres and sold each plot for a $2,000 mortgage that charged 5 percent interest. The company agreed to buy the cotton produced at market prices, but not more than $1 for a bale minus freight and expenses. In 1890s dozens of Italian families arrived with the hope of starting a new life for themselves. Unfortunately, one-third of the original migrants were in debt after the first harvest. The Italians were unhappy with the filtered Mississippi River water they had to drink and demanded that the plantation owners build a well to tap artesian waters, but the company refused to do so. Contract disputes were frequent—the Italians claimed that they had been overcharged for the land by at least 50 percent. In 1897 yellow fever killed 28 adults and 44 children among the Italians. By March of 1898, most of the immigrant families had left, complaining about the unhealthy climate and deceptive contracts. In the first decade of the twentieth century, the plantation owners returned to black laborers.

On either side of the lower Mississippi River, large plantations were the dominate form of agriculture. They controlled the best land and had ready access to the Mississippi River for transportation. But as you moved inland a few miles, smaller farms were the norm. In contrast to the farmlands of the upper Mississippi where farms either grew in size or stayed the same in the last decades of the nineteenth century, southern farmers generally owned less land over time. In Iowa, for example, between 1880 and 1900, the average farm increased from 134 acres to 151 acres. In Mississippi in the same period, farm sizes decreased from 156 acres to 83 acres, in Arkansas 128 to 93 acres, and in Louisiana from 171 acres to 95 acres. Although the per capita income of southern farmers grew between 1866 and 1880, it only grew at half the national rate. From 1880 to 1900, the per capita rate grew at the national average as cotton prices stabilized. Still, southern farmers remained poor compared to those of Iowa, Illinois, and Minnesota. When wheat prices decreased, farmers on the upper Mississippi diversified, utilized the newest technology to improve yields, and generally prospered. The combination of a hot and humid climate and an acidic soil gave southern farmers fewer options. As in antebellum times, cotton remained the most marketable and profitable crop for many southern farms. Corn was grown mostly for local consumption. Sugar required huge capital investments that only the largest plantation could afford. Moreover, animal husbandry never prospered in the South because parasites and diseases killed cattle and hogs at a high rate or kept the quality of the animals low. For similar reasons, horses and mules were most often imported from the north. Most southern farmers outside the immediate alluvial lands of the Mississippi scraped by, but any disaster such as drought, a flood, or an insect infestation of their crops proved disastrous.

The poverty of the South manifested itself in other ways. Generally, a laborer in a southern city made 30 to 50 percent less than a comparable worker in northern cities. Unskilled white labor made about as much as unskilled black laborers. The margin of difference decreases between northern and southern workers in more skilled occupations. Unfortunately, blacks were often excluded from these skilled occupations. The

An African American near Vicksburg, ca. 1936. Courtesy of the Library of Congress.

millions of eastern and southern Europeans who migrated to this country at the end of the nineteenth century generally avoided the South because of the low wages and limited opportunity. The lack of a state and local government commitment to education was another sign of the poverty of the South. In 1890 Louisiana was spending 50 percent of the national average expenditure per student, but state governments of Mississippi, Arkansas, and Tennessee were only spending 32 percent, 40 percent, and 27 percent, respectively. The percentages got worse for Louisiana, Arkansas, and Tennessee a decade later. Southern elites realized a sad truth about their region: if a southerner received a high school degree, they more often than not opted to leave the South for better economic opportunity elsewhere. Moreover, keeping the poor black and white population uneducated guaranteed a low-wage labor supply. As the economy of the South stagnated, the region experienced the highest fertility rates in the country. The population of the South increased 50 percent between 1865 and 1877, which assured that wages could be kept low even without poor immigrants flocking to the region.

LIFE ON THE UPPER MISSISSIPPI: ST. LOUIS AND MINNEAPOLIS

Once the Civil War was over, the businessmen of St. Louis found that the railroad companies in Chicago had diverted most of the trade from Minnesota and Wisconsin away from their city. In many ways, it was their own fault. The elites of St. Louis clung to the belief that steamboats and the Mississippi River trade would remain dominant for decades to come. They were wrong. While towns north of St. Louis built bridges over the Mississippi, the merchants of St. Louis delayed the building of the Eads Bridge until 1874, and by then it was too late. In 1875 less than 78,000 tons of grain reached St. Louis by steamboat. In contrast, railroads were shipping more than 1.6 million tons of grain over the 13 bridges that spanned the Mississippi. Steamboats remained dominate in the transport of cotton for a decade after the Civil War, but by 1880, trains carried 464,000 bales of cotton while steamboats only carried 33,132 bales. The transport of general merchandise told a similar story. Only 198,000 tons of goods came by river to St. Louis while railroads delivered 2.4 million tons across the bridges of the Mississippi.

In the late nineteenth century, St. Louis managed to thrive because what it lost in trade it had gained in manufacturing. In 1870 St. Louis was the third largest manufacturing center in the country. Its factories produced iron goods, beer, clothing, and furniture, and its grain mills converted wheat from surrounding regions into flour. The city's 500 clothing companies employed nearly 4,000 workers. In 1873 Anheuser Company became the first brewery to distribute its bottled beer nationally. New manufacturing facilities in the 1870s produced chemicals, medicines, paving bricks, sewer pipes, and white lead. In 1872 the first shoe plant opened in St. Louis, and by 1899, the city had 26 shoe factories employing 5,500 workers. St. Louis was home to one of the country's first skyscrapers, the 10-story Wainwright Building. Although a tornado wrecked havoc in the city in 1896 killing several hundred people, the damaged parts of the city were quickly rebuilt. By 1900 St. Louis had 575,238 people and was the fourth largest city in the country.

With the coming of industrialization, the life of workers along the Mississippi River changed forever. Artisans and craftsmen had worked in their own shops, often living behind or above them. They dictated when and how they worked, and how often their sons would help them. They would also take on apprentices who worked for free in return for training, housing, and food. After several years, apprentices became journeymen, and then masters. But mechanization and mass production changed work in cities and towns up and down the river. Steam power allowed machines to increase the quantity of production dramatically. Consequently, the highly skilled workers were losing their jobs to machine tenders, who were easily replaceable. With artificial lighting, factories could run 24 hours a day, and workers were now required to work 10- to 12-hour shifts, six or seven days a week. In the nineteenth century, few companies gave vacations, sick days, or any other benefits. Workers worked as long as they could make money for the factory owners. If an accident happened at the factory, employers usually cared enough to get the worker to a hospital, but if the injured person could not return to work, he would be laid off. With no government welfare programs, a debilitated worker had to depend on his family or a mutual aid society.

In the first decades after the Civil War, most workers still believed that they could escape the regimented life of factory work and either buy land and set up farms or save enough money to start their own businesses. Yet, increasingly workers realized that they would never have enough savings to leave the factory. With the massive immigration of Europeans after the 1870s and the flood of black migrants from the south, individual workers had little chance of negotiating for better working conditions and higher wages. Union activity offered workers a chance to collectively bargain factory owners for better wages and working conditions. When workers believed that owners had failed to meet their grievances, employees went on strike. The Great Railroad Strike of 1877 marked the beginning of a series of strikes in the country that pitted the union movement against the owners of industry who viewed workers as a commodity. The strike practically shut down all the major industries in St. Louis. Railway executives in the city convinced the courts to issue an injunction that protected the operation of the railroads, and the U.S. military intervened to arrest the leaders of the strike. Nevertheless, strikes remained a real threat throughout the rest of the nineteenth century in St. Louis and other cities along the Mississippi, and they did not always end unfavorably for workers—unions at St. Louis breweries went on strike in 1886 and won their workers a 10 hour-day and Sundays off.

The Jewish experience in St. Louis in many ways was similar to the Jewish experience in many other American cities. Before the Civil War, St. Louis Jews had mostly emigrated from the disunited German states of Europe. They were migrants who had lived in cities and towns and engaged in mercantile trade and crafts. During the Civil War, Jewish merchants like their American counterparts took advantage of the needs of the Union army and made profits. But anti-Semitism surfaced when General Ulysses Grant's headquarters reacted to price gouging by issuing General Order 11 that forbade Jews from doing business with the army. Because Jews were not allowed anywhere near Union camps, Jewish families who had settled near the Union army were forcibly removed. Jewish leaders protested to President Abraham Lincoln for being singled out, and a month later, Grant was forced to rescind the order. In the general prosperity after the Civil War, a rich mercantile elite developed within the Jewish community and they moved to some of the richest neighborhoods in St. Louis. Over time, many of the German Jews readily adopting American culture while maintaining a reform-minded Jewish tradition. Some Jews broke their religious ties altogether. With the rest of St. Louis, the Jewish community responded with charity toward the victims of the Chicago fire of 1871 that burnt much of the city and left 90,000 people homeless. For the first time, Jews from all over St. Louis organized in a common cause and established the United Hebrew Relief Fund, which provided assistance to Jews in need in Chicago and later for Jewish victims of the Yellow Fever Epidemic of 1878. However, the history of Jews in America changed in the 1890s with the arrival of migrants from Russia (mostly from Russian-controlled parts of Poland). East European Jews were generally poor, orthodox, and victims of violent pogroms. The sheer numbers of the migration, nearly a million people across the United States, suggested that the Jewish community of the twentieth century would be very different from that of the nineteenth. In the following decades, reform-minded Jews and the new orthodox migrants would clash over what it meant to be a Jew in America.

In contrast to the lands of the lower Mississippi, Minnesota thrived in the last half of the nineteenth century. Although the Dakota attack in 1862 killed 500 settlers, it gave the federal government the excuse to drive the Dakota from Minnesota and force the Ojibwe into reservations on the upper Mississippi. The entire state was now open to white settlers. As late as 1900, white people made up 99.2 percent of the state's population. Minnesota men served faithfully in the Civil War, and the state's women managed farms and raised funds for military hospitals. Although the minority of the state's residents who were sympathetic to Confederates suffered oppression, most residents of the state prospered during the war. There had been no railroads in the state in 1860, but by war's end

250 miles of track linked Minnesota to other Midwestern states. Between 1860 and 1865, the state's population grew from 172,000 to 250,000, wheat prices increased from 50¢ a bushel to $1.5 a bushel, and the state's wheat production increased from 4.5 million bushels to 9.5 million bushels.

The postwar economy grew at a frenzied pace. In 1869 there were 15 sawmills in the area near St. Anthony on the Mississippi River. By 1890 Minneapolis was cutting nearly a half billion feet of lumber a year, making it the most productive lumber market in the world and a center of the paper-making industry. Even when the lumber industry moved westward, Minneapolis maintained its importance as a distribution center with 50 lumber companies making their headquarters in the city. Wheat production in Minnesota continued to climb in the late nineteenth century. Temporary setbacks such as a grasshopper swarm in 1873 and periods of drought only made minor dents in the production of wheat. Between 1865 and 1870, the wheat crop doubled to 18 million bushels, and it more than doubled again by 1880. In 1890 the state was producing over 52 million bushels. The population of the state had grown to 1.3 million in 1890, with over 700,000 of them working in the countryside. When wheat prices went down, most Minnesota farmers diversified and planted corn and barley. The general prosperity of the state allowed farmers to invest in the latest agricultural technology, much of it manufactured in Minneapolis after 1870. In the late nineteenth century, horses replaced oxen as the primary draft animal, and farmers grew oats as feed. In 1880 the family farms of Minnesota not only harvested 52 million bushels of wheat, but also 23 million bushels of oats, 15 million bushels of corn, 3 million bushels of potatoes, and 5 million bushels of barley. The number of cows in the state increased from 275,000 to 500,000 from 1880 to 1890. Minnesota became a major producer of dairy products. Overall, the Minnesota farmer's life was characterized by hard work and a general level of prosperity that was the envy of small farmers in the southern states.

Most of the surplus of Minnesota's wheat harvest ended up in the mills of Minneapolis. In the late nineteenth century, Minneapolis became the flour capital of the world. The city's flour production increased from 20 million bushels in 1870 to 60 million bushels in 1890. To achieve this success, Minnesota's flour industry had to overcome several technological problems. Spring wheat had husks that easily broke apart and mixed in with the flour to create speckles. It also had an oily wheat germ that reduced the quality of the flour, and its glutinous cell, so important to preserve for quality baking flour, tended to get lost in the husking process. The Middling Purifier solved these problems by blowing air over the crushed grain, which blew out the husks. Then, mills granulated the wheat instead of milling it the traditional way to leave the wheat germ intact. The millstones were placed further apart and then rotated more slowly. Eventually the millstones were replaced altogether by chilled iron or steel rollers that produced superior flour at lower costs. To prevent fires, Minnesota mills adopted a new exhaust system that filtered the air of flour particles.

By the last decade of the nineteenth century, the flour industry in Minneapolis had consolidated. The new technology was expensive, and the larger firms were more capable of doing experimental research to improve their product, negotiating better prices for grain, getting better railroad rates to ship the grain and flour, and investing large amounts in marketing and advertising. The larger firms bought the wheat at the peak of harvest when prices were the lowest for the year and then stored wheat in grain elevators. Farmers, in turn, often thought that the mills were controlling prices and giving them a bad deal. Tensions between farmers and mill owners persisted into the twentieth century. Nevertheless, the mills generated business opportunities for related industries and created job opportunities for thousands. Mill owners invested in the Soo Line Railroad in order to bypass Chicago and move their flour through Wisconsin and Michigan to the East Coast. Manufacturing plants in Minneapolis built the machines that milled the grains and supplied equipment for the state's farmers. Food companies such as the Pettijohn California Breakfast Foods and Cream of Wheat took advantage of the close proximity of the city's mills, which lowered transportation costs. The ultimate measure of success of Minneapolis was the growth of the city's population: the city grew from 5,809 people in 1860 to 129,200 people in 1885 to 202,718 in 1900.

After the Civil War, the black community in Minnesota was concentrated in St. Paul. In 1864 St. Paul had segregated its black children into separate schools, but public funding for these schools was minimal—the classrooms were not well supplied and the buildings suffered from broken and boarded windows and falling plaster. Hostility from whites and the poor conditions at the schools forced most black families to keep their children at home so that by 1868, only 20 black students attended public schools in the city. That same year, the citizens of Minnesota approved a referendum that gave full voting rights to blacks, Native-Americans, and people of mixed races. However, the majority of the white citizens of St. Paul opposed suffrage for minorities. When blacks marched in the streets in celebration and thanked the Republican mayor of the city for his support, he lost the next election to a racist Democrat. Black community organizations continued to exert pressure for the desegregation of schools. In March of 1869, the state legislature compelled St. Paul to allow black students to enter white schools. White hostility and racism made many black parents wary of sending their children to white schools and only 13 African-American students were enrolled at the end of 1869. Although Jim Crow laws in the city kept whites and blacks from living in the same neighborhoods at the end of the century, blacks were not segregated in St. Paul's public school system.

In the late nineteenth century, Iowa's population was over 99 percent white and the majority of the people were farmers who specialized in corn production. Iowa farmer increased their yields of corn from 2.4 million bushels before the Civil War to 275 million bushels in 1880. Although the size of farms in Iowa fell slightly in the average number of acres from 165 acres in 1860 to 134 acres in 1870, they rose again to 151 acres by 1900. About 34.9 percent of the state's farmers were tenants, mostly younger men who did not have a family farm to inherit or farmers who had lost their land in a foreclosure. Eventually, most were able to save their money and purchase land for themselves. What made starting a farm more difficult in the late nineteenth century was the cost of new technology, which was becoming a necessity because as historian Allan G. Bogue writes, "[b]etween the 1830s and the late 1870s, machinery increased the production of the worker in the small-grain fields by perhaps four to six times, in the hay meadow by certainly as much, and in the corn field by perhaps twice."[1]

The second half of the nineteenth century saw important changes in the lives of rural women on the upper Mississippi. The management of the household was the most important activity to the survival of the family. While the men worked in the fields, women worked, as historian Glenda Riley points out, "as domestic artisans in their homes, which also served as their workplaces or factories." They were involved in "whitewashing cabin walls, making medicines, and treating the ill, making candles and soap, processing foods, cooking in open fireplaces or on small stoves, making cloth and clothing, and washing clothes 'on the board.'"[2] One day out of the week would be devoted to washing. A woman had to haul in the water from a well, heat it, and then wash the clothes with a scrubbing board. More water had to be hauled in to rinse the clothes. Another day of the week would be devoted to the chore of ironing, which meant that the iron would have to be heated on the stove and then the cotton clothes pressed. But rural women also had duties outside the house—they made butter, collected and sold eggs, kept chickens, and often took care of the pigs and cows. Of course, looking after children was a major part of their lives.

As mass-produced goods became widely available through the Sears' Catalogue in the late nineteenth century, women quickly bought items that made their life slightly easier. Sewing and washing machines allowed women to finish their chores more quickly. Kerosene lamps replaced candles that once had to be made by hand. Women also gained access to the latest fashions. Homespun hand-me downs were exchanged for inexpensive mass-produced clothes, and underpants and corsets no longer needed to be made by hand. On prosperous farms, families bought pianos and other musical instruments to entertain themselves. Women ordered books and magazines that appealed to their interests and needs. Although the role of women as a domestic artisan was diminished by the market economy, women still had to find ways of earning money to buy those goods. The selling of eggs, chickens, and the surplus of their gardens continued unabated.

Farmers in Iowa and Minnesota were dependent on railroads to move their grain to markets. In the late nineteenth century, steamboats on the upper Mississippi simply could not compete with railroads. The upper Mississippi was mostly unnavigable for several months of the year because of low water in the summer and ice in the winter. In contrast, railroads could operate year round, 24 hours a day. In 1878 the U.S. Congress authorized navigation improvements on the upper Mississippi to create a channel with a minimal depth of 4.5 feet for the entire length of the upper Mississippi. Unfortunately, for steamboat companies, the 4.5 foot channel was not completed until 1906, and even then the upper Mississippi was not navigable in extreme low water. Not surprisingly, railroads continued to take freight away from the Mississippi steamboats. Ferries still transported people and their animals across the river, but, in most cases, steamboats were no longer a viable mode of transportation.

CONCLUSION

Compared to steamboats, railroads offered a more flexible, reliable, and cheaper way to get products from one place to another. Although barges pulled by tugboats were just beginning to show their worth at the end of the century, a city or town along the Mississippi River no longer enjoyed the economic advantages they once did. Still, the alluvial lands of the Mississippi offered some of the best agricultural lands in the country, and those who farmed those lands prospered. Unfortunately, the story of the lives of the people of the Mississippi after the Civil War is a tale of the division between the North and South, and the rich and the poor. Planters along the lower Mississippi refused to give up control over their black labor supply. The state and local governments and white elites conspired to keep the black race subjugated in the South. Sharecropping allowed poor blacks and whites some control over their lives, but debt trapped increasing numbers in a seemingly endless cycle of poverty. In contrast, the farmers of the central and upper Mississippi prospered on family farms. Even though railroad rates were high and prices of grain fluctuated, few farmers along the upper Mississippi lived in the broken down shacks that still can be seen along the lower Mississippi in states like Louisiana. While New Orleans, Natchez, Memphis, and Vicksburg recovered from the war and tried to return to antebellum prosperity, St. Louis and Minneapolis forged ahead into the new industrial order. In the process, the regimented life of the factory became the lot of thousands of laborers who now had to toil in a workplace that they could never hope to own. Nonetheless, the products of the machine age provided mass-produced goods for millions in the emerging consumer culture, thereby raising the standard of living for many Americans. But most black and white sharecroppers and tenant farmers along the lower Mississippi did not share in this bounty. That dichotomy caused upheavals that would reverberate throughout the twentieth century.

NOTES

1. Allan G. Bogue, "Farming in the Prairie Peninsula, 1830–1890" *Iowa History Reader,* ed. Marvin Bergman (Ames: State Historical Society of Iowa in association with Iowa State University Press, 1996), 77.

2. Glenda Riley, "In or Out of the Historical Kitchen?: Minnesota Rural Women" *The North Star State: A Minnesota History Reader,* ed. Anne J. Aby (St. Paul: Minnesota Historical Society Press, 2002), 214.

8

1900–1945

From 1900 to 1917, midwestern farmers in Minnesota, Illinois, and Iowa experienced one of the most prosperous periods in U.S. agricultural history—prices for farm products were up, yields were high, and living standards of most farmers improved. Towns and cities along the river thrived as railroads and barges carried farm goods in and out of the Mississippi Valley at record levels. For nearly a generation, it seemed that the good life could be obtainable by all. But the southern states along the Mississippi weren't as lucky. The boll weevil devastated small farmers and absentee landlords on plantations who did not keep up with the latest eradication methods. Then in 1921, hard times came to the Midwest as well when grain and cotton prices fell by more than a third. Mechanization allowed ever greater production with less labor, but at the same time it did require a larger capital investment. Those farmers and planters who had overextended themselves with credit had to foreclose. Farms and plantations grew larger and decreased in number, and tenancy rates rose. In the South, African Americans continued an exodus from rural areas, which exploited them under an oppressive regime of debt peonage and Jim Crow. Along the lower Mississippi River, African Americans found solace in music—jazz in New Orleans and blues in the Mississippi Delta and Memphis. Disaster struck the central and lower Mississippi when the flood of 1927 broke through the levee system to inundate millions of acres of land leaving hundreds of thousands of people homeless. In the 1930s, the Great Depression hit the region. New Deal programs relieved some of the economic pain, but ill-conceived programs such as the Agricultural

Adjustment Act allowed planters and large corporate farms to expand their land holdings at the price of sharecroppers and tenants. World War II ended the Depression, and prosperity returned. Unfortunately, racism was as virulent in 1945 as it had been nearly a half century before. The atomic bombs dropped on Hiroshima and Nagasaki may have ended the war abroad, but the struggle for justice and equality at home had just begun.

RURAL LIFE VS. CITY LIFE

Beginning in 1900, it seemed that midwestern farmers had entered a golden age that they hoped would never end. In that year, farmers in Minnesota produced 95 million bushels of wheat, 74 million bushels of oats, and 47 million bushels of corn, and yields only got better as the years went by. In Iowa, dairy farmers were paying attention to the latest scientific data about breeding superior cows. In 1850 the average dairy cow produced 147.9 gallons per a year. In 1900 the average milk production of a cow had more than doubled to 376 gallons. By 1940 dairy cows were producing on average 555.8 gallons per year and the best of them could produce over 900 gallons of milk. As corn yields in Iowa went up, so too did the price of land. In 1900 an acre of farm land cost on average $36.35. Ten years later the price had risen to $82.58 an acre. Technology was one of the factors driving the improvement in production, and Iowa farmers eagerly embraced the latest harvesters and tractors. Between 1920 and 1940, the number of tractors used by Iowa farmers increased from just over 20,000 to 124,487. There were more tractors in Iowa than in any other state, and Iowa farmers were producing 15 percent of the world's supply of corn.

With the money farmers made on the upper Mississippi, farmers could purchase the latest consumer goods from the Sears catalogue. Homespun hand-me-downs were being replaced with machine-made clothes in the latest styles. For entertainment, farmers purchased phonographs, pianos, and later radios. The living standards of Iowa and Minnesota farmers were some of the highest for rural people in the entire country. Good prices and high yields tempted many farmers to expand their farms and purchase more farmland on credit. As long as the prices of their grain remained high, many farmers were willing to take risks.

Yet even with this prosperity, young people were leaving the farms and moving to towns and cities. Historian Thomas J. Morain eloquently explained what was happening:

> When the Jefferson woman joked that her mother would not let her date "farm kids," she was not implying that farming was not a respectable occupation. Good farmers commanded respect in town as well as in the country. Farming, however, was more than just a man's occupation. It was a way of life for the entire family. Before 1920 rural children were likely to attend one-room schools only through eighth grade. Before rural electrification began in the 1930s most farm homes

lacked indoor plumbing, running water, and household appliances that town homes had possessed for two or three decades. Farm wives kept flocks of chickens, raised large gardens, and usually did most of their own baking. The social highlight of the week was the Saturday night trip to town. Poets and politicians may have praised the farmer, but town mothers did not want their daughters to marry [farmers] and leave the amenities of town life.[1]

Despite the prosperity in the countryside, cities offered more economic opportunities and better access to the industrial consumer economy. Although the timber industry in Minnesota had collapsed in 1916, other businesses took root in the Twin Cities. Minneapolis remained the flour capital of the world into the 1930s. There were jobs to be had in Minnesota, and thousands of Swedes, Norwegians, and German immigrants flocked to Minneapolis and St. Paul. In 1900, 42 shoemakers had shops in Minneapolis. Like craftsmen elsewhere, shoemakers were overwhelmed by the power of mass production. In 1910 they just could not compete with the 18 shoe factories in the state that employed 3,000 people. In 1920 not a single shoemaker was listed in the city's directory. What hurt the shoemaker was a bonus for consumers: low-priced high quality shoes. The workers in these factories did not have the control over the workplace as the craftsmen had, but jobs were plentiful and the wages high enough to allow them to participate in the consumer economy.

Kuklok's threshing machine, ca. 1900. Stearns History Museum, St. Cloud, Minnesota, Photo number Shm012338.

In 1907 St. Louis was the third largest city in the nation with a population of over 600,000 people. The city did not experience the large immigration of eastern and southern Europeans as did the rest of the country. Most of the immigrants to St. Louis were either Irish or German, and they merged with well-established ethnic communities. These immigrants arrived to see a city with electric trolley cars and a purified water system. When the World's Fair of 1904 celebrated the one hundredth anniversary of the Louisiana Purchase in St. Louis, 20 million people visited the fairgrounds that extended over 272 acres. The World's Fair encouraged the construction of new hotels and other buildings throughout the city. St. Louis had become the world's largest producer of beer, shoes, and stoves. In the 1920s, the city of St. Louis grew by 13 percent but the surrounding areas in St. Louis County increased by 110 percent. As in other expanding cities, middle- and upper-class people in St. Louis moved out of the downtown district and into suburbs. Streetcars, automobiles, and paved roads made living in the suburbs of the city feasible.

St. Louis World's Fair, 1904–1905. Courtesy of the Library of Congress.

Henry Ford had pioneered the mass production of automobiles that brought the price of a car within the reach of a middle-class family. Automobiles gave people a measure of freedom to travel that they had never experienced before. Their conception of time and distance changed as the country became a smaller place, especially when local and state governments began to invest in paved roads in the 1920s. In 1909 there were only 7,000 cars and 4,000 motorcycles registered in Minnesota. Twelve years later, Minnesotans owned 333,000 motor vehicles, and the number doubled again only a few years later.

The people in the cities along the Mississippi River became tied more tightly to the consumption culture of modern America. They shopped in chain and department stores such as May's in St. Louis and Dayton's in Minneapolis, with glass windows that displayed all kinds of tempting items. They bought the latest styles of mass-produced clothes and shoes. The availability of cheap high quality soap like Ivory, toothpaste, and indoor plumbing allowed people to pay more attention to their hygiene than ever before. More and more people captured treasured memories with cameras. Packaged foods such as Quaker Oatmeal and Kellogg's Corn Flakes promised freshness and convenience. By the 1920s, most cities along the river had electricity, so consumers could purchase the latest appliances for their homes. Amusement parks and circuses were lit up in the night, encouraging families to leave their homes in the evening hours and enjoy themselves. For a nickel, people enjoyed motion pictures featuring actors and actresses who were becoming national celebrities. Afterwards, they could go to the fountain shops and drink carbonated sodas and ice cream in a variety of flavors. By the end of the 1920s, millions of Americans communicated through the telephone, listened to radios, and enjoyed records on their phonographs. The industrialized consumer society offered assistance to women in their roles as mothers and wives. Appliances such as refrigerators, vacuum cleaners, and toasters made the daily grind of cooking and cleaning easier for women. As members of a consumer society, people up and down the Mississippi River were subject to mass advertising that sought to make people's wants into the necessities of life, and owning brand name products became a status symbol.

LIFE DURING WORLD WAR I

World War I provided opportunities for women as never before. As historian William E. Parrish noted, "Missouri women made sacrifices and aided the war effort at home and abroad. They contended with 'wheatless Mondays,' 'meatless Tuesdays,' and 'lightless nights,' 'porkless Thursdays,' and 'war time' or daylight savings time. Women worked in factories and on farms; they served as nurses in hospitals and on battlefields; they rolled bandages and knit sweaters and socks; and they raised money for the war through various bond drives."[2] The important role of women in World War I on the home front convinced President Woodrow Wilson and the majority of men in the country that women had a right to vote. Nearly three-quarters of a century of activism by women for suffrage had finally come to fruition with the ratification of the Nineteenth Amendment in 1920.

But the patriotism of World War I also had a nastier side. The Espionage Act of 1917, the Enemy Act of 1917, and the Sedition Act of 1918 attacked those within the country whom the government suspected of disloyalty. Minnesotans of German descent were one of the largest ethnic groups in the state. Their civil organizations had supported Germany in World War I, and they expressed their displeasure as President Woodrow Wilson's administration became more and more sympathetic to Great Britain and France. When the United States declared war against Germany, Germans in Minnesota either declared their loyalty to the United States or remained silent. Encouraged by public opinion, the federal and state government saw the German community as a threat. The Minnesota Commission of Public Safety began a campaign of repression attacking the civil rights of German-Americans. All aliens had to register. German professors were dismissed from their jobs, German language books were banned from libraries, and most schools dropped their German language programs. Americans formed local councils to catch disloyal Americans and make difficult the lives of those who did not buy their fair share of Liberty Bonds. Many private schools were forced to change their primary language of instruction from German to English. German newspapers across the country were shut down and harassed. German identity in Minnesota and the rest of the country suffered. The number of German-speaking people in the United States fell from 9 million in 1910 to just under 5 million in 1940.

World War I also brought changes to the African American community along the Mississippi. Thousands of African American men from the Mississippi Valley served in the segregated U.S. Army. The feverish pace of industrial production in the war economy caused labor shortages in the cities and forced white factory owners to hire blacks, which further encouraged the migration of African Americans out of rural areas. Many blacks received decent wages for the first time in their lives. However, the reaction of working-class whites was often swift and violent. In East St. Louis, Illinois, on July 3, 1917, white mobs went on a killing spree. An article in the *St. Louis Dispatch* described the horrors:

> I saw man after man with hands raised, pleading for his life, surrounded by groups of men—men who had never seen him before and knew nothing about him except that he was black—and saw them administer the historic sentence of intolerance, death by stoning. I saw one of these men, almost dead from a savage shower of stones, hanged with a clothesline, and when it broke, hanged with a rope which held. Within a few paces of the pole from which he was suspended, four other negroes lay dead or dying, another having been removed, dead, a short

time before. I saw the pockets of two of these negroes searched, without the finding of any weapon.[3]

Violence by whites against blacks was a part of southern culture along the lower Mississippi River, but World War I increased tensions. Thousands of blacks had served in the military and were not satisfied to return to the peonage of the Jim Crow South, so they demanded economic and political changes. The white community made sure that the status quo continued. When black laborers in Phillips County, Arkansas, sought to unionize, a white mob attacked their meeting at a church. After the shootout, 200 black men and women lay dead. Whites blamed blacks for starting the so-called riot. Local courts indicted 122 blacks and sentenced 12 men to be executed. Thankfully, pressure from the NAACP and the public forced Arkansas to release the 12 condemned men, but intimidation and individual acts of violence against blacks continued.

AFRICAN AMERICANS ALONG THE MISSISSIPPI

The alluvial land along the Mississippi River had always been owned by white planters with large landholdings, and it remained so into the twentieth century. However, blacks did own about 7.3 percent of the newly deforested and drained lowlands of the Yazoo-Mississippi Delta. But floods in 1912, 1913, and 1927 devastated small black farms, and high land prices prevented most tenants from acquiring their own farms. In the first decades of the twentieth century, a white planter elite gained control of the most productive lands of the Delta. However, the number of plantations decreased as white landlords no longer managed their operations as in the past because they preferred to live in the towns and cities of the state. Over time, large corporate plantations came to dominate the local agriculture. The Mississippi Delta Planting Company, for example, owned 45,000 acres in Bolivar County. A thousand tenant families worked for the company, and they produced a million bales of cotton a year. Because of the cheap supply of black labor, significant mechanization in the cotton fields did not occur until the 1950s. In 1925 farmers in Illinois were using over 43,000 tractors, but farmers and planters in Mississippi owned only 1,871 tractors.

In the 1920s, sharecroppers farmed about three-quarters of the Yazoo Delta's land. Besides depending on the landlord for most of their farm implements, most of them were cash poor, so they relied on advances paid in goods from planters to get by before the cotton was picked and the shares paid out. As historian James C. Cobb explained, "a cropper living on advances was almost certain to be wearing the cheapest shoes and clothing available and subsisting on a diet of fat salt pork, cornbread, and canned goods, mostly beans. If the plantation operated a commissary, the decision as to whether a family received new shoes might be made by the overseer rather than the tenant himself."[4] Since most landlords marketed the crops of their sharecroppers, black sharecroppers almost always received less money than they deserved for their work, and since they depended on goods from the plantation store for everyday life, they were almost universally in debt to the storeowner. The trick for every planter was to pay a sharecropper just enough to keep them from leaving but not too much to ensure that they would remain in debt to the planter and be forced to stay on. To make matters worse, vagrancy laws assured that blacks who left farm work and sought to move to town would be arrested and then sent back to plantations to work as convict labor. In this atmosphere of oppression blacks turned to music, the blues, to reflect on their hardship. When life became abysmal, many blacks opted to leave the South and take their music and culture with them for opportunities elsewhere. Since train stations were patrolled by whites looking to arrest blacks on vagrancy charges, blacks who fled the region often had to do so at night. The rise of the Ku Klux Klan in the 1920s coupled with vigilante lynching kept the black population terrorized, which encouraged blacks to flee for their own safety. The Reverend W. Ho Booker of Mississippi expressed the frustration of many blacks:

> We have no law to protect us. The system of debt slavery rules in this country. If a negro is arrested, he is taken to jail and kept there a while then he is taken to a big man's farm and put to work with out any trial whatever. Whenever white man kills a negro he is taken buried and that is all there is to it . . . if a negro commits a crime against the state if he promises the white man that he will work for him in to the cotton field that settles the case.[5]

African Americans also suffered from discrimination in the school system. The 1896 Supreme Court case, *Plessy v. Ferguson,* had legitimized racial segregation in transportation on the so-called separate but equal principle. White southerners quickly used the decision as a constitutional cover to create an all-encompassing state-mandated system of racial segregation. The effects of such a system touched virtually every aspect of everyday life for blacks and whites. It was immediately and strikingly evident in such areas as education, where very separate and unequal facilities not only marked off racial boundaries, but kept down prospects for black advancement and even hope. In Mississippi, the entire public education system was woefully underfunded, but for blacks it was even more so. Although blacks made up 57 percent of Mississippi population, black schools only received 14 percent of the state's budget for education in the 1929 to 1930 school year. White children attended 975 consolidated schools that had replaced the one-room school house. In contrast, there were only 16 consolidated schools for black students. In 1919 only half the school-aged black children in Memphis attended school at all, and a third that did attend had no seats for them in their classrooms. In 1927 Tennessee spent $21.02 per white child on public education, but only $11.88 for every black child.

In the daily struggle of life, African Americans turned to their Bibles, their families, and the blues, a musical genre that originated in the Mississippi Delta in the 1890s and became influential in the taverns and clubs of Memphis. The blues was a working-class phenomenon in the black community that fused elements of religious spirituals, African rhythms, and field-work songs with themes that dealt with the harsh social and economic realities of black life. The blues expressed emotions, particularly disappointment and heartbreak but also a lingering rage at the injustice of life. Historian Clyde Woods explains other facets of the blues:

> Born in a new era of censorship, suppression, and persecution, the blues conveyed the sorrow of the individual and collective tragedy that had befallen African Americans. It also operated to instill pride in a people facing daily denigration, as well as channeling folk wisdom, descriptions of life and labor, travelogues, hoodoo, and critiques of individuals and institutions. It is often forgotten that the blues are also defined by those songs, music, stories, jokes, dances, and other visual and physical practices that raise the spirit of the audience to unimaginable heights. The men and women who performed the blues were sociologists, reporter, counselors, advocates, preservers of language and customs, and summoners of life, love, laughter, and much, much more.[6]

Before Beale Street in Memphis became a commercialized tourist spot in the late twentieth century, it was a vibrant blues center for the African-American community. Located on the Chickasaw Bluffs, Memphis was and remains a river town. But the yellow fever epidemic of 1878 killed thousands in the town and caused most of the white elite to abandon the city. Memphis survived by becoming one of the major destinations for thousands of black migrants fleeing the rural poverty of the Mississippi Delta. With their skills and hopes and dreams, many black migrants also brought with them their taste for the blues. Beale Street became a mecca for black music and food. Over time, crime and prostitution and its working-class origins made it a rough part of the town, but that roughness gave Memphis blues its gritty, defiant character that defined the genre for millions of Americans, both black and white. The blues would evolve in Chicago, Detroit, and Harlem and provide the foundation for the development of rock and roll. White people in the United States and around the world would imitate the sound, and some African American blues artists found success. Yet, the social and economic struggles of the working-class black communities all over the country provides the most fertile ground for the heart-felt, gut-wrenching music that is the blues.

CHANGES IN LOUISIANA

One of the states with the lowest standard of living in the country was Louisiana. Although the so-called Choctaw Club, an alliance of business people, controlled the state's politics and made sure there was minimal government regulation and taxation of their businesses, they did have a vision to making Louisiana an industrial center. They focused their attention at developing the state's timber and its natural deposits of oil, natural gas, and sulfur. Enormous forests of cypress, a wood impervious to water damage, enticed the lumber industry to come to Louisiana. By 1910 that state was second in the nation in the quantity of lumber produced. Unfortunately, the net result for the environment of Louisiana was deforestation that led to soil erosion. Swamps became a sea of stumps, and eventually the cypress industry collapsed. Thanks to New Deal programs, a reforestation campaign began in the 1930s, but the boom days of the timber industry in Louisiana were gone, and the ecology of the swamps forever changed. Indeed, the rapid stripping of Louisiana's woods was typical of the unregulated grab-as-many resources practices that polluted the waters, destroyed wetlands, and compromised eco-systems in other parts of the Mississippi River Valley.

Louisiana's politicians also looked to the oil industry to bring prosperity to their state. At the turn of the century, all the oil of Louisiana was processed elsewhere, but the Standard Oil Company found that the Mississippi River provided an excellent means of transporting crude oil to the refinery and shipping processed oil to markets. In 1909 Standard Oil Company built a refinery along the banks of the Mississippi River two miles north of Baton Rouge. In 1920 Louisiana was refining eight percent of the nation's oil production, and most of it was shipped to Baton Rouge for processing. By the 1930s, the plant was processing 90,000 barrels a day, but the spike in demand during World War II increased output to 137,000 barrels by 1945. Louisianans received good jobs; 700 people were employed at the refinery in 1909 and over 9,000 people in 1940. Concerns of the environmental cost of this oil boom would not occur until the 1960s.

Louisiana's most famous and notorious politician, Huey Long, continued on the path of developing the state with a mixture of demagoguery and genuine concern for the poor of Louisiana. During his administration, 2,400 miles of paved highways and two bridges over the Mississippi at Baton Rouge and New Orleans made possible east-west travel across the state in automobiles. Huey Long improved education in rural areas and offered free textbooks to students. Whatever the short-comings of the man and the corruption of his administration, many poor Louisianans benefited from their state government for the first time. His assassination on September 8, 1935 continues to be mourned by many of Louisiana's residents today.

Louisiana's sugar industry was also modernizing. Sugar production always involved a large capital investment, but technological advances meant planters needed to invest more money into a sugar mill if they wanted to compete successfully. Although the sugar industry was, and remains, protected by tariffs, the number of sugar refineries dropped significantly in the twentieth century because sugar planters sought to centralize operations to increase efficiency. In 1898 there had been 347 sugar factories in Louisiana, but only 12 years later their number had dropped to 214. In the 1920s, the mosaic disease attacked sugar cane and crops failed. Between 1922 and 1926, the number of sugar mills went down from 112 to 54, but went back up to 70 in 1930. The Great Depression took a further toll. As historian John B. Rehder argued, "processing fundamentals in the manufacture of raw sugar during the 1800s differed little from those in modern sugar making. Sugarcane stalks were ground at the mill; juice was extracted, clarified, boiled, and crystallized; and raw sugar was separated from molasses."[7] But the technology to accomplish these tasks had changed. Planters adopted steam power at the turn of the century, and it became universal by 1950. Although mechanization came to the sugar fields more slowly, it did begin to replace the highly skilled labor force. Tractors were used only for plowing the land. Laborers cut the sugar cane by hand until 1935, when the first sugar harvesters appeared. By 1946 machines cut 63 percent of Louisiana's sugar crops.

These changes strained labor conditions on sugar plantations. The hot humid climate coupled with backbreaking work had always made the lives of sugar workers difficult. Since sugar production was such a capital intensive industry, sharecropping never caught on in the region and nearly all laborers were wage earners. Unfortunately, sugar planters found ways to entrap their laborers. As late as the 1960s, there were still sugar laborers who were being paid in so-called script that could only be used at the company store, which sold its goods at inflated prices. Mill consolidation, the losses from the mosaic disease, and the Great Depression took their toll on the industry, and sugar laborers often found themselves without work. Many of them had no choice but to pack up and migrate to other regions of the country.

After the Civil War, railroads had taken much business away from New Orleans, but the city remained an important center of trade with Latin American countries. Commerce in the city recovered as New Orleans became an important railroad hub at the turn of the century. Moreover, as barges replaced steamboats as the most efficient way of moving goods on the Mississippi River, New Orleans thrived on the trade of bulk freight. When cotton prices rose through 1900 to 1918, the city benefited. In 1904 New Orleans had only exported 150 million dollars worth of goods and imported only 34 million dollars worth of goods, but by 1922 the trade had grown to 600 million dollars of exports and 300 million dollars of imports.

The loading and unloading of goods required the labor of thousands of people along the docks and railroads yards of New Orleans. Laborers unloading the city's railway freight were the lowest paid wage earners amongst transportation workers in New Orleans. In the 1920s, a railroad day laborer made $1.50 for 10 hours of work compared to longshoremen along the Mississippi river docks who made $4.00 per a day. Many of the railway workers were transients who worked for a season and then moved on to other jobs.

New Orleans' cotton trade depended on the labor of 10,000 dockworkers. Their work was hard, seasonal, and dependent on market swings. Wearing gloves to protect their hands and working in gangs of four, several thousand longshoremen transferred goods off and onto awaiting ships using winches to mechanically lift the cargo from the levee and put it onboard the ship. Unfortunately for workers, there were usually more laborers than the foremen needed, so a longshoreman sometimes worked only a few hours in a day or experienced unemployment for several weeks at a time. Most held another job in the off-season. Screwmen stowed the cotton on the ship in the most compact form possible and made sure the cargo was evenly distributed on the ship. Like other longshoremen, their jobs were seasonal, but their skill made them the highest paid dockworkers. All dockworkers faced dangers on the job. Cargo could shift or a rope could snap sending a 500-pound bale of cotton on them.

In 1907, as Jim Crow laws became prevalent in the South, the owners of ships and their agents demanded that dockworkers segregate according to race. Realizing their similar economic interests and refusing to allow owners of ships to use race to weaken their union, white and black dockworkers resisted segregation. When steamship agents demanded that each gang of screwmen load 200 bales of cotton instead of 160, 9,000 dockworkers went on strike. Blacks and whites stood together, even in the face of strikebreakers, who could not coordinate their efforts to do the job efficiently. Twenty days later, the strike ended with a compromise of 180 bales of cotton per gang. Unfortunately, the fortunes of dockworkers turned for the worse in the late 1910s and 1920s, when new steamships with larger cargo space and better cotton presses, cranes, and conveyors made the skills of the screwmen less necessary. In 1931 in the midst of a national depression, white union leaders and the city only allowed registered voters to work the docks, so blacks could no longer be employed. But the numbers of dockworkers further decreased after World War II, when cargo ships switched to standard containers.

The geography of New Orleans changed during the first half of the twentieth century. The city's waterfront along the Mississippi just opposite the French Quarter had been transformed to a two-mile long line of wooden warehouses. Business leaders viewed the ugly warehouses as symbols of New Orleans' prosperity. A railway called the Public Belt traversed 12 miles of the riverfront and handled over 100,000 cars a year. Poor residents of the city lived in so-called shotgun houses, long narrow homes, in over-crowded districts within the city. In the 1920s and 1930s, politicians and business leaders made the decision to reclaim the backwaters of the city along Lake Pontchartrain. A canal system was constructed, and pumps drained the swamps. Unfortunately, the newly reclaimed wetlands dropped below sea-level as they dried. Levees were then built higher to keep the waters of Lake Pontchartrain out, and pumps were installed to drain the streets after every rainfall. Thousands of poor residents settled on these lowlands, where housing was cheap. Builders found that the homes they had built sunk into the soft ground, so many buildings were built on pilings that looked like stilts. These newly created lowland districts were in serious danger from hurricanes because a tide surge could overtop the levees and drown the neighborhoods. Another expansion of the city occurred when the Levee Board of New Orleans built a seawall that extended 3,000 feet into the lake. In 1934 the water within the wall was drained, and an airport and lakefront homes were built on what had once been the bed of the lake.

The Mardi Gras festival became an increasingly important source of revenue for the city and its residents. The celebration of a festival before the Lenten season had been a tradition in the city since its founding. In the eighteenth century, the elites of New Orleans organized into krewes and staged balls and parades, and relegated the masses to the role of spectators. In the early twentieth century, white elites excluded blacks and Jews from their celebrations. The King of a Krewe, whether it be Rex or Comus, reigned over a ball with a queen who was attended to by beautiful debutantes. As historian Reid Mitchell describes:

> Reigning as queen or attending a queen as a maid was simultaneously a rite of passage, an act of submission, and a mark of honor. Participation in the Carnival courts was the outward and visible sign that a daughter was conforming to the demands that "society" placed upon her. The court image of the woman as debutante, dressed in virginal white, was in sharp contrast with the alternative image of the woman dressed in masculine attire that characterized Carnival on the streets. By the rules of Carnival hierarchy, the most for which a man could strive was to be a Carnival king, and the most for which a woman could hope was to be a Carnival queen. A man became king when he was mature, at the height of his power and ability; the honor crowned his career. A woman became a Carnival queen when she was a girl; queenhood ended her childhood. After she was queen she might go on to become a woman, a wife, a mother.[8]

In the eyes of participants, Mardi Gras harked back to an earlier nobler time. However, black New Orleans did not allow the white community to prevent them from celebrating Mardi Gras. In 1908 blacks dressed up as Indians and attacked white men during the festivities. The black Indians returned year after year, and tribes controlled certain neighborhoods within the city. Blacks turned against one another as well—African Americans from uptown fought African-Creoles from downtown on the streets. But the black and Creole elites of New Orleans were interested in more civil forms of entertainment. In 1912 the Krewe of Zulu staged its first parade. The Zulu King led a parade that celebrated music and dancing.

Every year, jazz bands competed with each other to make the greatest impact with the crowds. Generations of young people were inspired by what they heard. The Zulu parade brought jazz to the masses of tourists, who then spread their love of the art form across the nation and around the world. Other black krewes followed the example of the Zulu.

Prohibition and the Great Depression hurt the Mardi Gras festivals. Krewes could not afford to stage parades. Still, Mardi Gras came to symbolize the hope for better times. White businessmen created the Krewe of Hermes to attract tourists. White women organized the Krewe of Venus to get the female population involved in the celebrations. The Elks Krewe sought to democratize Mardi Gras by allowing all white New Orleanians to join their parade. By the end of World War II, blacks were still segregated, but they continued to have their own parades, often mocking the white parades. In the bleak years of the Depression, jazz music continued to echo in the streets of New Orleans.

THE FLOOD OF 1927

Flooding or the threat of it has always been a part of the daily life of people who lived along the Mississippi from Cape Giradeau to the Gulf of Mexico. Since ancient times, people settled along the river to take advantage of the rich alluvial soil that lay on either side of the Mississippi. This soil had been deposited there by floods. In some places, the alluvial soil was several feet thick. During a flood, the river waters that would flow over the banks dropped the heaviest sediment that the waters carried near the main channel. This accumulated sediment formed natural levees, which provided shelter from mild to moderate floods. Floods caused water to accumulate in lowlands on either side of the river. These swamps served as reservoirs that would absorb a portion of the flood waters coming down the main channel of the river. In Louisiana, the Mississippi River also flowed into outlets or bayous that took water out of the main channel and drained them into the Gulf of Mexico. Generally, outlets and swamps lowered the volume of water in the main channel of the river.

Since ancient times, people settled along the natural levees. The soil was fertile, and it provided moderate safety from floods. The first white settlers founded their towns and cities on these natural levees. But natural levees were never sufficient enough to protect against major floods, so white settlers reinforced the natural levees with artificial ones. The first levees were no more than hills of dumped dirt and garbage, so it should be of no surprise that these levees were easily breached by the river. The quality of the levee as well as the height was important for it to work effectively. People living along the river also learned that levees had to be extended over the length of the river for them to work properly. A breach in a neighbor's levee could flood one's farm or plantation as easily as a break on your own property. Since the 1700s, planters and farmers had organized themselves to construct and maintain levees for their mutual survival. Local governments levied taxes on property and created levee boards to administer the funds. Over time, a levee community was created up and down the lower Mississippi: the prosperity of everyone depended on controlling the Mississippi River, and that meant keeping its water within the main channel.

By the 1800s, local governments began to shut down bayous to prevent flood waters from entering them and inundating planters who lived along their banks. Swamp lands were also reclaimed. Farming in the Mississippi-Yazoo Delta after the Civil War meant draining the swamps, cutting down the trees, plowing up the land, and most importantly, constructing levees. Levees had to prevent the waters of the Mississippi from reaching the back swamps. The end result was that by the 1880s, the Mississippi River was almost wholly confined to a single channel. After the Civil War, the U.S. Army Corps of Engineers was responsibility for overseeing the levee system.

Since the 1830s, there had been a few engineers who expressed dire warnings about what the people along the Mississippi were doing to the river. State engineers in Louisiana had warned that confining the river to a single channel was raising the height of the flood waters. Without the volume of water being able to spread itself out into outlets and swamps, it had nowhere to go but down the main channel. In the early 1850s, Charles Ellet, Jr., criticized the levees-only policy that was being adopted by people on the lower Mississippi. Swamps, he wrote, served as natural reservoirs, but reclamation projects were severing the vital connection between the Mississippi and its lowlands. Moreover, Ellet warned that farming up and down the Mississippi and its tributaries increased run-off into river systems. The forest and grasslands had been able to absorb much of the local rainfall, but as farmers plowed up most of the natural landscape, they made sure their fields drained as quickly as possible into rivers. The net result, Ellet argued prophetically, was that more water was entering the Mississippi at a quicker rate than ever before and this would continue as long as people plowed up forests and grasslands. Andrew A. Humphrey and John Abbott's federal study of 1861 added a further warning that the Mississippi was not digging out a deeper channel for itself as levees-only supporters claimed. Still, they believed that the U.S. Army Corps of Engineers was capable of containing the Mississippi as long as the levees were built and maintained by properly trained engineers and a few outlets remained opened to siphon any excess water. In contrast, James Buchanan Eads called for the closing of all outlets. His jetties at the mouth of the river, he claimed, had proven that the confinement of the river would increase the volume and speed of the waters, and this would allow the river to dig a deeper channel. Eventually, higher levees would no longer be necessary. From 1881 to 1927, the U.S. Army Corps of Engineers, the Mississippi River Commission, and most of the people who lived along the Mississippi River put their trust into levees. Human ingenuity would conquer the river, and the Mississippi's rich alluvial lands could be fully exploited for the progress for humanity.

In 1927 that faith in levees was shattered. In the early spring months, record rainfall fell along the tributaries of the Mississippi. The high water mark of the Mississippi rose each day. Newspapers up and down the Lower Mississippi optimistically predicted that the levees would hold, and the U.S. Army Corps of Engineers assured the public that everything was under control. As the waters of the Mississippi grew higher and higher, armed parties patrolled levees for fear that someone on the other side of the river would sabotage the levee to save their own property. In Mississippi, sheriffs rounded up black men and forced them to help bolster levees. Thousands of volunteers, forced laborers, and convicts filled sand bags. About 3 million cubic feet of water per second was rushing down the main channel of the Mississippi south of the mouth of the Arkansas River. The Mississippi River normally carried one million cubic feet of water per second at that point.

The first break in the levee system along the Mississippi occurred at Dorena, Missouri, on April 16, 1927. Flood waters inundated 175,000 acres of land. Five thousand people were homeless and without food, and another 6,000 had fled to Helena for shelter. Another crevasse occurred on the Arkansas River at Pine Bluff and flooded another 150,000 acres. Some hoped that the breaks would relieve pressure on the Lower Mississippi, but the water kept rising as terrible storms from the west hit the region. On April 21, the levee at Mounds Landing in Mississippi broke. The crevasse developed into "a wall of water three-quarters of a mile wide and 100 feet high."[9] A conservative estimate of the number of blacks who were working to repair the levee at the time and were subsequently drowned was 100, but some claimed several hundred were swept away. The planter and writer William Alexander Percy described the devastation:

> The 1927 flood was a torrent ten feet deep the size of Rhode Island; it was thirty-six hours coming and four months going; it was deep enough to drown a man, swift enough to upset a boat, and lasting enough to cancel a crop year. The only islands in it were eight to ten tiny Indian mounds and the narrow spoil-banks of a few drainage canals. Between the torrent and the river ran the levee, dry on the land side and on the top. The south Delta became seventy-five hundred square miles of mill-race in which one hundred and twenty thousand human beings and one hundred thousand animals squirmed and bobbed.[10]

The wall of water ripped up trees, destroyed houses and cotton gins, and overwhelmed people and animals. Sam Huggins, a survivor from Mississippi, recalled the horror:

> When the levee broke, the water just come whooshing, you could just see it coming, just see big waves of it coming. It was coming so fast till you just get excited,

because you didn't have time to do nothing, nothing but knock a hole in your ceiling and try to get through if you could.... It was rising so fast till peoples didn't get a chance to get nothing.... People and dogs and everything like that on top of houses. You'd see cows and hogs trying to get somewhere where people would rescue them.... Cows just bellowing and swimming.... A lot of those farmhouses didn't have no ceiling that would hold nobody.[11]

Nearly 70,000 people were forced into refugee camps and another 87,668 had fled and lived wherever they could. About 30,000 people left the area permanently.

New Orleans was threatened with total inundation. The politicians and the elites of the city lobbied hard with the federal government to save the city by having the U.S. Army Corps of Engineers blow up a levee south of the city in St. Bernard Parish. The rural people of St. Bernard protested to no avail. The city of New Orleans promised relief and money to rebuild their flooded communities, but help from the city never came. After two centuries of building levees, people along the Mississippi River willfully destroyed a levee with dynamite on April 29, 1927. People in St. Bernard and Plaquemine Parishes had been forced to evacuate. The artificial crevasse took time to widen, but it eventually allowed 250,000 cubic feet of water per second to rush past. A day later, a crevasse occurred on the west bank of the Mississippi near New Orleans that made the artificial break unnecessary.

Although New Orleans was saved, the Central and Lower Mississippi Valleys were devastated. The Red Cross provided shelter for over 300,000 people and food for another 311,922 people. The homes of 900,000 people were inundated over an area of 27,000 square miles. Refugee camps set up by the Red Cross were still assisting people four months later. Official estimates of death range from 246 to 1000 people. The cost of lost property and production was in the tens of millions of dollars.

Debate in Congress and along the lower Mississippi questioned the levees-only policy that was supposed to protect the inhabitants along the river and control the Mississippi. A compromise of two plans eventually became federal policy: levees would be strengthened all along the river, but the Mississippi's waters would be allowed to escape the main channel through artificial spillways that would be opened in times of flood. About 30 miles north of New Orleans, the U.S. Army Corps of Engineers constructed the Bonnet Carré spillway that could siphon 250,000 cubic feet of water per second away from the river and direct it into Lake Pontchartrain. Further north, the Morganza Floodway was built in 1963 to seal off the Atchafalaya River from the Mississippi River and send 600,000 cubic feet of the Mississippi waters into the Atchafalaya Basin in times of flood. In the 1930s and 1940s, the Mississippi River Commission shortened the length of the river by 150 miles to increase its slope so the main channel could send water down to the Gulf of Mexico more quickly. Also, a floodway was built in Missouri that could create an artificial river 5 miles wide and 65 miles long to act as a reservoir and be able to handle 550,000 cubic feet of water per second in times of flood. Many argued, as they had in the past, that the human ingenuity had once again conquered the Mississippi.

THE BAD TIMES

People in rural areas up and down the Mississippi suffered when the prices for agricultural products fell drastically in 1920, and continued to be low for the next 20 years. Grain prices dropped by over 50 percent, and hog and cattle prices fell by a third. Cotton prices went from a high of 43¢ during World War I to between 13 and 15¢ in 1920, and they dropped down to a low of 4.6¢ in 1931. Stores in small towns along the Mississippi were dependent on the countryside for their business, and as farm prices plunged, fewer farmers could afford to purchase new agricultural implements, supplies, and luxury items. Businesses shut down, and local economies were in a deep recession throughout the 1920s.

Then, in 1929, the Great Depression hit the Mississippi River Valley. For farmers and planters, the bad times of the 1920s turned worse. The crash of the New York Stock Exchange in October 1929 seemed a distant affair because so few Americans along the Mississippi owned stock, but the crash created a cascade of economic disasters as confidence in the economy sank, consumer spending plummeted, and banks all over the country closed. Prices for everything nose-dived as the demand for them evaporated. And then a drought hit the western parts of the Midwest in 1931 that lasted the rest of the decade. The national unemployment rate would reach over 20 percent, but millions of people took huge cuts in salary, worked shorter hours, and felt that they could lose their job at any time. Freight tonnage on the upper Mississippi River dropped from 1,883,668 million tons in 1915 to 973,567 million tons in 1923 to 527,487 million tons in 1930. Minneapolis lost its supremacy in flour production as companies began to move out of the city in the 1930s. Without a federal welfare program, local and state government along with private charities struggled to provide relief.

President Franklin Delano Roosevelt's New Deal programs came to the aid of the people along the Mississippi. The Agricultural Adjustment Act tried to raise the price of farm products by paying farmers and planters not to plant a portion of their fields in an effort to decrease the supply of farm products on the market. The prices of farm products did go up, but the Agricultural Adjustment had unforeseen consequences. Farmers and planters found it profitable to take the lands of their tenants and sharecroppers out of cultivation in order to get the government allotments, causing undue hardship of the poorest elements of rural society. Those getting government payments used the money to mechanize their farms, which further cut the demand for agricultural laborers while also increasing productivity over time. The migration of the rural poor, both black and white, to towns and cities accelerated.

The New Deal did help some African Americans. In St. Paul, Minnesota, the local school system did not segregate segregated blacks, but the white community kept African Americans out of white neighborhoods and allowed them mostly to work in the service sector and on railroads. Under pressure from the St. Paul Urban League, automobile companies in St. Paul agreed to keep at least 10 black workers on their staff. In the 1930s, New Deal programs opened new economic avenues for blacks. The Civilian Works Administration hired the state's first black nurse, hospital clerk, and bookbinder. When the Roosevelt administration promised legal protection to unions attempting to organize and make collective bargaining agreements with employers, blacks joined with whites to form a hotel union in St. Paul. Still, a white worker earned as much as $50 a month more than a black worker for the same job at the Curtis Hotel. Anthony Brutus Cassius, a black man who had organized the local hotel union, sued the hotel. In 1940 the lawsuit coupled with bad publicity forced the hotel to pay equal wages for black and white workers. Equality was still decades away, but the blacks of Minnesota were making strides for a more equitable economic system.

Iowa farmers weathered the storm of depression better than most. In fact, government programs such as rural electrification actually increased the standard of living of many of the homes in rural Iowa during the 1930s. By 1940, the average Iowa and Illinois farmer had a higher standard of living than rural people anywhere else in the country. The lowest-rated counties in Iowa were better than the highest-ranking counties in nine other states. The number of tractors in Iowa doubled between 1930 and 1940, and Iowa farmers eagerly adopted hybrid corn and oats that were more resistant to drought and insects. Yields of corn on average increased from 40 bushels per acre in 1933 to 60 bushels per acre in 1943. Whereas only 1 percent of Iowan corn had been hybrid in 1933, only 10 years later hybrid corn represented 99 percent of the total production. Farm sizes increased from an average of 151 acres in 1900 to 160 in 1940, but the number of farms during that period dropped from only 228,622 to 213,318. At the same time, the value of Iowa's farms was more than double the national average in 1940. Farmers further benefited from federal government programs during the 1930s that promoted "soil conservation, balanced output, crop loans, marketing agreements, extended uses for farm products, crop insurance, and rural security."[12] The number of farms with electricity in Iowa increased from 25 percent in 1934 to 33 percent in 1944. By 1941, three-quarters of Iowa's rural publication had access to a public library.

WORLD WAR II

World War II revitalized the Mississippi Valley as the economy of the region was geared toward military production. In St. Louis, the McDonnell

Aircraft Corporation became the largest employer in the city. Thousands of Louisianans in New Orleans built ships, including the famous landing crafts that were used in the D-Day invasion and the Pacific campaign against Japan. Four billion dollars worth of defense contracts poured into Missouri alone. When the U.S. government initiated the Food for Victory Program, the prices for farm products shot up. The mechanization of agriculture continued to spread south—in the states bordering the lower Mississippi River, tractors had plowed only 16 percent of the arable land in 1939, but they plowed 42 percent in 1946. Electrification spread into rural areas as well—by 1945, half the farms in Iowa had electricity whereas only a third did two years earlier.

Nationwide, the income of the lowest-paid workers increased relatively faster than the income of the rich, but the rationing of meat and flour and other consumer products made every civilian a soldier on the home front. Women were encouraged to cook balanced meals with what little they had. Many of them planted victory gardens to help supplement their family's diets. As millions of men joined or were drafted in the military, women took their places on farms and in the factories. The percentage of farm women in Iowa doing daily chores rose from 60 percent in 1941 to 80 percent in 1943. During the war, about 13 percent of Iowa farm women were driving trucks and tractors and 29 percent were involved with livestock, which had once been the purview of males. Sales of poultry and eggs by farm women rose by 500 percent. Since rationing provided few opportunities for women to spend their money, the savings rates rose for American families up and down the river.

The Chinese community in Minnesota rallied in support of the war effort despite suffering decades of discrimination by the U.S. government. In Minneapolis and St. Paul, Chinese immigrants sent 20 percent of their men into the American armed forces. Four hundred Chinese businessmen formed the Twin Cities Chinese Emergency Relief Society and raised $45,000 for relief and $20,000 for military aid to the Chinese who battled against the Japanese invasion. Since China was now an ally of the United States in the war against Imperial Japan, Congress repealed the Exclusion Act that had limited Chinese immigration to this country. For the first time in a half a century, the Chinese felt welcomed in communities along the Mississippi River.

Although cotton prices increased, planters still found ways of keeping their tenant population in poverty. As historian Nan Elizabeth Woodruff has described, "planters continued to steal their tenants' parity checks, violate wage and crop arrangements, overcharge commissary accounts, and cheat them on cotton weights."[13] Tens of thousands of poor rural whites and blacks responded by taking advantage of the great demand for labor in the cities. Nineteen percent of the population of the Yazoo-Mississippi Delta left the region. One of every 10 blacks sought opportunities elsewhere. Many of those who stayed decided to work for wages instead of signing sharecropping agreements. In Arkansas and Mississippi, planters succeeded in getting the state government to pass wage ceilings. Still, the great demand for labor in the countryside and the cities allowed most blacks to achieve better wages for their work than ever before.

CONCLUSION

When World War II ended in 1945, the people along the Mississippi River were on the verge of great societal and economic changes. The mechanization of cotton agriculture would end the exploitive plantation economy that had shaped the history of the lower Mississippi River for three centuries. The prosperity during two world wars only heightened expectations among poor whites and blacks that better times were possible if they were given real opportunities to improve their lives. The battle for civil rights was already occurring on a small scale before the war and would become a sweeping movement in the 1950s. The industrialization of the cities and towns along the Mississippi would continue into the 1970s. Louisiana would attract even more oil and chemical plants to the banks of the Mississippi for the betterment of some, and to the detriment the health of those who lived along the river between Baton Rouge and New Orleans. In 1993 a devastating flood in the central Mississippi Valley would remind all the Mississippi River was not yet tamed, so much so that the federal government was paying people to not rebuild on the flood plain. Although New Orleans had it saved itself from the Flood of 1927, Hurricane Katrina in 2005 would show the folly of the city's expansion into the swamplands of Lake Pontchartrain.

NOTES

1. Thomas J. Morain, "To Whom Much Is Given: The Social Identity of an Iowa Small Town in the Early Twentieth Century," *Iowa History Reader,* ed. Marvin Bergman (Ames: Iowa State University Press, 1996), 315.
2. William E. Parrish, et. al. *Missouri: The Heart of the Nation* (St. Louis: Forum Press, 1980), 284.
3. "Post-Dispatch Man, an Eye-Witness, Describes Massacre of Negroes" *St. Louis,* eds. Selwyn K. Troen and Glen E. Holt (New York: New Viewpoints, 1977), 151.
4. James C. Cobb, *The Most Southern Place on Earth: The Mississippi Delta and the Roots of Regional Identity* (New York: Oxford University Press, 1992), 102.
5. Quoted in Nan Elizabeth Woodruff, *American Congo: The African American Freedom Struggle in the Delta* (Cambridge: Harvard University Press, 2003), 130.
6. Clyde Woods, *Development Arrested: The Blues and Plantation Power in the Mississippi Delta* (New York: Verso, 1998), 17.
7. John B. Rehder, *Louisiana's Vanishing Plantation Landscape* (Baltimore: Johns Hopkins University Press, 1999), 133.
8. Reid Mitchell, *All on a Mardi Gras Day: Episodes in the History of New Orleans Carnival* (Cambridge: Harvard University Press, 1995), 105.

9. John M. Barry, *Rising Tide: The Great Mississippi Flood of 1927 and How It Changed America* (New York: Simon and Schuster, 1997), 202.

10. William Alexander Percy, *Lanterns on the Levee: Recollections of a Planter's Son* (Baton Rouge: Louisiana State University Press, 2005), 249.

11. Quoted in John M. Barry, *Rising Tide: The Great Mississippi Flood of 1927 and How It Changed America* (New York: Simon & Schuster, 1997), 204.

12. Earle D. Ross, *Iowa Agriculture: An Historical Survey* (Iowa City: The State Historical Society of Iowa, 1951), 176.

13. Nan Elizabeth Woodruff, *American Congo: The African American Freedom Struggle in the Delta* (Cambridge: Harvard University Press, 2003), 196.

9

Life along the Mississippi, 1945–2005

When historians Stephen E. Ambrose and Douglas G. Brinkley describe the Mississippi as an industrial river, they were recognizing how drastically the river had been altered by human beings. Ships no longer fear to sail to New Orleans because they could pass through jetties at the mouth of the river or bypass the winding river altogether by traveling the 66 miles of the Mississippi River-Gulf Outlet Canal. About 16,000 miles of levees protect human settlement. Barge traffic up and down the river carries as much tonnage as steamboats ever did in the antebellum era. The myriads of sugar plantations that once existed on the lower Mississippi had been transformed into a handful of large conglomerates that produce more sugar than ever before. A fifth of the country's petrochemical industry makes its home along the Mississippi between New Orleans and Baton Rouge. Just north of Louisiana's capital, one will find plantations, but these mechanized entities look very different from the plantations of old. Neither slave nor tenant nor sharecropper labor inhabit the fields anymore. The roar of diesel engines drowned out human voices that once were heard among the rows of cotton. In the Upper Mississippi Valley, farms are as efficient as they have ever been. Although the number of farms has declined, their agricultural produce feeds the United States and hundreds of millions of others around the world.

Nevertheless, industrial development does not necessarily mean prosperity. In what some call cancer alley between New Orleans and Baton Rouge, a noxious odor hangs over what is left of the antebellum mansions along River Road. These relics serve as tourist attractions that attempt to preserve a by-gone era, which some cherish and others want to forget. The agricultural towns along the central and lower river are, if not decaying, at least trapped in stagnation. Neither Natchez nor Vicksburg is a thriving town, but both towns make great stops for tourists and river casinos may rejuvenate their local economies. Mark Twain's Hannibal, Missouri, survives as a tourist attraction, where inhabitants dress like their nineteenth-century ancestors. Nauvoo, Illinois, is a Mormon open-aired museum, which ignores the darker aspects of what once occurred there. The most prosperous neighborhoods along the river now exist in the suburbs, while the major cities are struggling. New Orleans has held the dubious honor of being referred to as one of the most dangerous cities in the United States, but in October 2006, Morgan Quinto Press gave that distinction to St. Louis because New Orleans had been largely abandoned after Hurricane Katrina. A large portion of St. Louis and New Orleans have become poor ghettos, while middle- and upper-class residents live in the surrounding suburbs. Urban renewal projects have attempted to revive both cities, but often such attempts displace the poor from one area to another without dealing with the fundamental causes of poverty. In Memphis, the city has converted Beale Street, once the heart of the black community, into a tourist spot celebrating a sanitized version of jazz and blues, and hundreds of thousands of pilgrims make their way to Graceland to pay homage to Elvis Presley. The city is the center of the cotton exchange, but the rest of the city struggles economically.

The floods of 1993 and 2001 reminded everyone of the dangers of living along the Mississippi River. In 2005 Hurricane Katrina swamped New Orleans, and its future remains uncertain. The very levees that protect people on the Mississippi contributed to the destruction of wetlands, which once had minimized the storm surges. Recent events only confirm that the river is more than a drainage ditch that can be molded to fit human needs on a whim. The Mississippi is alive. To forget that puts all of the residents along the river in peril.

But not everything is so bleak. Agricultural communities remain prosperous along the river in Iowa, Illinois, Wisconsin, and Minnesota. The Twin Cities of Minneapolis and St. Paul have big city problems, but they remain jewels of urban life along the Mississippi. In the last 50 years, the civil rights movement has made incredible inroads into creating racial equality and harmony in the country. As the grandchildren of the millions of immigrants of the nineteenth century have nearly totally assimilated into American culture, new immigrants from Asia, Latin America, and the Middle East have added their traditions to the medley of American life. Even though most of the consumer products the people of the Mississippi Valley buy and use are no longer produced in the United States, the American consumer society continues to evolve. Televisions homogenized Americans as never before, and provided new outlets for religious outreach, mass sporting events, information on many subjects, and entertainment. Almost daily, computers are revolutionizing every aspect of our lives, from work to play to education. As the twentieth-first century begins, the people along the Mississippi continually adapt to the dynamic society that evolves around them.

UPHEAVALS IN AGRICULTURE

Before World War II, cotton plantations on the lower Mississippi were beginning to adopt tractors to plow up the fields, but they were still dependent on thousands of low-paid tenants and sharecroppers to pull weeds and pick the cotton. A majority of these people were African Americans. Jim Crow laws and customs kept the black population socially segregated and economically deprived, and discrimination at the polling booths across the South kept them from political power. Vigilante violence terrorized the black population into subservience. For many African Americans, a cycle of debt kept most families at the subsistence level, but an increasing number were fleeing the region to change their fortunes in the cities.

The introduction of mechanized cotton pickers and new herbicides altered the economic dynamics of the plantation. In 1958 machines picked just over a quarter of the cotton harvest. Only six years later, diesel-powered contraptions harvested 81 percent of the cotton crop. Herbicides were

Tenant's house near levee in Louisiana, ca. 1940. Courtesy of the Library of Congress.

introduced in the 1950s, but it was not until the successful introduction of DuPont's diuron that hand weeding became obsolete. In 1955 only 5 percent of the cotton fields had been treated with herbicides, but ten years later 80 percent of the cotton crop was being sprayed with weed-killing chemicals. These changes had a profound impact on the physical landscape of the cotton lands along the Mississippi. As historian Charles S. Aiken explains:

> Because houses scattered across fields were obstacles to efficient use of the new machinery, those that were abandoned were razed, and the remaining ones were moved to form a line of dwellings near plantation headquarters. . . . High, open-sided buildings for storage of tractors and mechanical pickers replaced mule and horse barns. . . . Plantation commissaries and furnish merchant stores were closed, and the buildings were razed or converted to other uses. Even cotton ginneries vanished from many plantations as large, expensive high-capacity plants capable of rapidly processing machine-harvested cotton replaced small obsolete plants.[1]

Mechanization was a boom to production, but it had human costs. Small farmers could not compete with the larger agribusiness operations, which with more access to capital were able to lease the newest equipment. By the 1970s, economic strains had wiped out small farmers in Louisiana, and those that managed to hang on usually had a full-time job in the industrial sector. Throughout the lower Mississippi Valley, hundreds of thousands of sharecroppers and tenants were now hired as seasonal wage laborers. The poverty that had been the lot of a majority of these rural workers only deepened because modern agriculture no longer needed them. As a result, a mass migration to cities and towns followed. The population of Poinsett County, Arkansas, for instance, decreased by 31.7 percent between 1950 and 1970, but the rural population of the county had gone down a startling 62.5 percent. Entire rural communities disappeared, and so did their churches and the stores that supplied them. Throughout the South, horses and mules could once be found on every farm—Poinsett County had almost 5,000 of them in 1949—but 20 years later there were only a few hundred left in the entire county.

Sugar plantations had always required a large capital investment in equipment. Still, black laborers were needed in the fields and in the sugar-producing factories. These laborers had been some of the most skilled workers in the southern agricultural economy. They lived in housing provided to them by the plantation owner, but they had managed to resist becoming sharecroppers or tenants, and commanded decent wages. In the twentieth century, sugar plantations adopted technologies that were expensive, but boosted production. Those plantations that did not buy the new machinery could not compete with their neighbors that did. In 1969, 44 sugar factories and 1,687 farms produced sugar in Louisiana. During the fuel crisis of the 1970s, competition for laborers from the petrochemical industry and consolidation of the industry changed the sugar plantation landscape drastically. By 1999 there were only 19 sugar factories left and the number of sugar farms had dropped to 690. In the same period, the production and processing of sugar nearly doubled. As on cotton plantations, the skilled black field hand had become obsolete. A few laborers drove tractors and operated machinery, but the need for large numbers of workers had diminished. Temporary unskilled Mexican laborers now supply seasonal needs.

The exodus of blacks from rural areas accelerated in the 1950s. Most headed to cities of the Midwest and the North where they faced new forms of segregation. Blacks crowded into neighborhoods with poor housing, inadequate public services, and all the social ills that come from poverty, illness, and isolation. The squalor of the countryside was replaced with the squalor of the black urban ghetto. White policemen patrolled these neighborhoods, and white landlords owned most of the buildings. Except for a small percentage of black professionals, most blacks took jobs in the low-paying service sector, and open discrimination kept them from obtaining the better paying jobs in the factories. Still, for many blacks, leaving rural areas offered the hope of great opportunities. Claude Walton explained his decision of leave the rural life of the South:

> Leaving was the best thing that ever happened to me. Literally the single most important thing in my life. More important than meeting your mother, joining the service, whatever. Forty years ago there was nothing here for black folks but oppression. Leaving brought our whole family out of darkness and deprivation. Living in a shack as sharecroppers, existing on the meager things that were available to us. Always the minimum. It never allowed us to be totally free to do what we desired to do or go where we wanted to go, have what we wanted to have. It was just existence, that's all it was. We existed—and we, my brothers and sisters, seemed to have been trapped by the fact that our parents did not seem to think they could do anything else. By me getting out I think it led to them thinking *they* could get out. They saw one doing better and it encouraged them.[2]

In Missouri, Illinois, Iowa, and Minnesota, farms continued to get larger as the number of individual farms decreased. Those who could not compete moved into the cities. Corn and soybean production per acre improved. In 1939 a Missouri farmer averaged 30 bushels of corn per acre. By 1977 that yield had increased to 76 bushels per acre. In 2004 yields reached a record 162 bushels per acre. After World War II, Missouri farmers began switching from corn to soybeans, and by 1968 they were growing more soybeans than corn, but that balance changed year to year depending on the market price of each crop. In Iowa, the average yield of corn reached 180 bushels per acre in 2004 for a state total of 2.2 billion bushels. Iowa farmers also produced 477 million bushels of soybeans in 2004, and yields of soybeans had increased from 14 bushels per acre in the 1920s to 43 bushels in the 1990s. Although less numerous than in the past, the farms of the Upper Mississippi Valley are models of efficient production, and their owners have some of the highest living standards of Americans in rural areas.

THE CIVIL RIGHTS MOVEMENT

Before the late 1960s, southern blacks were racially segregated by law from the white population in almost every aspect of everyday life. When a Greyhound bus reached the state line of Mississippi, blacks were required to move to the back of the bus or face arrest. Blacks did not eat in white restaurants or cafeterias. All public facilities were divided along the color line: bathrooms, drinking fountains, and waiting areas. Black men almost never had a conversation with white women as equals. All white people were to be addressed as Mr. or Mrs. or Miss, as the case might be, but never by first name only. Black men usually kept their eyes down when they walked past a white woman for fear of being accused by white men of so-called eye rape. Black children attended all-black schools, which were always more poorly funded than white schools. There was the black part of town and the white part of town—a railroad track, the business district, or a river often would divide the two, but in every town people knew who belonged where regardless of physical barriers.

In the southern countryside, most black tenant farmers and sharecroppers lived in a perpetual state of debt. Mechanization forced them to become wage laborers, which worsened their economic condition as work became seasonal. Health conditions for blacks were abysmal, and child mortality rates were high. Still, there were black farmers who owned land, but they had to make sure that their prosperity did not catch the attention of poor white people who often retaliated against them. White men would poison a black farmer's livestock, physically attack blacks, and even lynch a black person who seemed to be uppity in their eyes.

Blacks resisted Jim Crow in many ways, often by building their own institutions, such as churches, and refusing to accept white depictions of them as inferior. After World War II, blacks increasingly challenged the racial segregation of the South overtly. Thousands of black veterans returned from fighting Nazis only to encounter similar racism throughout the United States, but they did not readily bow down to white authority. The NAACP provided one means in the struggle to change the system. The organization filed lawsuits at the local, state, and federal level challenging discrimination in the schools and workplace, with each such challenge based on the courage and willingness of black families to bring such suits and resist the pressure to back down. A major victory occurred in 1954 with the U.S. Supreme Court decision in *Brown v. Board of Education,* which declared that racially segregated schools were not equal. In 1955 the Court ordered desegregation as quickly as possible, but provided no timetable. Blacks were left to fight for desegregation compliance district by district.

Many within the white community mobilized in response to *Brown v. Board of Education*. The governor of Mississippi openly fought against integration. Mobs of whites harassed black students who attempted to enter white schools. Middle-class whites organized White Citizen Councils to maintain what they referred to as racial integrity. The councils would often publish in local newspapers the names of blacks who attempted to join a civil rights organization, so white employers could promptly fire them. In town after town, white-controlled police departments intimidated and beat those blacks who tried to stand up for their rights. Arrests were common for the slightest provocation. All-white juries made sure that blacks were punished, but white perpetrators of violence against blacks usually were not. From the state to the local government and the sheriff, the entire apparatus of government was used to prevent blacks from achieving their rights as American citizens.

At first, the civil rights movement embraced the ideology of nonviolence. The goal was to bring national attention to the injustices in the South through the nation's media. Civil rights organizers hoped that public opinion in the country at large would become sympathetic to the black victims and force the federal government to intervene on their side. The press did capture images in photographs and film black protesters being beaten, bit by police dogs, and hosed down by firemen. The Freedom Riders challenged segregation on the buses by refusing to get out of the front seat of buses when the vehicles entered segregated southern states. The Student Non-Violent Coordinating Committee (SNCC) staged sit-ins to integrate lunch counters in Tennessee and other states. In Mississippi, SNCC aligned themselves with other civil rights organizations to begin a voter registration campaign. Young African Americans were mobilized to go house-to-house and encourage blacks to register. Unfortunately, the barriers to registration were many. Whites in local governments used a literary and understanding test, among several devices, to keep blacks from the polls. The police and local citizens also did not hesitate to resort to violence and intimidation to stop African Americans from registering to vote. Some whites fired their black employees who had decided to register.

The murder of Medgar Evers in the driveway of his house galvanized the black community to even greater sacrifice. Thousands of black citizens went to civil rights meetings, lined up to be registered, and marched in protest when their rights were denied. They risked their lives and their livelihood for a greater cause. In 1964 Bob Moses, SNCC's leader in Mississippi, in cooperation with other civil rights organizations launched Freedom Summer, an initiative that brought northern volunteers, white and black, to Mississippi to register black voters. Mississippi's state government called these volunteers "invaders" who were threatening the very fabric of society. The murder of James Chaney, Andrew Goodman, and Michael Schwerner drew national attention and an investigation by the FBI. Despite the violence, hundreds of volunteers spread across Mississippi to convince blacks to register and garner support from the white community.

In 1964 President Lyndon Johnson signed the Civil Rights Act that banned discrimination in public areas, education, and employment. The Voting Rights Act of 1965 made it illegal to require tests of voters and put the process of registering into the hands of the Federal government. Although African Americans could now vote, real economic and social problems remained, and racism continued to impact the everyday lives of African Americans.

On April 4, 1968, Martin Luther King was in Memphis to give a speech at a rally in support of black garbage workers who were striking for better wages. When a white assassin killed King, the civil rights movement had lost its most prominent leader, a man who had made nonviolence the centerpiece of the struggle for justice and earned him the Nobel Peace Prize. His assassination unleashed feelings of anger across the United States as blacks in urban ghettos burned down buildings and looted businesses. Stokely Carmichael of SNCC and other leaders had already been moving toward a more militant stance to fight white oppression. Black Power was both a cry for racial pride and a statement of independence from the white liberal establishment who had been allies of the civil rights movement. Whatever the mistakes of the Black Power movement, it did reflect the frustration at the realities of black life at the end of the 1960s and early 1970s. Black Power never received the complete support of African Americans and alienated the sympathetic white community, but it did send a signal to whites that violence against blacks would not be tolerated.

Although schools along the Mississippi River had become desegregated by the 1970s, the victory was a chimera. As blacks moved into public schools, whites moved out by sending their children to private schools, which operated with public support. The public schools in cities like New Orleans and Memphis became were almost exclusively black. The whites that did attend were usually from poor white families who could not afford to send them to private schools. Martin Luther King's dream of white children walking hand-in-hand with black children was still to be realized.

Despite having the right to vote, the black community was hampered by the tactics of white politicians. As Anthony Walton has explained, "Cracking was the splitting of heavy black concentrations, stacking was putting a large number of blacks in a district with even more whites, and packing involved, in the rare instance where blacks could not otherwise be silenced, drawing the district so that it was totally black, thus ensuring that neighboring areas would provide safe white seats."[3] But black candidates continued to challenge the white establishment. As more and more whites came to accept black leadership, blacks gained political power.

Between 1978 and 2004, New Orleans, Vicksburg, Memphis, Minneapolis, Natchez, and Greenville elected black mayors.

CITY LIFE

Bustling cities and towns had always been a part of life along the Mississippi. Boatmen, steamboat pilots, gamblers, prostitutes, wharf workers, traders, and others mingled on the river's banks and exchanged goods, money, and gossip. With the passing of steamboats, trade on the Mississippi withered because of the competition from railroads. The barges pushed by diesel-powered towboats revived shipping along the river. But for many towns along the river, this trade did not save them from economic decline. New Orleans remained an important port, but St. Louis stumbled as the gateway to the West. In contrast, Minneapolis and St. Paul thrived after World War II.

For many reasons, the racial riots that spread across American cities in the 1960s did not occur in the cities along the Mississippi. The black and white community had managed to compromise just enough to keep the poor black ghettos from exploding in violence. In the Lower and Central Mississippi Valley, as elsewhere in the country, whites moved out into the suburbs and African Americans moved into the inner city. St. Louis actually suffered a decline in population after World War II. Whereas over 800,000 people had lived within the city limits in 1950, only 622,236 did so in 1970, and the population fell to 344,362 in 2005. At the same time, the metro area of St. Louis grew from 1.2 million people in 1970 to 1.8 million people by 2004.

For nearly three decades after World War II, the United States experienced economic prosperity. From 1945 to 1964, the birth rate soared. The GI Bill had given loans to 1.3 million veterans of World War II to purchase homes and to have money for college to 2.2 million ex-soldiers. For the first time, colleges were accessible to most middle-class American families. The number of college students in Missouri increased from 16,539 in 1952 to 154,270 in 1975 to over 303,000 in 2005. More and more Americans became middle-class and could afford to purchase new homes in the expanding suburbs.

The so-called cookie-cutter tract homes of the suburbs attracted families who sought houses with garages, large yards for children to play in, and safe neighborhoods. Suburbs bred conformity, and many people found solace and safety in rows of identical houses occupied by white middle-class people just like them. The new schools, parks, churches, and malls of the suburbs meant better living conditions for their residents compared to the crowded and debilitated old neighborhoods within the cities. Crime rates were lower in the suburbs, and the public education better because of the stronger tax base. In the 1950s, church attendance was at its high. Women were encouraged to be good wives and mothers, and the men were supposed to be the breadwinners. Because jobs were readily available and unions remained strong, the world of the middle-class life became possible for millions of blue-collar factory workers. Middle-class Americans embraced consumerism, especially the new technology of television, whose programming and commercials spread middle-class values to nearly every home along the Mississippi, as elsewhere. Electrical appliances provided conveniences as never before because most middle-class people could afford them. The creation of the interstate highway system in the 1950s and the growth of the automobile industry facilitated these changes by making traveling to work in the cities easier.

Moving to the suburbs had its costs. Driving into the city meant sitting in traffic jams at rush hour. The problems were compounded in New Orleans because suburbs were either across the Mississippi or across Lake Pontchartrain, and the bridges became congested very quickly. Moreover, keeping-up-with-the-Joneses became a national obsession as materialism became the defining characteristic of success. The suburbs were also bastions of whiteness that openly discriminated against African Americans. Real estate agents kept blacks and other minorities out of white neighborhoods. The anti-communist hysteria of the 1950s also found strong roots there.

In towns and cities along the river, middle-class evangelicals took their children out of public schools and placed them in parochial schools. The new suburban churches reflected the general conservatism of their membership. Evangelicals decried liberals, the teaching of evolution, and the secularization of society, but they also created a supportive community and an arena for spiritual contentment. From Baton Rouge, Jimmy Swaggart became one of the leading televangelist in the 1980s until two sexual scandals weakened his influence. Although Jerry Falwell's Moral Majority united evangelicals politically, and issues like abortion and gay marriage may still stir evangelicals to action, the movement's strength is at the local level in providing real-life solutions to the everyday problems of life—despair, drug addiction, alcoholism, homelessness, and poverty. The waters of the Mississippi continue to provide a very large baptismal fountain for thousands.

Conformity bred resentment among many. Poets, novelists, and artists rallied against the blandness of the suburban living. In 1963 Betty Friedan's *The Feminine Mystique* inspired suburban women to look beyond the confines of the kitchen and their roles of wives and mothers and seek educational and career opportunities elsewhere. Elvis Presley brought black music and dancing to white teenagers across the country, and made it cool. His dance gestations on stage may have been censored when he appeared on the Ed Sullivan Show, but millions of young people thrilled at the evocative display of sexuality. The Beatles added fuel to the cultural fire. The counter-culture movement of the 1960s empowered young people to break with past traditions and their definitions of morality and seek new avenues of enlightenment and fulfillment. With the availability of effective birth control pills, young unmarried people engaged in sex as never before. Drugs, such as LSD and marijuana, were another way to experience a new consciousness. By 1968 the excesses of the counter-culture movement were becoming evident as famous rock & roll celebrities like Jimi Hendrix and Janis Joplin overdosed, and tens of thousands of young people became drug addicts. Open sexuality led to unwanted pregnancies and near-epidemic spread of venereal diseases. It would take the AIDS epidemic that began in the 1980s to put a damper on the sexual revolution, but high rates of teen pregnancies and single-mother households continue to plague communities up and down the Mississippi River.

The people of the inner cities were not enjoying the middle-class lifestyle that they saw on television. White flight from the cities left old neighborhoods to the poor. Just as the overall population of the city was decreasing, the black population of St. Louis increased from 18 percent in 1950 to 41 percent in 1970 to 51 percent in 2000. With the tax base depleting, city resources became strained. Garbage pick-up, sewer services, and street maintenance were dismal. The malls, which suburbanites enjoyed, did not open up in the poor neighborhoods. The grocery chains avoided building stores in the inner cities. Black residents had to purchase their food from small stores that charged high prices and contained little fresh produce. Inner-city schools were habitually poor compared to suburban schools. Unemployment for blacks in the inner-city was often twice the rate of that of whites. The counter-culture had popularized drug use, and some of the poor saw that the only way to participate in the consumerism of middle-class culture was to turn to a life of drug dealing. Those who fell in despair turned to drugs or alcohol to relieve their burdens.

New Orleans had its own set of problems. The expansion of the city during the twentieth century into the swamplands offered affordable housing for the city's poor, but it made the neighborhoods liable to flooding. As geographer Pierce F. Lewis describes:

> Subsidence is a nagging and expensive problem everywhere. New houses are commonly built on concrete pads, laid on sand, and undergirded by thirty-foot piles sunk into the mush on four-foot centers and held firm by a process delicately known as "skin friction." Such heroic tactics add considerably to the cost of building and they prod developers into selling property as quickly as possible, even though it might be wiser to let it settle for a few years. As a result a new owner often has the enriching prospect of watching yard, driveways, and sidewalks sink, while his or her house stands firm, supported by skin friction. (If the water mains or sewers are sheared away, it becomes even more exciting.) By the time the area is ditched and sprayed against mosquitoes, there may be nothing more than a broken driveway to remind the owner that he or she is living in a reclaimed swamp. Memories are short.[4]

The majority of the houses in the poor black neighborhoods of New Orleans were rentals. Landlords failed to make improvements, and tenants did not care or have the money to make their own. In recent years, as many as 37,000 houses were vacant in the city—becoming home to drug dealers and homeless people. The central retail district steadily lost its share of retail sales to suburban stores. In 1948 stores in the central business district controlled 42 percent of the sales in the city, but that had fallen to only 24 percent in 1963.

To remake the cities, politicians and urban planners called for urban renewal. St. Louis bulldozed its central city, dislocating the poor in the hopes of attracting the middle and upper classes with condos and new retail establishments. The results have been mixed. In contrast, New Orleans preserved the French Quarter, even if it became more of a tourist attraction rather than a functioning neighborhood. In 1940 there had been 11,000 residents in the French Quarter, but by 2000, only 4,000 people called the French Quarter their home. Still, the French Quarter attracts hundreds of thousands of visitors from around the world and it has provided the city with much needed revenue.

The national campaigns of the 1950s and 1960s for affordable and safe public housing were filled with good intentions, but often ended in dismal failure. Creating affordable housing has plagued the cities along the Mississippi throughout history. The poor have crowded into slum areas because that is all they could afford. Government-sponsored housing seemed like a solution. In St. Louis, the Pruitt Apartments and the Igoe Apartments, a total of 40 eleven-story buildings, served for a time as models of public housing projects. In the 1950s, city planners had hoped the 2,870 affordable apartments would encourage white residents to stay in St. Louis. But the Supreme Court ended racial discrimination in public housing in 1954, and poor blacks migrated into the apartments instead of whites. Nearly all of the 11,500 residents of the complexes were black, and conditions quickly deteriorated. Like public housing projects elsewhere, the poor residents were stuffed into a small area together away from the rest of the population. The governing authorities did not screen residents, so criminal elements found refuge in the cheap housing. Gangs ruled the stairways and outdoor areas. Limits on income kept middle-class families out, and those residents who could afford to get out did so. The apartments became a symbol of everything wrong with public housing: wasteful government spending and poor management that perpetuated poverty instead of alleviating it. In the early 1970s, both apartment complexes were razed. More recent housing projects have aimed to mix subsidized housing with rentals, and these have had greater success.

Since World War II, Minneapolis and St. Paul have been the most prosperous cities along the Mississippi River, but they have suffered many of the same problems that faced St. Louis and New Orleans. The suburban population increased dramatically to over 1.6 million just as the population of Minneapolis had decreased from a high of 521,718 in 1950 to 382,618 in 2000. Generally, the black community has been more prosperous in the Twin Cities than in southern cities along the river. In the 1970s, 18 percent of the black community worked as professionals, and although the black unemployment rate there was 9.2 percent, which was nearly double that of whites, it was only one-third of the rate of blacks in Memphis. In the 1990s, 110,000 minorities entered the Twin Cities while the white population declined by 81,000. Hmong, Vietnamese, Chinese, Tibetan, and Somali immigrants moved in, and Asians numbered nearly 7 percent of the population of Minneapolis and 12.36 percent of the population of St. Paul in 2000.

The life of an immigrant was often characterized by hard work and the ambition to succeed in their new home. One daughter of a Chinese immigrant recalls:

> My first memories of visiting my dad at work was when he worked at the Shelling Café...We'd always go to the back door of the restaurant, which was a screen door. And, my dad was always dressed in white and he had his long apron on and his cook's hat, which I just loved, the puffy chef's hat...When he worked at the Snelling, he'd go to work at five-thirty or six in the morning to get all the American food, the roasts and chicken, whatever, going early in the morning. Then, he'd come home at three. He would nap for an hour, go to Kee's Chow Mein at four and work till eight. He did that six days a week, and every other Sunday, he worked an afternoon at Kee's.[5]

First-generation immigrants tended to move into neighborhoods where most of the residents were of their own ethnicity. They worked at jobs, attended religious services, and shopped at stores with people who spoke their language and shared their culture. New technological innovations like international telephone networks, commercial airlines, and e-mail have allowed them to keep in close contact with relatives back home. Immigrants who came to the United States as single people tended to marry within their ethnic group, and often would return to their home country to get a husband or a wife. By the end of the twentieth century, only a small number of the descendants of German and Scandinavian immigrants could speak the language of their ancestors, but they continued to celebrate their heritage in food, religion, and music. In many ways, they are indistinguishable from other midwestern people in social and political attitudes and how they spend their daily lives.

Still, the Twin Cities have experienced economic convulsions. Beginning in the 1960s, factories began to move their production to foreign lands in order to reduce their cost of labor. For example, thousands of good-income shoemaking jobs have left Minnesota. At the same time, older industries have adapted and prospered. The food industry continues to be a significant employer in the Minneapolis and St. Paul area. The farms of the upper Mississippi are some of the most efficient anywhere in the world, and Minnesota has benefited in the sale and processing of its produce. In the 1990s high tech health companies have located in the Twin Cities area. In 1997 the annual average pay of workers in the Twin Cities was $4,000 over the national average. Between 1990 and 1998, the Twin Cities experienced a growth rate in jobs of just over 5 percent. With a low unemployment rate, an impressive array of college and universities, the largest shopping extravaganza known as called the Mall of America, and excellent cultural amenities, the Twin Cities remain the gems of the upper Mississippi River.

THE SAGA OF LOUISIANA

For nearly a century, Louisiana's government has staked much of its economic future on the development of the petrochemical industry along the Mississippi River. Tax incentives and lax government regulations encouraged companies to move to Louisiana and offer its residents tens of thousands of good-paying jobs. Scores of Cajuns and other rural Louisianans left their tight-knit rural communities to take jobs in the industry. By 2000, 158 chemical plants along the Mississippi and over a hundred others throughout the state produced one-fifth of the world's chemical products. Hundreds of millions of tax dollars are pumped into the economy of Louisiana parishes. Unfortunately, the factories also pump their waste into the Mississippi. In 2002 industries dumped 126 million pounds of waste into Louisiana's air, ground, and water. As historian John B. Rehder explains, "Little wonder that on the banks of the Mississippi one now saw grotesquely contorted pipes, tanks, and metal structures with vents spewing noxious fumes, flames, and steam and smoke clouds into Louisiana skies. Some 350 legally permitted outfall pipes would discharge untold thousands of gallons of waste fluids into the river. Industry meant money. It was the way progress in Louisiana would be measured, and it meant that a plantation landscape dominance along this hundred-mile stretch of the Mississippi would be no more."[6] The long-term health problems of the residents are hotly debated, but when oil prices fall, as they did in the 1980s, the economy of Louisiana, one of the poorest states in the country, suffers. But recent hikes in oil prices have once again brought prosperity to the petroleum industry.

Since World War II, New Orleans has struggled. The gaps between rich and poor, black and white are clearly visible along St. Charles Avenue. A trolley car ride allows a tourist to enjoy the beautiful mansions, Tulane University, Audubon Park, and massive oak trees that line the street. However, a short walk from the boulevard showcase reveals some very poor neighborhoods. Crime is a constant problem for residents and tourists. A visitor is warned not to walk in the historic cemeteries alone. As Pierce F. Lewis explains, in describing the late 1990s and early twenty-first century, "Muggings and robberies were commonplace, and many citizens were terror-stricken, especially affluent whites who lived near the boundaries of poor black neighborhoods. Across the city, and not just in affluent areas, razor-wire appeared atop household walls, and throughout the city heavy padlocked chains were wrapped around the ornate iron gates that barred the entrance to private dwellings. And in a city that was looking to tourism to rescue its economy, there were too many muggings of affluent tourists to escape the notice of the national media."[7] In 2000 New Orleans had the highest black poverty rate in the country at 33 percent. Despite all the problems, most of the city's residents are fiercely proud of their city and its heritage. The middle and upper class who chose to live in the city have rejected suburban living for the excitement of the city.

Carnival in New Orleans had always been an important cultural barometer of what was going on in the city. Into the 1990s, the organizers of parades, called krewes, remained segregated. Since some of the oldest krewes like Momus and Comus excluded blacks, the black community staged their own parades. One black krewe called Zulu dressed up as African tribesmen and black-faced themselves. When in 1961, the black leaders of the civil rights movement called for a boycott of Carnival parades to protest segregation, the organizers of Zulu decided to go on with the parade anyway. Zulu became the target of civil rights activists who criticized it for perpetuating black stereotypes. Taverns owned by African Americans refused to uphold the tradition of toasting the king of Zulus as he passed by. By 1969 reformers gained control of Zulu and altered the traditional Zulu parade to reflect the changing sensibilities within the black community.

By 1991 the majority of the population of the city of New Orleans was African American and so were its local politicians. Finally, by city ordinance Carnival was desegregated to the dismay the white krewes of Comus and Momus. In protest, both groups refused to march anymore because they saw the ordinance as government interference in their private affairs. They also believed that with their withdrawal, Carnival would falter and the city would suffer economically. But they had misread what had become of the Mardi Gras celebrations. Carnival had transformed itself into a national and international festival that did not depend on Momus or Comus or any other krewe. In 1992 the number of people participating in Carnival was larger than ever before despite the absence of two of the oldest krewes. In fact, newer krewes such as Bacchus and Endymion had long ago become more popular with the crowds because they used skillful marketing, attracted celebrities to ride with them, decorated their floats extravagantly, and threw generous amounts of colorful beads to the crowds lining the parade route. The festival had become a public celebration open to all. The private balls of Comus and Momus were no longer a necessity. In many ways, Mardi Gras had become democratized as never before. The open discrimination against blacks, Jews, and women that had characterized Carnival for two centuries would no longer be tolerated by society. In response to the changes, Rex, the king of Carnival, invited three blacks to his krewe in a sign of compromise. Not even Hurricane Katrina could stop Carnival, which did go on several months later, albeit in an abbreviated form.

Since the 1980s, New Orleans had banked a lot of its financial future on the success of tourism. Unlike the central business districts of other cities, the French Quarter remained a thriving area at night. In 1969 residents and local business leaders successfully fought against a proposed federal highway that would have been built along the waterfront and cut off the Mississippi River from the residents of the city. Instead, the Mississippi River levee and the river became part of the tourist attraction of French Quarter. In 1960, the city had 4,160 hotel rooms. In 2000 the number of hotel rooms had risen to 33,000. In the 1990s the number of jobs in hotels, bars, and restaurants increased by more than a third for a total of 67,300 jobs—more than all the factory and petrochemical jobs in the city combined. Unfortunately, these jobs pay less, have fewer benefits, and are more seasonal than factory work. The better paying management jobs often go to people living outside the city. The devastation of Hurricane Katrina has hurt tourism, but more than three-quarters of the tourist jobs were back by July 2006, and jobs in the petrochemical industry had increased by 20 percent because of the high oil prices. Nonetheless, predictions in 2007 are that 60 percent of small businesses in the city will not survive the hurricane.[8]

The disaster of Hurricane Katrina was not an unforeseen event. Hurricane Betsy in 1965 had flooded St. Bernard Parish because of a storm surge. As Katrina neared, the lowlands south of New Orleans were flooded, but the levees protecting New Orleans appeared to hold. On August 29, 2005, Hurricane Katrina hit Louisiana, but since the eye had missed New Orleans, it seemed that the city had been spared the worst. However, at 4:30 A.M., waters leaked through gates in the industrial canal that linked New Orleans with the Intercoastal Waterway. A storm surge from Lake Borgne overtopped the levees that protected St. Bernard Parish, and a 21 foot wall of water from the Gulf literally crossed the Mississippi to flood Plaquemine Parish south of New Orleans. Then another surge of water at 6:30 A.M. overtopped the levees that protected eastern New Orleans and the entire area went underwater. The flood traveled into the industrial canal and overtopped levees on both sides. At 7:30 A.M., a levee wall on the west side of the industrial canal collapsed and flooded the upper 9th Ward of the city. Two sections of the levees wall of the east side of the canal broke and the lower 9th Ward was flooded. A surge from Lake Pontchartrain added more water into east New Orleans. Waters finally equalized with Lake Pontchartrain on September 1. The swamp lands that had been filled to make way for housing in the early twentieth century had been reclaimed by the sea.

The impact of Hurricane Katrina was devastating. Eighty percent of the city of New Orleans was flooded, and at least 1,800 people lost their lives. By January 1, 2006, New Orleans had lost 63.8 percent of its population, while the more rural St. Bernard Parish lost 94.8 percent of its population. Entire neighborhoods were condemned as uninhabitable. Businesses struggled to reopen in the French Quarter for a lack of a labor force. Tourists stayed away from the city. Tulane University had to lay off hundreds of professors, and many of its students had to enroll elsewhere. The city hospitals and other important institutions suffered significant damage and struggled to reopen. Vital urban infrastructure was destroyed or so severely compromised that city leaders worried that reopening and upgrading schools, public utilities and sewers, and other essential facilities would cost in the billions of dollars. In September 2006, the city council of New Orleans reviewed a plan for rebuilding the city that would cost over 2 billion dollars. The full damage to Louisiana cost 22 billion dollars as of 2006. Estimates are that 200,000 people were left homeless and 300,000 people lost their jobs in Louisiana.

The hurricane revealed fundamental flaws in public responses to disaster. There is enough blame to share at the local, state, and federal government level. Mayor Ray Nagin had hesitated to call for a mandatory evacuation of the city. Thousands of poor New Orleanians had been told to head to the Superdome for shelter, but sanitary conditions quickly deteriorated, and crime was rampant there because there was no one in charge of managing the relocation. Despite individual heroism and determined effort by many police, fire, and health care personnel, the city government had abandoned its poorest citizens and state and federal authorities proved incompetent to meet the crisis, which swamped not only the New Orleans area, but also the Gulf coast of Mississippi. Hundreds of thousands of people either went to live with relatives or were sent to cities like Houston on public assistance. For thousands, a trailer became their home. As of November 2006, of the 79,000 families who have applied for federal assistance to rebuild their homes, only 22 families have received their share of the 7.5 billion dollars allocated by Congress for Hurricane Katrina relief.[9] The geographic fact that much of New Orleans lies below sea level had finally caught up to the city. The flooding was inevitable; the sorry response by government officials on all levels was not.

THE RIVER AWAKENS

In the last half century, as in the centuries before, human efforts to control the great river have compromised and complicated the natural renewing process of nature. Two centuries of levee-building cut the Mississippi off from its wetlands. In the past, the Mississippi had spilled over its banks as it leached lower Mississippi and added soil and fresh water to coastal areas. But when people built the levees, the river could no longer aid in the fight against salt water intrusion. The Caernarvon project was just the beginning of a major effort to bring Mississippi waters once again into the wetlands. Congress still has not adopted the Louisiana Coastal Area Ecosystem Restoration plan to restore the wetlands. Hurricane Katrina further worsened the destruction of wetlands by converting another 217 square miles of coastal wetlands into sea.

Dams have stimulated trade of the upper Mississippi. Barges carried only 2.4 million tons of goods in 1940, 27 million tons in 1970, 76 million tons in 1980, and 90 million tons in 2005. Grain represents half of the cargo that barges ship from the Midwest to the rest of the nation and the world. The recreation business on the Mississippi has taken advantage of the placid upper Mississippi and created 18,000 jobs. Unfortunately, the prosperity is coming at a cost. Through a series of canals, the waters of the Mississippi are connected with the Atlantic Ocean. Invasion of foreign fish and mollusks threaten local species. The dams have disrupted the breeding habits of native fish. The flood of 1993 actually helped the population of native fish by flooding wetlands.

The flood of 1993 reminded everyone that levees have not totally tamed the Mississippi. The disaster cost between 15 and 20 billion dollars, damaged or destroyed 50,000 houses, and forced the evacuation of 54,000 people.[10] Flood stage was reported at 500 points on the upper Mississippi River system, and records were broken on 44 forecast points on the upper

Lock and Dam no. 13, Whiteside County, IL. Courtesy of the Library of Congress.

Mississippi. At St. Louis, the previous record had been set in 1973 at 43.3 feet, but on August 1, 1993, the river reached a height of 49.58 feet above flood level. The Mississippi flooded 75 towns and 20 million acres of land in Missouri, Iowa, Illinois, and Minnesota. Forty of the 229 federal levees and 1,043 of 1,347 non-federal levees were overtopped or damaged. In flooded areas the harvest of 1993 was destroyed. Estimates are that 600 billion tons of top soil had been eroded by the flood waters. In response to this disaster, the federal government initiated a program that bought out homes in flood-prone areas along the Mississippi and its tributaries. So far, 13,000 homes have been sold to the federal government and their residents have abandoned living along the Mississippi. However, some residents refused to leave and rebuilt their homes without insurance protection.

The flood of 2001 on the upper Mississippi broke a levee at La Crosse, Wisconsin, reaching 4.41 feet above flood stage, flooding neighborhoods and streets. Davenport, Iowa, experienced flooding as well, and when the river reached the waste treatment plant, it contaminated the water in the streets. Except for one, all dams on the upper Mississippi had their gates up to allow the river to flow freely in order to lessen the height of the water. Nonetheless, 10 counties along the Mississippi in Iowa were declared disaster areas by the governor, Red Rock Island was flooded, and many dams were damaged. Four hundred miles of the river were closed to barge traffic, and 2,000 barges were stuck for several days. In St. Paul, four parks and a downtown airport flooded. Damages amounted to hundreds of millions, but thankfully, thousands of residents on low-lying areas had already abandoned their homes after the flood of 1993, so the damage in 2001 was not as extensive. Also, the waters receded more quickly in 2001 than they had in 1993.

CONCLUSION

As they have for centuries, people along the Mississippi River await each spring with a feeling of anticipation and even dread. Perhaps this year the river will produce its worst flood ever? Perhaps this year the river will sweep away the Old River Structure and move its main channel into the Atchafalaya Basin? Or will the Mississippi finish the demolition of New Orleans that Hurricane Katrina started? The future is uncertain. Allowing the river to reclaim its wetlands on the upper and lower river looks promising, but no one knows whether such efforts will be successful when the great hurricane comes. Pollution is an ever increasing concern of those who live next to the river. The industrial waste within the waters of the Mississippi is not only harming residents along the river, it also is creating a dead zone within the Gulf of Mexico where no fish can live. But industry means a livelihood for thousands. If government regulation becomes too burdensome, will the chemical companies just move away? By making year-round navigation possible, the dams on the upper Mississippi River have greatly benefited the economy of the upper Midwest. Yet, the long-term consequences to the environment are still being studied. The loss of wetlands has hurt the small fishermen and makes storm surges from hurricanes even more devastating. Levees remain the primary way of keeping the water out of the cities along the Mississippi, and behind those levees, challenges exist that plague most American cities: crime, corruption, racism, and poverty. But other American cities do not have to grapple with the threat of destruction by the largest river in North America. Whatever problems communities along the river face, they cannot forget that "Ole Man River" is flowing past their homes, and one day it may demand to have its alluvial lands returned to it.

NOTES

1. Charles A. Aiken, *The Cotton Plantation South since the Civil War* (Baltimore: Johns Hopkins University Press, 1998), 111.
2. Anthony Walton, *Mississippi: An American Journey* (New York: Alfred A. Knopf, 1996) 285.
3. Ibid., 251.
4. Pierce F. Lewis, *New Orleans: The Making of an Urban Landscape,* 2nd edition, (Santa Fe: Center for American Places, 2003), 81–82.
5. Sheila Chin Morris, "Personal Account: My Father, Harry Chin," in *Chinese in Minnesota,* ed. Sherri Gebert Fuller (St. Paul: Minnesota Historical Society Press, 2004), 85.
6. John B. Rehder, *Delta Sugar: Louisiana's Vanishing Plantation Landscape* (Baltimore: Johns Hopkins University Press, 1999), 296.
7. Lewis, *New Orleans,* 128.
8. Peter Henderson, "New Orleans Regains 70 pct of jobs since Katrina," *Red Orbit,* Web site, July 26, 2006.
9. Leslie Eaton, "Slow Home Grants Stall Progress in New Orleans," *The New York Times,* November 11, 2006.
10. National Oceanic and Atmospheric Administration, and National Weather Service, *Natural Disaster Survey Report: The Great Flood of 1993* (Rockville, MD: U.S. Department of Commerce, 1994), xvii.

Glossary

Abraders—Stones used to sharpen tools.

Acadians—French immigrants to Nova Scotia who were expelled in the 1750s by the English. Several thousand of them settled in Louisiana.

Adena—Between 600 B.C.E. and 200 B.C.E. the Adena people settled in the Ohio Valley and buried their dead in mounds.

American Bottom—The alluvial lands on the opposite side of the Mississippi River from what today is St. Louis.

Archaic Period—From 8500 B.C.E. to 600 B.C.E., Native Americans settled in small communities along the Mississippi River.

Arkansas Post—The French trading post located near the mouth of the Arkansas River.

Awl—A tool with a spike that can be used to be make holes.

Barge—A huge container vessel that is flat-bottomed and pushed or pulled by other ships.

Black Code—Racist laws regulating the lives of African Americans.

Cabildo—The Spanish administrative building in New Orleans.

Cajun—The name given to Acadians after they became Americanized.

Casqui—A Native people who occupied a fortified village in Arkansas and convinced Hernando De Soto to assist them in an attack against the neighboring village of Pacaha.

Chenopodium—A flowery plant that can be eaten.

Chickasaw—A warrior tribe that inhabited central Mississippi and Tennessee, but their hunting territories extended to the banks of the Mississippi River. During the Colonial Era, they often sided with the English against the French and their allies.

Clovis point—A fluted point made out of stone that was used by Paleolithic peoples along the Mississippi.

Compromise of 1877—A deal made by Republicans and Democrats after the presidential election of 1876 yielded no candidate with a majority in the electoral college. Southern Democrats got Republican candidate Rutherford B. Hayes to agree to pull federal troops out of the South for their support.

Consumerism—Defining social and economic status in terms of the accumulation of manufactured goods in an industrial economy.

Cotton gin—A mechanical device that removed the seed from cotton.

Cotton press—A mechanical device that pressed cotton into a bale or square, which was then tied with ropes. Steamboat charged by the bale, not by weight, so the more cotton you could press into the bale, the cheaper the transportation costs.

Creole—Originally the term referred to people with mixed French and African American blood. Sometimes used by whites in Louisiana to refer to people with French ancestry before the American takeover in 1803.

Crevasse—A break in a levee.

Dakota—A Siouan-speaking people who moved into central Minnesota around 800 C.E.

Dalton point—A non-fluted stone point, generally larger than the Clovis, that emerged in the Archaic Period.

Ecosystem—The vast interconnection between biological organisms and the environment.

Enemy Act of 1917—The U.S. government could enact economic sanctions against foreign countries and their citizens.

Espionage Act of 1917—U.S. citizens could be arrested if the government suspected that they had given out information that harmed the U.S. Army.

Evangelicals—Fundamentalist Christians who take the Bible and its teachings literally and actively seek to convert others.

Flatboat—A flat-bottomed boat that carried freight.

Food for Victory Program—The U.S. government encouraged citizens to plant gardens to supply their families with food so as not to impair the food supply to the U.S. armed forces.

Fort Rosalie—The French fort at Natchez that was destroyed in the uprising in 1729.

Fort Snelling—An American fort at the confluence of the Mississippi and Minnesota Rivers.

Freedom Riders—Black volunteers who challenged the policy of segregating buses in Mississippi by refusing to move to the back of the bus.

Gourd—A plant whose fruit can be dried and used for storage.

Great Depression—The greatest economic calamity in U.S. history, which lasted from 1929 to 1939.

Hoecake—A simple, thin cornbread.

Hoghead—A barrel that contained at least 63 gallons.

Hominy—Finely ground corn.

Hopewell—Native peoples who lived in the Ohio Valley from 200 B.C.E. to 400 C.E. and buried their dead in mounds.

Ioway—A Native American tribe that lived in what today is Iowa and northern Arkansas.

Jim Crow—Racist laws that abridged the civil rights of African Americans.

Keelboat—A vessel that carried freight. It had a large wooden beam that ran in the middle of its bottom, upon which the entire structure of the boat was built. Boats with keels cut through the water more efficiently than flatboats.

Krewe—Organization that staged parades and balls during Mardi Gras in New Orleans.

Levee—An earthen mound that runs parallel with a river bank to prevent flooding.

Louisiana Purchase of 1803—The United States bought the colony of Louisiana from Napoleon.

Mardi Gras—A celebration that takes place before the Christian religious season of Lent.

Mesquakie—An Algonquian-speaking people whom the French referred to as the Fox.

Mississippian Period—From 700 C.E. to 1400, some Native American societies created chiefdoms with large ceremonial centers. They relied on cultivated plants as their main source of food.

NAACP—The National Association for the Advancement of Colored People is a civil rights organization founded in 1909.

Natchez—A Native American tribe organized as a chiefdom along the Mississippi. When they rebelled against French intrusion and massacred hundreds of men, women, and children in 1729, they were eliminated as a tribe by a French force.

New Deal—Franklin Delano Roosevelt's program to end the Great Depression.

Ojibwe—Europeans referred to this Native American tribe as the Chippewa. They moved into Minnesota and pushed the Dakota out. They still have a reservation near the Mississippi at Mille Lacs Lake.

Oneota—From 1300, the Oneota established villages in the upper and central Mississippi Valley.

Pacaha—A native village that was attacked by Hernando De Soto and the Casqui. The village no longer existed when the French arrived more than 140 years later.

Paleolithic—Also referred as the Old Stone Age, this period witnessed people using stone tools in hunting/gathering societies.

Palisade—A wall of upright logs.

Plessy v. Ferguson—In 1896, the Supreme Court stated that separate but equal public facilities for blacks and whites were allowable.

Presbytere—A public building in Jackson Square, New Orleans.

Quapaw—A tribe in what is today Arkansas that allied itself with the French, but the Americans forced them to cede their lands and relocate to Oklahoma.

Quizquiz—One of the native villages that fought against Hernando De Soto. They were ancestors of the Tunica.

Reaper—A mechanical device that cut down crops during harvest.

Rex—One of the kings of Mardi Gras.

Sauk—An Algonquin-speaking people who under their leader Black Hawk were defeated by American forces.

Sedition Act of 1918—The U.S. government prohibited criticism of itself and its policies during World War I.

Seven Year's War—From 1756 to 1763, France and England fought a war. At its conclusion, England gained control of Canada and France gave its Louisiana colony to Spain.

Sharecropper—A person who farmed someone else's land and gave the landlord a share of the crop.

Smallpox—A highly contagious disease that is spread by a virus.

SNCC—The Student Nonviolent Coordinating Committee organized young people to peacefully protest the injustices of racism.

Tenant Farmer—A farmer who rents his land from a landlord.

Thresher—A mechanical device that separated grain from the stalk.

Tunica—A native tribe that allied itself with the French. By moving its main village and adapting to new technology, the tribe managed to survive wars with the English and other tribes. Today, they are known as the Tunica-Biloxi.

Wharf—A wooden platform along a body of water that allows the unloading and loading of ships.

White League—A racist white organization that used violence and intimidation to keep blacks subjugated.

Woodland Period—From 600 B.C.E. to 400 C.E., natives along the Ohio and Mississippi River buried their dead in elaborate mounds, adopted the bow for hunting, and practiced agriculture.

World's Fair—In the nineteenth and twentieth centuries, this event celebrated technology and science, and it was a major tourist draw for cities that hosted it.

Yellow Fever—A disease spread by the mosquito that plagued the lower Mississippi Valley until the end of the nineteenth century.

Selected Bibliography

GENERAL WORKS

Aby, Anne J. *The North Star State: A Minnesota History Reader.* St. Paul: Minnesota Historical Society Press, 2002.

Ackerknecht, Erwin H. *Malaria in the Upper Mississippi Valley, 1760–1900.* Reprint. New York: Arno Press Inc., 1977.

Ambrose, Stephen E., Douglas G. Brinkley, and Sam Abell. *The Mississippi and the Making of a Nation: From the Louisiana Purchase to Today,* Washington, D.C.: National Geographic, 2002.

Anderson, Philip J., and Dag Blanck. *Swedes in the Twin Cities: Immigrant Life and Minnesota's Urban Frontier.* St. Paul: Minnesota Historical Society Press, 2001.

Anfinson, John O. *The River We Have Wrought: A History of the Upper Mississippi.* Minneapolis: University of Minnesota Press, 2003.

Ashmore, Harry S. *Arkansas: A Bicentennial History.* New York: W. W. Norton & Company, Inc., 1978.

Baker, Vaughan Burdin, ed. *Visions and Revisions: Perspectives on Louisiana Society and Culture.* The Louisiana Purchase Bicentennial Series in Louisiana History. Vol. 15. Lafayette: Center for Louisiana Studies, University of Louisiana at Lafayette, 2000.

Becnel, Thomas A. *Agriculture and Economic Development in Louisiana.* The Louisiana Purchase Bicentennial Series in Louisiana History. Vol. 16. Lafayette: Center for Louisiana Studies, University of Louisiana at Lafayette, 1997.

———. *Labor, Church, and the Sugar Establishment: Louisiana, 1887–1976.* Baton Rouge: Louisiana State University Press, 1980.

Blegen, Theodore C. *Minnesota: A History of the State.* 2nd ed. Minneapolis: University of Minnesota Press, 1975.

Carpenter, Barbara, ed. *Ethnic Heritage in Mississippi.* Jackson: University Press of Mississippi, 1992.

Carrigan, Jo Ann. *The Saffron Scourge: A History of Yellow Fever in Louisiana, 1796–1905.* Lafayette: Center of Louisiana Studies, University of Southwestern Louisiana, 1994.

Clinton, Catherine, ed. *Half Sisters of History: Southern Women and the American Past.* Durham: Duke University Press, 1994.

Clinton, Catherine, and Michele Gillespie, eds. *The Devil's Lane: Sex and Race in the Early South.* New York: Oxford University Press, 1997.

Cobb, James C. *Industrialization and Southern Society, 1877–1984.* Lexington: University Press of Kentucky, 1984.

Collins, R. *New Orleans Jazz: A Revised History: The Development of American Music from the Origin of the Big Bands.* New York: Vantage Press, 1996.

Colten, Craig E. *An Unnatural Metropolis: Wresting New Orleans from Nature.* Baton Rouge: Louisiana State University Press, 2005.

Corbett, Katharine T. *In Her Place: A Guide to St. Louis Women's History.* St. Louis: Missouri Historical Society Press, 1999.

———, ed. *Transforming New Orleans and Its Environs.* Pittsburgh: University of Pittsburgh Press, 2000.

Cummins, Light Townsend, et al. *Louisiana: A History.* 2nd ed. Arlington Heights, IL: Forum Press, Inc., 1990.

Dodd, Donald B., and Wynelle S. Dodd. *Historical Statistics of the South, 1790–1970.* Tuscaloosa: University of Alabama Press, 1973.

Dominguez, Virginia R. *White By Definition.* New Brunswick: Rutgers University Press, 1986.

Dorman, James H. *The People Called Cajuns: An Introduction to Ethnohistory.* Lafayette: The Center for Louisiana Studies, University of Southwestern Louisiana, 1983.

Ehrlich, Walter. *Zion in the Valley: The Jewish Community of St. Louis: The Twentieth Century.* Vol. II. Columbia: University of Missouri Press, 2002.

Faherty, S. J., William Barnaby. *The St. Louis Irish: An Unmatched Celtic Community.* St. Louis: Missouri Historical Society Press, 2001.

Finley, Randy, and Thomas A. DeBlack. *The Southern Elite and Social Change: Essays in Honor of Willard B. Gatewood, Jr.* Fayetteville: University of Arkansas Press, 2002.

Folwell, William Watts. *A History of Minnesota.* Vol. 1–4. St. Paul: Minnesota Historical Society, 1956.

Fremling, Calvin R. *Immortal River: The Upper Mississippi in Ancient and Modern Times.* Madison: University of Wisconsin Press, 2005.

Fuller, Sherri Gebert. *Chinese in Minnesota.* St. Paul: Minnesota Historical Society Press, 2004.

Gill, James. *Lords of Misrule: Mardi Gras and the Politics of Race in New Orleans.* Jackson: University Press of Mississippi, 1997.

Gilman, Rhoda R., and June Drenning Holmquist. *Selections from "Minnesota History": A Fiftieth Anniversary Anthology.* St. Paul: Minnesota Historical Society, 1965.

Holmquist, John Drenning, ed. *They Chose Minnesota: A Survey of the State's Ethic Groups.* St. Paul: Minnesota Historical Society Press, 1981.

Hurley, Andrew, ed. *Common Fields: An Environmental History of St. Louis.* St. Louis: Missouri Historical Society Press, 1997.

Kelman, Ari. *A River and Its City: The Nature of Landscape in New Orleans.* Berkeley: University of California Press, 2003.

Lass, William E. *Minnesota: A History.* 2nd edition. New York: W. W. Norton & Company, 1998.

LeMaster, Carolyn Gray. *A Corner of the Tapestry: A History of the Jewish Experience in Arkansas, 1820s–1990s.* Fayetteville: University of Arkansas Press, 1994.

Lewis, Peirce F. *New Orleans: The Making of an Urban Landscape,* 2nd ed. Santa Fe: Center for American Places, 2003.

Lichtenstein, Grace, and Laura Dankner. *Musical Gumbo: The Music of New Orleans.* New York: W. W. Norton & Company, 1993.

Long, Alecia P. *The Great Southern Babylon: Sex, Race and Respectability in New Orleans, 1865–1920.* Baton Rouge: Louisiana State University Press, 2004.

Matson, Madeline. *Food in Missouri: A Cultural Stew.* Columbia: University of Missouri Press, 1994.

McKinney, Louise. *New Orleans: A Cultural History.* New York: Oxford University Press, 2006.

McLemore, Richard Aubrey. ed. *A History of Mississippi,* Vol. I. Hattiesburg: University & College Press of Mississippi, 1973.

Members of the Staff of the Iowa State College and the Iowa Agricultural Experiment Station. *A Century of Farming in Iowa, 1846–1946.* Ames: Iowa State College Press, 1946.

Mitchell, Reid. *All on a Mardi Gras Day: Episodes in the History of New Orleans Carnival.* Cambridge: Harvard University Press, 1995.

Nager, Larry. *Memphis Beat: The Lives and Times of America's Musical Crossroads.* New York: St. Martin's Press, 1998.

Parrish, William E., Charles T. Jones Jr., and Lawrence O. Christensen, eds. *Missouri: The Heart of the Nation.* St. Louis: Forum Press, 1980.

Ravenswaay, Charles Van. *St. Louis: An Informal History of the City and Its People, 1764–1865.* Edited by Candace O'Conner. St. Louis: Missouri Historical Society Press, 1991.

Regan, Ann. *Irish in Minnesota.* St. Paul: Minnesota Historical Society Press, 2002.

Ross, Earle D. *Iowa Agriculture: An Historical Survey.* Iowa City: The State Historical Society of Iowa, 1951.

Sandweiss, Eric. *St. Louis: The Evolution of an American Urban Landscape.* Philadelphia: Temple University Press, 2001.

Sparks, Randy J. *Religion in Mississippi.* Jackson: University Press of Mississippi, 2001.

Sternberg, Mary Ann. *Along the River Road: Past and Present on Louisiana's Historic Byway.* Baton Rouge: Louisiana State University Press, 1996.

Taylor, David Vassar. *African Americans in Minnesota.* St. Paul: Minnesota Historical Society Press, 2002.

Taylor, Joe Gray. *Louisiana: A Bicentennial History.* New York: W. W. Norton & Company, Inc., 1976.

Taylor, William Banks. *Brokered Justice: Race, Politics, and Mississippi Prisons, 1798–1992.* Columbus: Ohio State University Press, 1993.

Thompson, Julius E. *Black Life in Mississippi: Essays on Political, Social, and Cultural Studies in a Deep South State.* Lanham: University Press of America, Inc., 2001.

Troen, Selwyn K., and Glen E. Holt, eds. *St. Louis.* New York: New Viewpoints, 1977.

Tucker, David M. *Arkansas: A People and Their Reputation.* Memphis: Memphis State University Press, 1985.

Turitz, Leo E. and Evelyn Turitz. *Jews in Early Mississippi.* Jackson: University Press of Mississippi, 1995.

Twain, Mark. *Life on the Mississippi.* New York: New American Library, 2001.

Tyler, Pamela. *Silk Stockings & Ballot Boxes: Women & Politics in New Orleans, 1920–1963.* Athens: University of Georgia Press, 1996.

Vujnovich, Milos M. *Yugoslavs in Louisiana.* Gretna: Pelican Publishing Company, 1974.

Waal, Carla, and Barbara Oliver Korner. *Hardship and Hope: Missouri Women Writing About Their Lives, 1820–1920.* Columbia: University of Missouri Press, 1997.

Whayne, Jeannie M., ed. *The Arkansas Delta: Land of Paradox.* Fayetteville: University of Arkansas Press, 1993.

———, ed. *Shadows over Sunnyside: An Arkansas Plantation in Transition, 1830–1945.* Fayetteville: University of Arkansas Press, 1993.

Whayne, Jeannie M., Tom DeBlack, George Sabo, and Morris S. Arnold, eds. *Arkansas: A Narrative History.* Fayetteville: University of Arkansas Press, 2002.

Wilkie, Laurie A. *Creating Freedom: Material Culture and African American Identity at Oakley Plantation, Louisiana, 1840–1950.* Baton Rouge: Louisiana State University, 2000.

Wingerd, Mary Lethert. *Claiming the City: Politics, Faith, and the Power of Place in St. Paul.* Ithaca: Cornell University Press, 2001.

Wyatt-Brown, Bertram. *The House of Percy: Honor, Melancholy, and Imagination in a Southern Family.* New York: Oxford University Press, 1994.

NATIVE AMERICANS BEFORE 1492

Ahler, Steven R. ed. *Mounds, Modoc, and Mesoamerica: Papers in Honor of Melvin L. Fowler.* Illinois State Museum Scientific Papers Series. Vol. 27. Springfield: Illinois State Museum, 2000.

Barton, C. Michael, Geoffrey A. Clark, David R. Yesner, and Georges A. Pearson, eds. *The Settlement of the American Continents: A Multidisciplinary Approach to Human Biogeography.* Tucson: University of Arizona Press, 2004.

Blaine, Martha Royce. *The Ioway Indians.* Norman: University of Oklahoma Press, 1979.

Bonnichsen, Robson, and Karen L. Turnmire, eds. *Ice Age People of North America: Environments, Origins, and Adaptations.* Corvallis: Oregon State University, 1999.

Broyles, Bettye J., and Clarence H. Webb. *The Poverty Point Culture.* Morgantown: Southeastern Archaeological Conference, 1975.

Byrd, Kathleen M., ed. *The Poverty Point Culture: Local Manifestations, Subsistence Practices, and Trade Networks.* Geoscience and Man series, vol. 29. Baton Rouge: Department of Geography and Anthropology, Louisiana State University, 1991.

Caldwell, Joseph R., and Robert L. Hall, eds. *Hopewellian Studies.* Scientific Papers Vol. 11. Springfield: Illinois State Museum, 1964.

Chappell, Sally A. Kitt. *Cahokia.* Chicago: The University of Chicago Press, 2002.

Claassen, Cheryl, and Rosemary A. Joyce, eds. *Women in Prehistory: North America and Mesoamerica.* Regendering the Past Series. Philadelphia: University of Pennsylvania Press, 1997.

Cobb, Charles R. *From Quarry to Cornfield: The Political Economy of Mississippian Hoe Production.* Tuscaloosa: University of Alabama Press, 2000.

Dalan, Rinita A., William I. Woods, John A. Koepke, and George R. Holley. *Envisioning Cahokia: A Landscape Perspective.* DeKalb: Northern Illinois University Press, 2003

Davis, Hester A. *Arkansas Before the Americans.* Fayetteville: Arkansas Archeological Survey Research Series No. 40, 1991.

Dragoo, Don W. *Mounds for the Dead: Analysis of the Adena Culture.* Annals of the Carnegie Museum Vol. 37. Pittsburgh: The Carnegie Museum of Natural History, 1963.

Fagan, Brian M. *Ancient North America: The Archaeology of a Continent.* 3rd edition. New York: Thames & Hudson, 2000.

Frison, George C. *Survival by Hunting: Prehistoric Human Predators and Animal Prey.* Berkeley: University of California Press, 2004.

Gibson, Jon L. *The Ancient Mounds of Poverty Point.* Gainesville: University Press of Florida, 2000.

Greber, N'omi B., and Katherine C. Ruhl. *The Hopewell Site: A Contemporary Analysis Based on the Work of Charles C. Willoughby.* Boulder: Westview Press, 1989.

Haynes, Gary. *The Early Settlement of North America: The Clovis Era.* Cambridge: Cambridge University Press, 2002.

Iseminger, William R. "Culture and Environment in the American Bottom: The Rise and Fall of the Cahokia Mounds." In *Common Fields: An Environmental History of St. Louis.* Edited by Andrew Hurley. St. Louis: Missouri Historical Society Press, 1997, 38–57.

Mainfort, Jr., Robert C., ed. *Middle Woodland Settlement and Ceremonialism in the Mid-South and Lower Mississippi Valley: Proceedings of the 1984 Mid-South Archaeological Conference Pinson Mounds, Tennessee-June, 1984.* Archaeological Report No. 22. Jackson: Mississippi Department of Archives and History, 1989.

Mainfort, Jr., Robert C., and Lynne P. Sullivan, eds. *Ancient Earthen Enclosures of the Eastern Woodlands.* Gainesville: University Press of Florida, 1998.

McKusick, Marshall. *Men of Ancient Iowa as Revealed by Archeological Discoveries.* Ames: Iowa State University Press, 1964.

McNutt, Charles H, ed. *Prehistory of the Central Mississippi Valley.* Tuscaloosa: University of Alabama Press, 1996.

Mehrer, Mark W. *Cahokia's Countryside: Household Archaeology, Settlement Patterns, and Social Power.* DeKalb: Northern Illinois University Press, 1995.

Morse, Dan F., and Phyllis A. Morse. *Archaeology of the Central Mississippi Valley.* New York: Academic Press, 1983.

Muller, Jon. *Mississippian Political Economy.* New York: Plenum Press, 1997.

Nassaney, Michael S., and Charles R. Cobb. *Stability, Transformation, and Variation: The Late Woodland Southeast.* New York: Plenum, 1991.

Neusius, Sarah W., ed. *Foraging, Collecting, and Harvesting: Archaic Period Subsistence and Settlement in the Eastern Woodlands.* Carbondale: Center for Archaeological Investigations, Southern Illinois University at Carbondale, Occasional Paper No. 6, 1986.

O'Brien, Michael J., and Robert C. Dunnel, eds. *Changing Perspectives on the Archaeology of the Central Mississippi River Valley.* Tuscaloosa: University of Alabama Press, 1998.

Page, Jake. *In the Hands of the Great Spirit: The 20,000 Year History of American Indians.* New York: Free Press, 2003.

Phillips, James L., and James A. Brown, eds. *Archaic Hunters and Gatherers in the American Midwest.* New York: Academic Press, 1983.

Rogers, J. Daniel, and Bruce D. Smith, eds. *Mississippian Communities and Households.* Tuscaloosa: University of Alabama Press, 1995.

Scarry, John F., ed. *Political Structure and Change in the Prehistoric Southeastern United States.* Gainesville: University Press of Florida, 1996.

Schoolcraft, Henry R. *Information Respecting the History, Condition and Prospects of the Indian Tribes of the United States: collected and Prepared Under the Direction of the Bureau of Indian Affairs, Per Act of Congress of March 3rd, 1847.* Reprint. New York: Paladin Press, 1969.

Shaffer, Lynda Norene. *Native Americans Before 1492: The Moundbuilding Centers of the Eastern Woodlands.* Armonk, NY: M. E. Sharpe, 1992.

Smith, Bruce D. *Middle Mississippi Exploitation of Animal Populations.* Anthropological Papers. No. 57. Ann Arbor: Museum of Anthropology, University of Michigan, 1975.

Struever, Stuart, and Felicia Antonelli Holton. *Koster: Americans in Search of their Prehistoric Past.* Garden City, NY: AnchorPress/Doubleday, 1979.

Toth, Alan. *Archaeology and Ceramics at the Marksville Site.* Archaeological Papers, No. 56. Ann Arbor: Museum of Anthropology, University of Michigan, 1974.

Toth, Edwin Alan. *Early Marksville Phases in the Lower Mississippi Valley: A Study of Culture Contact Dynamics.* Archeological Report No. 21. Jackson: Mississippi Department of Archives and History, 1988.

Webb, Clarence H. *The Poverty Point Culture.* 2nd revised edition. Geoscience and Man Series. vol. XVII. Baton Rouge: Louisiana State University School of Geoscience, 1982.

NATIVE AMERICANS AFTER 1492

Anderson, Gary Clayton. *Kinsmen of Another Kind: Dakota-White Relations in the Upper Mississippi Valley, 1650–1862.* Lincoln: University of Nebraska Press, 1984.

Anderson, Gary Claytion, and Alan R. Woolworth, *Through Dakota Eyes: Narrative Accounts of the Minnesota Indian War of 1862.* St. Paul: Minnesota Historical Society Press, 1988.

Arnold, Morris S. *The Rumble of a Distant Drum: The Quapaws and Old World Newcomers, 1673–1804.* Fayetteville: University of Arkansas Press, 2000.

Atkinson, James R. *Splendid Land, Splendid People: The Chickasaw Indians to Removal.* Tuscaloosa: University of Alabama Press, 2004.

Bataille, Gretchen M., David Mayer Gradwohl, and Charles L. P. Silet. *The Worlds between Two Rivers: Perspectives on AmericanIndians in Iowa.* Ames: Iowa State University Press, 1978.

Black Hawk. *Black Hawk: An Autobiography.* Edited by Donald Jackson. Urbana: University of Illinois Press, 1964.

Blaine, Martha Royce. *The Ioway Indians.* Norman: University of Oklahoma Press, 1979.

Bossu, Jean-Bernard. *Travels in the Interior of North America, 1751–1762.* Edited and translated by Seymour Feiler. Norman: University of Oklahoma Press, 1962.

Brain, Jeffrey. *Tunica Archaeology.* Cambridge: Peabody Museum of Archaeology and Ethnology Harvard University, 1988.

Brasseaux, Carl D., ed. and trans. *A Comparative View of French Louisiana, 1699 and 1762: The Journals of Pierre Le Moyne d'Iberville and Jean-Jacques-Balise d'Abbadie.* Revised edition. Lafayette: Center of Louisiana Studies, University of Southwestern Louisiana, 1981.

Carson, James Taylor. *Searching for the Bright Path: The Mississippi Choctaws from Prehistory to Removal.* Lincoln: University of Nebraska Press, 1999.

Catlin, George. *Letters and Notes on the Manners, Customs, and Condition of the North American Indians,* vol. II, reprint. Minneapolis: Ross & Haines, Inc., 1965.

Charlevoix, Pierre F. X. *Charlevoix's Louisiana: Selections from the History and the Journal.* Edited by Charles E. O'Neill. Baton Rouge: Louisiana State University Press, 1977.

Crosby, Alfred W. *The Columbian Exchange: Biological and Cultural Consequences of 1492.* Westport, CT: Greenwood Press, 1972.

Cushman, H. B., *History of the Choctaw, Chickasaw, and Natchez Indians.* Edited by Angie Debo. Greenville, TX: Headlight Printing House, 1999.

Davis, Hester A., ed. *Arkansas Before the Americans.* Fayetteville: Arkansas Archeological Survey Research Series No. 40, 1991.

Eastman, Mary. *Dahcotah or, Life and Legends of the Sioux Around Fort Snelling.* New York: Arno Press, 1975.

Ethridge, Robbie, and Charles Hudson, eds. *The Transformation of the Southeastern Indians, 1540–1760.* Jackson: University Press of Mississippi, 1998.

Ford, Richard I., ed. *Prehistoric Food Production in North America.* Anthropological Papers. No. 75. Ann Arbor: Museum of Anthropology, University of Michigan, 1985.

Gibbon, Guy. *The Sioux: The Dakota and Lakota Nations.* Malden, MA: Blackwell Publishing, 2003.

Gibson, Arrell M. *The Chickasaw.* Norman: University of Oklahoma Press, 1971.

Green, Michael D. "We Dance in Opposite Directions: Mesquakie (Fox) Separatism from the Sac and Fox Tribes." In *Iowa History Reader.* Edited by Marvin Bergman. Ames: Iowa State University Press, 1996.

Hudson, Charles, and Carmen Chaves Tesser, eds. *The Forgotten Centuries: Indians and Europeans in the American South, 1521–1704.* Athens: University of Georgia Press, 1994.

Johnston, Basil. *Ojibway Heritage.* New York: Columbia University Press, 1976.

Kidwell, Clara Sue. *Choctaws and Missionaries in Mississippi, 1818–1918.* Norman: University of Oklahoma Press, 1995.

Le Page, M. du Pratz. *The History of Louisiana: Translated from the French of M. Le Page du Pratz.* Edited by Joseph G. Tregle, Jr. Baton Rouge: Louisiana State University Press, 1975.

McNeill, William H. *Plagues and Peoples.* Garden City, NY: Doubleday Anchor, 1976.

McWilliams, Richebourg Gaillard, ed. and trans. *Fleur de Lys and Calumet: Being the Pénicaut Narrative of French Adventure in Louisiana.* Tuscaloosa: University of Alabama Press, 1988.
Pond, Samuel W. *The Dakota or Sioux in Minnesota As They Were in 1834.* St. Paul: Minnesota Historical Society Press, 1986.
Ramenofsky, Ann F. *Vectors of Death: The Archaeology of European Contact.* Albuquerque: University of New Mexico Press, 1987.
Sabo III, George. *Paths of Our Children: Historic Indians of Arkansas.* Revised edition. Fayetteville: Arkansas Archeological Survey, Popular Series No. 3, 2001.
Swanton, John R. *Indians of the Southeastern United States.* Reprint. Washington: Smithsonian Institution Press, 1979.
Thorne, Tanis C. *The Many Hands of My Relations: French and Indians on the Lower Missouri.* Columbia: University of Missouri Press, 1996.
Thornton, Russell. *American Indian Holocaust and Survival: A Population History Since 1492.* Norman: University of Oklahoma Press, 1987.
Usner, Jr., Daniel H. *American Indians in the Lower Mississippi Valley: Social and Economic Histories.* Lincoln: University of Nebraska Press, 1998.
———. *Indians, Settlers, Slaves in a Frontier Exchange Economy: The Lower Mississippi Valley before 1783.* Chapel Hill: University of North Carolina Press, 1992.
Vere, David L. *The Caddo Chiefdoms: Caddo Economies and Politics, 700–1835.* Lincoln: University of Nebraska Press, 1998.
Wallace, Anthony F. C. *Prelude to Disaster: The Course of Indian-White Relations Which Led to the Black Hawk War of 1832.* Springfield: Illinois State Historical Society, 1970.
White, Richard. *The Middle Ground: Indians, Empires, and Republics in the Great Lakes Region, 1650–1815.* Cambridge: Cambridge University Press, 1991.
Woods, Patricia Dillon. *French-Indian Relations on the Southern Frontier, 1699–1762.* Ann Arbor: UMI Research Press, 1980.

THE COLONIAL ERA

Banner, Stuart. *Legal System in Conflict: Property and Sovereignty in Missouri, 1750–1860.* Norman: University of Oklahoma Press, 2000.
Brasseaux, Carl. A. *The Founding of New Acadia: The Beginnings of Acadian Life in Louisiana, 1765–1803.* Baton Rouge: Louisiana State University Press, 1987.
Christian, Shirley. *Before Lewis and Clark: The Story of the Chouteaus, the French Dynasty That Ruled America's Frontier.* New York: Farrar, Straus, and Giroux, 2004.
Clark, John G. *New Orleans 1718–1812: An Economic History.* Baton Rouge: Louisiana State University Press, 1970.
Conrad, Glenn R. ed. *The French Experience in Louisiana.* Vol. I. The Louisiana Purchase Bicentennial Series in Louisiana History. Lafayette: Center for Louisiana Studies University of Southwestern Louisiana, 1995.
Din, Gilbert C. *Spaniards, Planters, and Slaves: The Spanish Regulation of Slavery in Louisiana, 1763–1803.* College Station: Texas A&M University Press, 1999.
———. *The Spanish Presence in Louisiana, 1763–1803.* The Louisiana Purchase Bicentennial Series in Louisiana History. Vol. 2. Lafayette: Center for Louisiana Studies, University of Louisiana at Lafayette, 1996.
Ekberg, Carl J. *Colonial Ste. Genevieve: An Adventure on the Mississippi Frontier.* Gerald, MO: The Patrice Press, 1985.

———. *French Roots in the Illinois Country: The Mississippi Frontier.* Urbana: University of Illinois Press, 1998.
Galloway, Patricia K. *La Salle and His Legacy: Frenchmen and Indians on the Lower Mississippi Valley.* Jackson: University Press of Mississippi, 1982.
Hall, Gwendolyn Midlo. *Africans in Colonial Louisiana: The Development of Afro-Creole Culture in the Eighteenth Century.* Baton Rouge: Louisiana State University Press, 1992.
Hanger, Kimberly S. *Bounded Lives, Bounded Places: Free Black Society in Colonial New Orleans, 1769–1803.* Durham: Duke University Press, 1997.
Libby, David J. *Slavery and Frontier Mississippi, 1720–1835.* Jackson: University Press of Mississippi, 2004.
Malone, Ann Patton. *Sweet Chariot: Slave Family and Household Structure in Nineteenth-Century Louisiana.* Chapel Hill: University of North Carolina Press, 1992.
McDonald, Roderick A. *The Economy and Material Culture of Slaves: Goods and Chattels on the Sugar Plantations of Jamaica and Louisiana.* Baton Rouge: Louisiana State University Press, 1993.
Moore, John Hebron. *Emergence of the Cotton Kingdom in the Old Southwest: Mississippi, 1770–1860.* Baton Rouge: Louisiana State University Press, 1988.
Poole, Stafford, C. M., and Douglas J. Slawson, C. M. *Church and Slave in Perry County, Missouri, 1818–1865.* Lewiston: Edwin Mellen Press, 1986.
Owens, Jeffrey. 1999. "Holding Back the Waters: Land Development and the Origins of Levees on the Mississippi, 1720–1845." Ph.D. diss., Louisiana State University.
Riley, Glenda. *Frontierswomen: The Iowa Experience.* Ames: Iowa State University Press, 1981.
Schwartz, Marie Jenkins. *Born in Bondage: Growing Up Enslaved in the Antebellum South.* Cambridge: Harvard University Press, 2000.
Young, Gloria A. and Michael P. Hoffman, eds. *The Expedition of Hernando de Soto West of the Mississippi, 1541–1543: Proceedings of the De Soto Symposia 1988 and 1990.* Fayetteville: University of Arkansas Press, 1993.

THE ANTEBELLUM ERA: RURAL LIFE

Bankole, Katherine. *Slavery and Medicine: Enslavement and Medical Practices in Antebellum Louisiana.* New York: Garland Publishing, Inc. 1998.
Blassingame, John W. *Slave Testimony: Two Centuries of Letters, Speeches, Interviews and Autobiographies.* Baton Rouge: Louisiana State University, 1977.
———. *The Slave Community: Plantation Life in the Antebellum South.* Revised edition. New York: Oxford University Press, 1979.
Bolton, S. Charles. *Arkansas, 1800–1860: Remote and Restless.* Fayetteville: University of Arkansas Press, 1998.
———. *Territorial Ambition: Land and Society in Arkansas, 1800–1840.* Fayetteville: University of Arkansas Press, 1993.
Bowen, Elbert R. *Theatrical Entertainments in Rural Missouri before the Civil War.* Columbia: University of Missouri Press, 1959.
Brasseaux, Carl A. *Acadian to Cajun: Transformation of a People, 1803–1877.* Jackson: University Press of Mississippi, 1992.

Burlend, Rebecca, and Edward Burlend. *A True Picture of Emigration,* Edited by Milo Milton Quaife. Lincoln: University of Nebraska Press, 1987.

Burnett, Robyn and Ken Luebbering. *German Settlement in Missouri: New Land, Old Ways.* Columbia: University of Missouri Press, 1996.

Clayton, Ronnie W. *Mother Wit: The Ex-Slave Narratives of the Louisiana Writers' Project.* New York: Peter Lang, 1990.

Cook, Florence. 1992. "Growing Up White, Genteel, and Female in a Changing South, 1865 to 1915." Ph. D. diss., University of California at Berkeley. Ann Arbor: UMI Dissertation Services, 1994.

Davis, Ronald L. F. *Good and Faithful Labor: From Slavery to Sharecropping in the Natchez District, 1860–1890.* Westport, CT: Greenwood Press, 1982.

Dempsey, Terrell. *Searching for Jim: Slavery in Sam Clemens's World.* Columbia: University of Missouri Press, 2003.

Follett, Richard J. *The Sugar Masters: Planters and Slaves in Louisiana's Cane World, 1820–1860.* Baton Rouge: Louisiana State University Press, 2005.

Fox-Genovese, Elizabeth. *Within the Plantation Household: Black and White Women of the Old South.* Chapel Hill: University of North Carolina Press, 1988.

Franklin, John Hope, and Loren Schweninger. *Runaway Slaves: Rebels on the Plantation.* New York: Oxford University Press, 1999.

Frazier, Harriet C. *Slavery and Crime in Missouri, 1773–1865* Jefferson, NC: McFarland & Company, Inc., 2001.

Genovese, Eugene D. *Roll, Jordan, Roll: The World the Slaves Made.* New York: Vintage Books, 1976.

Gould, Virginia Meacham, ed. *Chained to the Rock of Adversity: To Be Free, Black, & Female in the Old South.* Athens: University of Georgia Press, 1998.

Gutman, Herbert G. *The Black Family in Slavery and Freedom, 1750–1925.* New York: Vintage Books, 1977.

Heitmann, John Alfred. *The Modernization of the Louisiana Sugar Industry, 1830–1910.* Baton Rouge: Louisiana State University Press, 1987.

Hilliard, Sam Bowers. *Hog Meat and Hoecake: Food Supply in the Old South, 1840–1860.* Carbondale: Southern Illinois University Press, 1972.

Jewett, Clayton E., and John O. Allen. *Slavery in the South: A State-by-State History.* Westport: Greenwood Press, 2004.

Johnson, Walter. *Soul By Soul: Life Inside the Antebellum Slave Market.* Cambridge: Harvard University Press, 1999.

Kilbourne, Jr., Richard Holcombe. *Debt, Investment, Slaves: Credit Relations in East Feliciana Parish, Louisiana, 1825–1885.* Tuscaloosa: University of Alabama Press, 1995.

King, Wilma, ed. *A Northern Woman in the Plantation South: Letters of Tryphena Blanche Holder Fox 1856–1876.* Columbia: University of South Carolina Press, 1993.

Malone, Ann Patton. *Sweet Chariot: Slave Family and Household Structure in Nineteenth-Century Louisiana.* Chapel Hill: University of North Carolina Press, 1992.

McDonald, Roderick A. *The Economy and Material Culture of Slaves: Goods and Chattels on the Sugar Plantations of Jamaica and Louisiana.* Baton Rouge: Louisiana State University Press, 1993.

McNeilly, Donald P. *The Old South Frontier: Cotton Plantations and the Formation of Arkansas Society, 1819–1861.* Fayetteville: University of Arkansas Press, 2000.

Moore, John Hebron. *Agriculture in Ante-Bellum Mississippi.* New York: Octagon Books, 1971.
Morris, Christopher. *Becoming Southern: The Evolution of a Way of Life, Warren County and Vicksburg, Mississippi, 1770–1860.* New York: Oxford University Press, 1995.
O'Brien, Frank G. *Minnesota Pioneer Sketches: From the Personal Recollections and Observations of a Pioneer Resident.* Minneapolis: H.H.S. Rowell, Publisher, Housekeeper Press, 1904.
Owens, Jeffrey. 1999. "Holding Back the Waters: Land Development and the Origins of Levees on the Mississippi, 1720–1845." Ph.D. diss., Louisiana State University.
Sanfilippo, Pamela K. *Agriculture in Antebellum St. Louis: A Special History Study.* St. Louis: Ulysses S. Grant Historic Site, 2000.
Taylor, Yuval, ed. *I Was Born a Slave: An Anthology of Classic Slave Narratives.* Vol. 2. 1849–1866. Chicago: Lawrence Hill Books, 1999.
Winters, Donald L. *Tennessee Farming, Tennessee Farmers: Antebellum Agriculture in the Upper South.* Knoxville: University of Tennessee Press, 1994.
Wyman, Mark. *Immigrants in the Valley: Irish, Germans, and Americans in the Upper Mississippi Country, 1830–1860.* Chicago: Nelson-Hall, 1984.

THE ANTEBELLUM ERA: CITY LIFE AND THE TRANSPORTATION REVOLUTIONS

Adler, Jeffrey S. *Yankee Merchants and the Making of the Urban West: The Rise and Fall of Antebellum St. Louis.* New York: Cambridge University Press, 1991.
Allen, Michael. *Western Rivermen, 1763–1861: Ohio and Mississippi Boatmen and the Myth of the Alligator Horse.* Baton Rouge: Louisiana State University Press, 1990.
Baldwin, Leland D. *The Keelboat Age on Western Waters.* Pittsburgh: University of Pittsburgh Press, 1980.
Buchanan, Thomas C. *Black Life on the Mississippi: Slaves, Free Blacks, and the Western Steamboat World.* Chapel Hill: University of North Carolina Press, 2004.
Burnett, Robyn, and Ken Luebbering. *German Settlement in Missouri: New Land, Old Ways.* Columbia: University of Missouri Press, 1996.
Carr, Kay J. *Belleville, Ottawa, and Galesburg: Community and Democracy on the Illinois Frontier.* Carbondale: Southern Illinois University Press, 1996.
Clamorgan, Cyprian. *The Colored Aristocracy of St. Louis.* Edited by Julie Winch. Columbia: University of Missouri Press, 1999.
Davis, Edwin Adams, and William Ransom Hogan. *The Barber of Natchez: Wherein a Slave is Freed and Rises to a Very High Standing; Wherein the Former Slave Writes a Two-Thousand-Page Journal about His Town and Himself; Wherein the Free Negro Diarist is Appraised in Terms of His Friends, His Code, and Community's Reaction to His Wanton Murder.* Port Washington, NY: Kennikat Press, 1972.
De Latte, Carolyn E., ed. *Antebellum Louisiana, Part A, 1830–1860,* Louisiana Purchase Bicentennial Series in Louisiana History. Vol. 4. Lafayette: The Center for Louisiana Studies, University of Southwest Louisiana, 2004.
Duffy, John. *Sword of Pestilence: The New Orleans Yellow Fever Epidemic of 1852.* Baton Rouge: Louisiana State University Press, 1966.

Flanders, Robert Bruce. *Nauvoo: Kingdom on the Mississippi.* Urbana: University of Illinois Press, 1965.

Gerstäcker, Friedrich. *Wild Sports in the Far West; The Narrative of a German Wanderer beyond the Mississippi, 1837–1843.* Reprint. Durham: Duke University Press, 1968.

Greenberg, Amy S. *Cause for Alarm: The Volunteer Fire Department in the Nineteenth-Century City.* Princeton: Princeton University Press, 1998.

Haites, Erik F., James Mak, and Gary M. Walton. *Western River Transportation: The Era of Early Internal Development, 1810–1860.* Baltimore: Johns Hopkins University Press, 1975.

Hallwas, John E., and Roger D. Launius, eds. *Cultures in Conflict: A Documentary History of the Mormon War in Illinois.* Logan: Utah State University Press, 1995.

Hogan, William Ransom and Edwin Adams Davis, eds. *William Johnson's Natchez: The Ante-Bellum Diary of a Free Negro.* Baton Rouge: Louisiana State University Press, 1993

Hunter, Louis C. *Steamboats on the Western Rivers: An Economic and Technological History.* New York: Dover Publications, Inc., 1993.

Johnson, Walter. *Soul by Soul: Life Inside the Antebellum Slave Market.* Cambridge: Harvard University Press, 1999.

Kanes, Adam I. *The Western River Steamboat.* College Station: Texas A&M University Press, 2004.

Keillor, Steven J. *Grand Excursion: Antebellum America Discovers the Upper Mississippi.* Afton, MN: Afton Historical Society Press, 2004.

Kein, Sybil. *Creole: A History and Legacy of Louisiana's Free People of Color.* Baton Rouge: Louisiana State University Press, 2000.

Labbie, Delores Egger. *The Louisiana Purchase and Its Aftermath, 1800–1830.* The Louisiana Purchase Bicentennial Series in Louisiana History. Vol. 3. Lafayette: Center for Louisiana Studies, University of Louisiana at Lafayettte,1998.

Launius, Roger D., and John E. Hallwas, eds. *Kingdom on the Mississippi Revisited: Nauvoo in Mormon History.* Urbana: University of Illinois Press, 1996.

Madsen, Carol Cornwall, ed. *In Their Own Words: Women and the Story of Nauvoo.* Salt Lake City: Deseret Book Company, 1994.

Merrick, George Byron. *Old Times on the Upper Mississippi: The Recollections of a Steamboat Pilot from 1854 to 1863.* St. Paul: Minnesota Historical Society Press, 1987.

Mueller, Edward A. *Upper Mississippi River Rafting Steamboats.* Athens: Ohio University Press, 1995.

Northup, Solomon. "Twelve Years a Slave. Narrative of Solomon Northup, A Citizen of New York, Kidnapped in Washington City in 1841, and Rescued in 1853, From a Cotton Plantation Near the Red River." In *I Was Born a Slave: An Anthology of Classic Slave Narratives.* Vol. II, 1849–1866. Edited by Yuval Taylor. Chicago: Lawrence Hill Books, 1999.

Penick, Jr., James. *The New Madrid Earthquakes of 1811–1812.* Columbia: University of Missouri Press, 1976.

Petersen, William J. *Steamboating on the Upper Mississippi.* New York: Dover Publications, Inc., 1995.

Roseman, Curtis C., and Elizabeth M. Roseman. *Grand Excursions on the Upper Mississippi River.* Iowa City: University of Iowa Press, 2004.

Shippee, Lester B., ed. *Bishop Whipple's Southern Diary, 1843–1844.* New York: Da Capo Press, 1968.

Suppiger, Joseph, Salomon Koepfli, and Kaspar Koepfli. *Travel Account of the Koepfli and Suppiger Family to St. Louis on the Mississippi and the Founding of New Switzerland in the State of Illinois.* Edited by John C. Abbott. Translated by Raymond J. Spahn. Carbondale: Southern Illinois University Press, 1987.

Willis, Jocelyn. *Boosters, Hustlers, and Speculators: Entrepreneurial Culture and the Rise of Minneapolis and St. Paul, 1849–1883.* St. Paul: Minnesota Historical Society Press, 2005.

THE CIVIL WAR ALONG THE MISSISSIPPI

Balfour, Emma. *Vicksburg,A City Under Siege: Diary of Emma Balfour May 16, 1863–June 2, 1863.* Phillip C. Weinberger, 1983.

Ballard, Michael B. *Vicksburg: The Campaign that Opened the Mississippi.* Chapel Hill: University of North Carolina Press, 2004.

Bearss, Edwin C. *Rebel Victory at Vicksburg.* Reprint. Wilmington: Broadfoot Publishing Company, 1989.

Bercaw, Nancy. *Gendered Freedoms: Race, Rights, and the Politics of Household in the Delta, 1861–1875.* Gainesville: University Press of Florida, 2003.

Bettersworth, John K. "The Home Front 1861–1865." *A History of Mississippi.* Vol. 1. Edited by Richard Aubrey McLemore. Hattiesburg: University & College Press of Mississippi, 1973.

East, Charles, ed. *Sarah Morgan: The Civil War Diary of a Southern Woman.* New York: Simon & Schuster, 1992.

Frankel, Noralee. *Freedom's Women: Black Women and Families in Civil War Era Mississippi.* Bloomington: Indiana University Press, 1999.

Gerteis, Louis S. *Civil War St. Louis.* Lawrence: University Press of Kansas, 2001.

Gower, Herschel. *Charles Dahlgren of Natchez: The Civil War and Dynastic Decline.* Washington: Brassey's, Inc., 2002.

Grimsley, Mark. *The Hard Hand of War: Union Military Policy toward Southern Civilians, 1861–1865.* New York: Cambridge University Press, 1997.

Messner, William F. *Freedmen and the Ideology of Free Labor: Louisiana 1862–1865.* Lafayette: Center for Louisiana Studies, University of Southwestern Louisiana, 1978.

Roland, Charles P. *Louisiana Sugar Plantations during the American Civil War.* Reprint. Baton Rouge: Louisiana State University Press, 1997.

Shea, William L. Shea, and Terrence J. Winschel. *Vicksburg Is the Key: The Struggle for the Mississippi River.* Lincoln: University of Nebraska Press, 2003.

RECONSTRUCTION AND LIFE ALONG THE MISSISSIPPI: 1865–1900

Aiken, Charles S., *The Cotton Plantation South since the Civil War.* Baltimore: Johns Hopkins University Press, 1998.

Arnesen, Eric. *Waterfront Workers of New Orleans: Race, Class, and Politics, 1863–1923.* Urbana: University of Illinois Press, 1994.

Bercaw, Nancy. *Gendered Freedoms: Race, Rights, and the Politics of Household in the Delta, 1861–1875.* Gainesville: University Press of Florida, 2003.

Blassingame, John W. *Black New Orleans, 1860–1880.* Chicago: University of Chicago Press, 1973.

Bloom, Khaled J. *The Mississippi Valley's Great Yellow Fever Epidemic of 1878.* Baton Rouge: Louisiana State University Press, 1993.

Brandfon, Robert L. *Cotton Kingdom of the New South: A History of the Yazoo Mississippi Delta from Reconstruction to the Twentieth Century.* Cambridge: Harvard University Press, 1967.

Cobb, James C. *The Most Southern Place on Earth: The Mississippi Delta and the Roots of Regional Identity.* New York: Oxford University Press, 1992.

Davis, Ronald L. F. *Good and Faithful Labor: From Slavery to Sharecropping in the Natchez District, 1860–1890.* Westport, CT: Greenwood Press, 1982.

Finley, Randy. *From Slavery to Uncertain Freedom: The Freedmen's Bureau in Arkansas, 1865–1869.* Fayetteville: University of Arkansas Press, 1996.

Kriedberg, Marjorie. *Food on the Frontier: Minnesota Cooking from 1850 to 1900 with Selected Recipes.* St. Paul: Minnesota Historical Society Press, 1975.

Moneyhorn, Carl H. *Arkansas and the New South.* Fayetteville: University of Arkansas Press, 1997.

Pabis, George S. "Delaying the Deluge: The Engineering Debate over Flood Control on the Lower Mississippi, 1846–1861." *Journal of Southern History.* Vol. 64 (August 1998): 421–454.

———. "Subduing Nature through Engineering: Caleb G. Forshey and the Levees-only Policy, 1851–1881." In *Transforming New Orleans and Its Environs: Centuries of Change.* Edited by Craig E. Colten. Pittsburgh: University of Pittsburgh, 2001, 64–83.

———. "The Destiny of a River: James Buchanan Eads, the U.S. Army Corps of Engineers and the Mississippi, 1865–1881." *The Journal of the Georgia Association of Historians.* Vol. 22, (2001): 100–141.

Rodrigue, John C. *Reconstruction in the Cane Fields: From Slavery to Free Labor in Louisiana's Sugar Parishes, 1862–1880.* Baton Rouge: Louisiana State University Press, 2001.

Rousey, Dennis C. *Policing the Southern City: New Orleans, 1805–1889.* Baton Rouge: Louisiana State University Press, 1996.

Saikku, Mikko. *This Delta: An Environmental History of the Yazoo-Mississippi Floodplain.* Athens: University of Georgia Press, 2005.

Somers, Dale A. *The Rise of Sports in New Orleans, 1850–1900.* Baton Rouge: Louisiana State University Press, 1972.

Taylor, Joe Gray. *Louisiana Reconstructed, 1863–1877.* Baton Rouge: Louisiana State University Press, 1974.

Tunnel, Ted. *Crucible of Reconstruction: War, Radicalism, and Race in Louisiana, 1862–1877.* Baton Rouge: Louisiana State University Press, 1992.

Vandal, Gilles. *Rethinking Southern Violence: Homicides in Post-Civil War Louisiana, 1866–1884.* Columbus: Ohio State University Press, 2005.

Wayne, Michael, *The Reshaping of Plantation Society: The Natchez District, 1860–80.* Urbana: University of Illinois Press, 1990.

Wharton, Vernon Lane. *The Negro in Mississippi, 1865–1890.* Reprint. Westport, CT: Greenwood Press, 1984.

White, Walter. *Rope and Faggot: A Biography of Judge Lynch.* Reprint. New York: Arno Press and the New York Times: 1969.

Willis, Jocelyn. *Boosters, Hustlers, and Speculators: Entrepreneurial Culture and the Rise of Minneapolis and St. Paul, 1849–1883.* St. Paul: Minnesota Historical Society Press, 2005.

Willis, John C. *Forgotten Time: The Yazoo-Mississippi Delta after the Civil War.* Charlottesville: University Press of Virginia, 2000.
Winters, Donald L. *Farmers without Farms: Agricultural Tenancy in Nineteenth-Century Iowa.* Westport, CT: Greenwood Press, 1978.
Woodward, C. Vann. *Origins of the New South, 1877–1913.* Baton Rouge: Louisiana State University Press, 1967.
———. *The Strange Career of Jim Crow.* New York: Oxford University Press, 1966.
Wright, Gavin. *Old South, New South: Revolutions in the Southern Economy since the Civil War.* Baton Rouge: Louisiana State University Press, 1996.

PEOPLE ALONG THE MISSISSIPPI, 1900–1945

Barry, John M. *Rising Tide: The Great Mississippi Flood of 1927 and How It Changed America.* New York: Simon & Schuster, 1997.
Bernard, Shane K. *The Cajuns: Americanization of a People.* Jackson: University Press of Mississippi, 2003.
Cobb, James C. *The Most Southern Place on Earth: The Mississippi Delta and the Roots of Regional Identity.* New York: Oxford University Press, 1992.
Daniel, Pete. *Deep'n As It Come: the 1927 Mississippi River Flood.* Fayetteville: University of Arkansas Press, 1996.
———. *The Shadow of Slavery: Peonage in the South, 1901–1969.* New York: Oxford University Press, 1973.
Detjen, David W. *The Germans in Missouri, 1900–1918: Prohibition, Neutrality, and Assimilation.* Columbia: University of Missouri Press, 1985.
Fairclough, Adam. *Race & Democracy: The Civil Rights Struggle in Louisiana, 1915–1972.* Athens: University of Georgia Press, 1995.
Holley, Donald. *Uncle Sam's Farmers: The New Deal Communities in the Lower Mississippi Valley.* Urbana: University of Illinois Press, 1975.
Johnson, Ben F. *Arkansas in Modern America, 1930–1999.* Fayetteville: University of Arkansas Press, 2000.
Lemann, Nicholas. *The Promised Land: The Great Black Migration and How It Changed America.* New York: Vintage Books, 1992.
Percy, William Alexander. *Lanterns on the Levee: Recollections of a Planter's Son.* Baton Rouge: Louisiana State University Press, 2005.
Rehder, John B. *Louisiana's Vanishing Plantation Landscape.* Baltimore: Johns Hopkins University Press, 1999.
Rosenberg, Daniel. *New Orleans Dockworkers: Race, Labor, and Unionism, 1892–1923.* Albany: State University of New York Press, 1988.
Rudick, Elliot. *Race Riot at East St. Louis, July 2, 1917.* Urbana: University of Illinois Press, 1982.
Stockley, Grif. *Blood in Their Eyes: The Elaine Race Massacres of 1919.* Fayetteville: University of Arkansas Press, 2001.
Strahan, Jerry E. *Andrew Jackson Higgins and the Boats that Won World War II.* Baton Rouge: Louisiana State University Press, 1994.
Wailoo, Keith. *Dying in the City of the Blues: Sickle Cell Anemia and the Politics of Race and Wealth.* Chapel Hill: University of North Carolina Press, 2001.
Whayne, Jeannie M. *A New Plantation South: Land, Labor, and Federal Favor in Twentieth-Century Arkansas.* Charlottesville: University Press of Virginia, 1996.

Woods, Clyde. *Development Arrested: The Blues and Plantation Power in the Mississippi Delta.* New York: Verso, 1998.

LIFE ALONG THE MISSISSIPPI: 1945–2006

Andrews, Kenneth T. *Freedom Is a Constant Struggle: The Mississippi Civil Rights Movement and Its Legacy.* Chicago: University of Chicago Press, 2004.

Brinkley, Douglas. *The Great Deluge: Hurricane Katrina, New Orleans, and the Mississippi Gulf Coast.* New York: Morrow, 2006.

Capeci, Jr., Dominic J. *The Lynching of Cleo Wright.* Lexington: University Press of Kentucky, 1998.

Cheseborough, Steve. *Blues Traveling: The Holy Sites of Delta Blues.* Jackson: University Press of Mississippi, 2001.

Cobb, James C., ed. *The Mississippi Delta and the World: The Memoirs of David L. Cohn.* Baton Rouge: Louisiana State University Press, 1995.

Dittmer, John. *Local People: The Struggle for Civil Rights in Mississippi.* Urbana: University of Illinois Press, 1994.

Duffy, Timothy. *Music Makers: Portraits and Songs from the Roots of America.* Athens, GA: Hill Street Press, 2002.

Early, Gerald, ed. *"Ain't But a Place": An Anthology of African American Writings about St. Louis.* St. Louis: Missouri Historical society Press, 1998.

Fairclough, Adam. *Race & Democracy: The Civil Rights Struggle in Louisiana, 1915–1972.* Athens: University of Georgia Press, 1995.

Hallowell, Christopher. *People of the Bayou: Cajun Life in Lost America.* Gretna: Pelican Publishing Company, 2003.

Hay, Fred J., ed. *Goin' Back to Memphis: Conversations with the Blues.* Athens: University of Georgia Press, 2001.

Hendrickson, Paul. *Sons of Mississippi: A Story of Race and Its Legacy.* New York: Alfred A. Knopf, 2003.

Horne, Jed. *Breach of Faith: Hurricane Katrina and the Near Death of a Great American City.* New York: Random House, 2006.

Lee, Chana Kai. *For Freedom's Sake: The Life of Fannie Lou Hamer.* Urbana: University of Illinois Press, 1999.

Lipsitz, George. *A Life in the Struggle: Ivory Perry and the Culture of Opposition.* Philadelphia: Temple University Press, 1995.

Metress, Christopher. *The Lynching of Emmett Till: A Documentary Narrative.* Charlottesville: University of Virginia Press, 2002.

National Oceanic and Atmospheric Administration. U.S. Dept. of Commerce. *Natural Disaster Survey Report: The Great Flood of 1993.* Rockville, MD: U.S. Dept. of Commerce, 1994.

Newman, Mark. *Divine Agitators: The Delta Ministry and Civil Rights in Mississippi.* Athens: University of Georgia Press, 2004.

Palmer, Robert. *A Tale of Two Cities: Memphis Rock and New Orleans Roll.* Brooklyn: Institute for Studies in American Music, Dept. of Music, School of Performing Arts, Brooklyn College of the City University of New York, 1979.

Raban, Jonathan. *Old Glory: A Voyage Down the Mississippi.* New York: Vintage Books, 1998.

Tidwell, Mike. *Bayou Farewell: The Rich Life and Tragic Death of Louisiana's Cajun Coast.* New York: Vintage Books, 2004.

Wald, Elijah, and John Junkerman. *River of Song: A Musical Journey Down the Mississippi.* New York: St. Martin's Press, 1998.

Walton, Anthony. *Mississippi: An American Journey.* New York: Alfred A. Knopf, 1996.

Whitfield, Stephen J. *A Death in the Delta: The Story of Emmett Till.* New York: Free Press, 1988.

Williams, Johnny E. *African American Religion and the Civil Rights Movement in Arkansas.* Jackson: University Press of Mississippi, 2003.

Woodruff, Nan Elizabeth. *American Congo: The African American Freedom Struggle in the Delta.* Cambridge: Harvard University Press, 2003.

Index

About the Author

GEORGE S. PABIS is Associate Professor of History at Georgia Perimeter College, Lawrenceville, GA. He holds a Ph.D. in U.S. history from the University of Illinois at Chicago. He has published several scholarly articles and book chapters focusing on the Mississippi River.

Recent Titles in the
Greenwood Press Daily Life in the United States series

Immigrant America, 1870–1920
June Granatir Alexander

DISCARD